THE TEXTUAL LIFE OF DICKENS'S CHARACTERS

The Textual Life of Dickens's Characters

James A. Davies

Lecturer in English Literature
University College, Swansea

BARNES & NOBLE BOOKS
Savage, Maryland

First published in the United States of America 1990 by
BARNES & NOBLE BOOKS
8705 Bollman Place
Savage, Maryland 20763

Library of Congress Cataloging-in-Publication Data
Davies, James A.
  The Textual Life of Dickens's Characters
  Bibliography: p.
  Includes index.
  1. Dickens, Charles, 1812–1870—Characters.
2. Dickens, Charles, 1812–1870—Technique.
3. Characters and characteristics in literature.
I. Title.
PR4589.D37 1990   823'.8   85–13438
ISBN 0–389–20588–5

Printed in Great Britain

To Jen

Contents

Acknowledgements

I am grateful to my colleague, Neil Reeve, for reading and commenting on Chapter 5.

Part of Chapter 2 first appeared in the *Durham University Journal,* LXX (1977–8). A version of Chapter 6 first appeared in the *Dickensian* LXXII (1976).

1

Introduction – Some *Sketches By Boz*

INTRODUCTION: THE 'JANUS-FACED CRITIC'

My aim, to put matters at their simplest, is to examine a number of Dickens's characters in order to interpret the works in which they feature. If this sentence has a slightly defensive tone it is because what might be described as the age of A.C. Bradley has long been overtaken by the world of modern literary criticism and in the latter not only is an approach through character hardly common but that literary criticism has an interpretative function can no longer be taken for granted. Both character and interpretation, it hardly needs stressing, have been amongst the casualties – though not, I believe, among the fatalities – of the modern movement away from mimetic to semiotic notions of literature. So far as 'character' is concerned Barthes's famous pronouncement, 'What is obsolescent in today's novel is not the novelistic, it is the character . . .'[1] has been, rightly or wrongly, highly influential, particularly given the anti-humanist bias of structuralist thinking. As for 'interpretation': that a leading contemporary theorist, whose clarity and cogency has done much to disseminate structuralist and post-structuralist thinking, can entitle his first chapter, 'Beyond Interpretation' and argue that of the 'many tasks that confront criticism', tasks concerned 'to advance one's understanding of the conventions and operations of an institution, a mode of discourse', the 'one thing we do not need is more interpretations',[2] speaks for itself though not always persuasively. For the semiotic view of literature, insisting on the arbitrary relationship of signifier to signified, of sound-image to concept, has posited a literary work freed from context, a complex example of a language that is self-defining and self-regulating. Regarding the work as self-contained artifact leads to a concern with 'literariness' rather than with literature that has meant the investigation of how works come into being and the

1

nature of that being. Since character is literature's supreme means of making statements about the real world, and so central to mimetic theory, the downgrading and comparative neglect of this mimetic function come as no surprise.

The separation of the mimetic and the semiotic is only one aspect of modern literary theory. A second, a product of narrative theory, needs to be outlined briefly. This is the distinction between 'story' and 'text' most conveniently described by Rimmon-Kenan: 'Story designates the narrated events ... together with the participants in these events. Whereas "story" is a succession of events, "text" is a ... written discourse which undertakes their telling.'[3] Story, then, has a mimetic thrust, text a semiotic one.

Even the most cursory and arbitrary glance at the history of literary criticism shows a concern with story to be the dominant preoccupation. From Aristotle to Arnold Bennett to A.J. Greimas, those who conceive of characters as functional entities invariably do so in relation to the story. Hence Aristotle's famous pronouncement that characters are 'for the sake of the action',[4] Bennett's that a 'character has to be conventionalized. It must somehow form part of the pattern, or lay the design of the book',[5] and Greimas's exclusive concern with how characters participate in what Barthes calls 'a sphere of action'.[6] When Greimas classifies characters as subject, object, indirect object and adjunct, and, as such, participating in 'three main semantic axes ... which are communication, desire (or quest) and ordeal',[7] though he does not intend to focus on the novel's mimeticism he clearly implies that his province is the story.

Work on Dickens has the same emphasis. Space hardly allows much engagement with such a vast amount of criticism but, to cite two critics of very different periods and persuasions: John Forster, in noting Dickens's zealous endeavours 'to keep the leading characters ... under some strictness of discipline' and that to 'confine exaggeration within legitimate limits was an art he laboriously studied',[8] considers how the Dickensian character performs appropriately within the story; the hostile Robert Garis implies the same when insisting that Dickens's characters 'perform their identities. They perform their natures.'[9] The standard bibliographical summary of work up to the mid-1970s on Dickens's 'characterisation', taking no cognizance of the modern tendency to attach 'character to 'story' and 'characterisation' to 'text', points only to work on such story-linked topics as psychological depth and complexity, methods of character revelation, and character types.[10]

The separation of mimetic from semiotic criticism exposes the inadequacy of each on its own as a way of approaching character, a fact that has not gone unobserved. Weinsheimer, for example, concluding an important article on the ultimate semiotic argument that characters are no more than segments of texts, asks for a

> Janus-faced critic who can do justice to both texts and per-sons. . . . Semiotic criticism cannot explain the integrity of char-acters; mimetic criticism cannot explain their integration. . . . Characters are both people and words.[11]

Seymour Chatman, drawing on A.J. Greimas, outlines the formal-ist/structuralist belief that since characters 'are, in short, partici-pants or *actants* rather than *personnages* . . . it is erroneous to consider them as real beings', but then notes that such seminal modern critics as Todorov and Barthes came to recognise 'a more open, afunctional notion of character'.[12] This, argues Chatman, is inevitable simply on grounds of common sense: 'The equation of characters with "mere words" is wrong. . . . Too often do we recall fictional characters vividly, yet not a single word of the text in which they came alive'.[13] Chatman may, here, be slipping away from character-*function*, but not from characters in relation to mimesis and story.

The important points are two in number. Firstly, far less atten-tion has been paid to 'characterisation' than to 'character'. Second-ly, though the former requires attention, it should not be, as Weinsheimer realises, at the expense of the latter. This present study begins with Greimas's (and Chatman's) concept of character as '*actant*', but applies this idea of character-function to the 'text' whilst taking into account its role in the 'story' through a concern with the works' interpretations of real experience. To put this basically: this study's examination of the textual life of Dickens's characters makes characterisation a central though not a sole concern.

Five basic textual functions of Dickens's characterisations are discussed: the modifying summariser of much or all of the whole work's thematic material, by which I mean a characterisation that not only embodies those main themes but also adds to them; Narrator; implied or intended reader and a Re-reader at least partly implied; vehicle for ideas; shaping or structuring device. For the sake of clarity each role is examined separately but I am well aware that each rarely excludes the others.

Characters are examined and assessed as textual constructs, Weinsheimer's 'segments'.[14] To put this another way, 'character-isations', the wordy shapes and structures through which characters foreground themselves against the dense, allusive mass of Dickens's writing, are, as has been said, my central concern. Dickens's work is particularly suited to such an approach because his is a highly semiotic, textually-conscious, writerly art; text dominates story to a far greater extent than, say, in Jane Austen or George Eliot. In his fiction as, indeed, though to a lesser degree, in such character-dominated non-fiction as letters and travel-writings, Dickens is far less concerned with the *process* of psychological change than are either of those female writers. Rather, it hardly needs to be said, his characters tend to move from one psychological peak to another. For Austen and Eliot strove for realism whereas Dickens, to quote Eigner, was a creator of ro-mances and 'the romancer uses his characters; he does not render or develop them much more than his thematic purposes require'.[15] It follows that the reader generates meaning by apprehending the structure of the characterisation through relating part to part, through understanding a system of comparisons and contrasts not only with other characters but also within the characterisation, and the patterns made by a series of key-scenes or by, as it were, spatial form, appearances in and disappearances from the text.

This study endorses Weinsheimer and Chatman's dissatisfaction with purely semiotic criticism by only *beginning* with the idea of character as wordy construct. Most of this book is formalistic textual analysis and exegesis. But since it is convinced of the ultimate inadequacy of the anti-humanist approach and that literary texts are more than structures of arbitrary signs it is also concerned with the textual life of Dickens's characters in its widest sense. For literature relates text to the real world, as unavoidable references to 'theme' and 'thematic purpose' make plain, and semiotic awareness is only the textual means to a 'supra-textual' interpretative end that relates text to story as the only way to understand the literary work.

Progress to that end is achieved through a selective approach that reflects the organic nature of great literature, possibly forced upon all critics by the sheer range and scope of Dickens's work but here, in any case, adopted deliberately. This selectivity is not random: chapters examine characters from early, middle and late Dickens, and from minor as well as major works, from letters and non-fiction, as well as the great novels on which most stress is placed. To illustrate the belief that a characterisation can often have a textual function that is far more important than the role played by the relevant character in the story, some minor characters are given as much detailed attention as some of Dickens's most complex creations. No apology would be required for interpreting, say, *Great Expectations* through the character of Pip, or *Our Mutual Friend* through John Harmon; none will be forthcoming for approaching *The Pickwick Papers* through the Fat Boy, and *Martin Chuzzlewit* through Young Bailey. To demonstrate the potential of major characterisations for the expressing of ideas and the structuring of complex works, Chapters 5 and 6 each concentrate on a single figure in a major novel.

SKETCHES BY BOZ: 'LABORATORY CONDITIONS'

Initial demonstration of this book's procedures and of the five basic character-functions it explores, draws, for convenience, on *Sketches By Boz*, Dickens's first published volume and one of his simpler texts. It provides, as it were, characterisations in 'laboratory conditions', as distinct from those enmeshed in the complexities of the later, greater texts. This early and, in some ways, apprentice work contains, in clarifying miniature, the whole range of Dickensian characterising procedures.

(i) Modifying Summaries in 'A Parliamentary Sketch'[16]

Characters functioning as modifying summaries can be seen, in a simple, basic way, in 'A Parliamentary Sketch', Dickens's careful merging and revising of two earlier pieces. Its setting is the House of Commons during the post-Reform years of the 1830s as parliamentary business begins at 4.30 in the afternoon and a few spectators observe the Members entering for a debate. Brief descriptions of parliamentary characters then follow: the 'conservator of the peace', the 'stranger', assorted Members, in particular 'ferocious-looking gentleman' and 'a county Member'. A brief encounter with the door-keeper to the Strangers' Gallery, and references to the House crowded for a debate, precede a longer account of Nicholas, the old 'butler of Bellamy's', which is the refreshment room, a few quick cameos of Members dining, then one of Jane, 'the Hebe of Bellamy's'. Two members eat a meal before the division bell rings and all dash away.

This 'Sketch' is essentially satirical, and the satire is hard-edged. Parliament is seen as a private club contemptuous of the general public; its reactionary members, scornful of the present, wish only to call back an idealised yesterday. Three are treated in detail. The 'conservator of the peace', who controls visiting spectators, is a hoarse-voiced and incessant talker ingratiating to his social superiors but angrily concerned to bully and repel all visitors. His slightly archaic dress, in particular his 'queer-crowned hat' and 'great boots', links him to that yesterday preferred by most members. He is pompously obsessed with the dignity of Parliament, the latter fuelling his exchange with the public that moves through annoyance at 'very irreverent behaviour' and a pettish response to uninformed questions, to the violent exclusion of a recalcitrant stranger. He is succeeded by the 'ferocious-looking gentleman' who carries a 'bundle of dirty papers ... which are generally supposed to be the miscellaneous estimates for 1804'. The ferocity is invariably directed against the public and is expressed verbally, when he objects to a person in the Strangers' Gallery viewing him through an eye-glass and threatens to complain to the Speaker, and physically when he objects to members of the public eating in the Members' dining-room by 'sitting with his booted leg on the table at which they were supping'. The 'county Member' wears 'a costume one seldom sees nowadays, and when the few who wear it have died off, it will be quite extinct'. He is obsessed with the past and 'can tell you long stories of Fox, Pitt, Sheridan, and Canning, and how much better the House was managed in those times'. Now he 'has a great contempt for all young Members of Parliament'. They are no more than a 'throng of Exquisites' not to be compared with 'the old House, in days gone by' when 'wit, talent, and patriotism flourished more brightly'. But he remains fascinated by the procedures of the House, discussed by him as an end in themselves, and shows little regard for what Parliament does for the public it should serve.

Nicholas, the 'Butler of Bellamy's', has controlled the Members' refreshment room for as long as anyone can remember. He has 'a great idea of the degeneracy of the times', and patronises those who venture 'deferential questions about Sheridan, and Percival, and Castlereagh'. To him the present metropolitan Members are no better than 'rascals' because they dine at home. As for Irish Members: they ate too much and drank only table beer, refusing wine and returning to their lodgings for whisky-and-water. '"And what was the consequence?"', snaps the old man. '"Why, the concern lost – actually lost, sir – by his patronage."' He may be too old to contemplate physical violence against his customers, so substitutes vituperation.

Among those lounging in Bellamy's is a 'small gentleman with the sharp nose'. His only memorable moment was in the recent past: he was 'remarkably active' when Parliament burned down, meaning that he ran about a great deal, but he has retained a great sense of his own importance and bravery. Among those working in Bellamy's is '"Jane": the Hebe of Bellamy's', who has 'a thorough contempt for the great majority of her visitors', a gleeful disdain for the younger Members whose attempts at drunken conversation with her she repels by digging forks into their arms, and much respect for Nicholas.

The Sketch ends with two Members – one of the Lords, the other of the Commons – having dinner. The peer is a Falstaffian character, and a fine trencherman, eating and drinking in a manner that once again suggests the long-gone age of 'Sheridan's parliamentary carouses'. His companion is a 'spare, squeaking old man' who damns everyone in his conversation. Whilst the one consumes, the other 'damns and drinks, and drinks and damns, and smokes'. Together their behaviour and old age enable them to function in the same manner as each character of substance throughout the sketch: as summaries of the thematic gesturing of the whole piece. Such characters, through appearance, behaviour and conversation, demonstrate either overtly or implicitly a general and invariably violent contempt for others, reactionary behaviour, and unthinking nostalgia for the glamorous past. Each is structured accordingly.

The effect is, of course, a simple one but not simple repetition. The contempt for the public shown so readily by the 'great conservator' is taken to extremes of discourtesy by the 'ferocious-looking gentleman'; the 'county Member' extends his contempt to include his fellow-Members; the fork-wielding 'Hebe of Bellamy's' repeats the violent tendencies of the Members but gives such behaviour a sexual edge. Thus, in miniature and in undeveloped characterisations, Dickens uses his figures as modifying summaries. These hint at a developing complexity through the eschewing of simple repetition but only occasionally is the single appearance sufficiently structured to suggest what this character-function can achieve. The conservator, for example, is presented, initially, in relation to the public – they laugh at him, he 'expostulates' with them – and through the very different relations he has with parliamentary dignitaries, before a sequence that dramatises these two contrasting attitudes. The organisation of the characterisation in itself has thematic force.

(ii) Narrator and Reader in 'Shabby-Genteel People'[17]

Sketches By Boz is a work in which the Narrator is always a strong presence but in some of the pieces, including those reflecting a metropolitan knowingness, the Narrator is the most important character. One example is 'Shabby-Genteel People', the tenth chapter of the section entitled 'Characters'. For a 'shabby-genteel' person is found only in London; he is always a man, in early middle-age, down on his luck, to say the least, but attempting to keep up appearances. He is 'a strange compound of dirty-slovenliness and wretched attempts at faded smartness'. The Narrator concentrates on one example, a shabby-genteel man first sighted in the British Museum Reading Room. His appearance is described, as are his attempts to hide his poverty; he is seen eating his frugal lunch, and appearing in obviously 'revived' (that is, cheaply dyed) clothes before the rain quickly returns them to shabby normality. The sketch ends with general descriptions of the haunts and occupations of that unfortunate group.

The first paragraph is of crucial importance:

There are certain descriptions of people who, oddly enough, appear to appertain exclusively to the metropolis. You meet them, every day, in the streets of London, but no one ever encounters them elsewhere; they seem indigenous to the soil, and to belong as exclusively to London as its own smoke, or the dingy bricks and mortar. We could illustrate the remark by a variety of examples, but, in our present sketch, we will only advert to one class as a specimen – that class which is so aptly and expressively designated as 'shabby-genteel'.

The passage begins with a first sentence in which attempts at a streetwise assurance give way to an 'appear' connoting a tentativeness not wholly concealed by the uneasy dignity of the language. That mixture is repeated in sentence two: the categorical assertion is partly undermined by the uncertainty of 'seem'. Sentence three defiantly, if not convincingly, asserts the Narrator's wide-ranging knowledge and power, an impression aided by the change from the second person plural of sentence two to the first person plural of sentence three. Through this change the Narrator excludes the reader from those, including himself, who know more.

But the Narrator's assumption of superiority is made too insistently. He struggles to make sense of his experiences and cannot hide the persisting uncertainty. The change of person emphasises the obviousness of that insistence by enabling him to include himself in a superior class of sketch-writers, one of whom is now at work.[18] The abruptness of the shift has the effect of demonstrating not the Narrator's wisdom, but a desperate search for authority through association with those other writers assumed to be knowing but about whom nothing is known.

Both aspects of paragraph one are developed through the remainder of this short sketch. Thus paragraph two, in avoiding the conditional mode – when 'may' is used its meaning, here, is 'can' – is confident and aware in its assertions about the shabby-genteel and about the London *milieu*. But paragraph three begins with a sense of difficulty evident in the inelegant language: 'We will endeavour to explain our conception of the term which forms the title of this paper'. And the persisting attempt, through this paragraph, to locate the shabby-genteel person and to be precise about him, is part of a dogged and awkward struggle towards some kind of definition. The opening conditional – 'If you meet a man lounging up Drury Lane, or leaning with his back against a post in Long-acre . . .' – leads to a detailed description of a man who, though shabby, is not genteel and so is eliminated as a subject. This false start is followed by a further sustained conditional: 'But, if you see hurrying along a by-street . . . if you observe, too, that his yellowish-white neckerchief is carefully pinned up . . . you may set him down as a shabby-genteel man.' The mode detracts from the force of the assertion, as does the qualification in the final sentence of that third paragraph: 'A glance at that depressed face, and timorous air of conscious poverty, will make your heart ache – always supposing that you are neither a philosopher nor a political economist.' 'Always supposing' is hardly suggestive of confidence and the categorical.

The rest of the sketch continues to undermine the Narrator's further attempts at those allusive, confidently categorical assertions with references to his own inadequate knowledge. Thus, in the British Museum Reading Room: 'When we first saw this poor object, we thought it quite impossible that his attire could ever become worse. . . . We knew nothing about the matter; he grew more and more shabby-genteel every day.' When the man disappears 'we thought he was dead'. The Narrator is quickly proved wrong and then further deceived, at least initially, by the 'revived' clothes. The final references to haunts and occupations stress the continuing problems of definition: 'It would be a task of equal difficulty, either to assign any particular spot for the residence of these beings, or to endeavour to enumerate their general occupations.' Persisting attempts at worldly wisdom – 'the miserably poor man . . . is one of the most pitiable objects in human nature', for example – would have more force if not preceded by that endemic uncertainty. Even the final sentence – 'Such objects, with few exceptions, are shabby-genteel people.' – has its slight force further reduced by the qualifying clause.

The Narrator, then, for all his street-wisdom and knowledge of London, is essentially an uncertain observer. In the second half of the sketch, as the 'we' form takes over, he constantly aligns himself with his fellow-writers to become part of a shadowy, neo-Kafkaesque group sharing the same urban experience and viewing the shabby genteel in a manner close to the intimidatory. That too-eager aligning betrays the extent to which he remains a distinct, troubled character who seeks confidence in numbers. His uncertainty about other urban inhabitants, in this case the 'shabby-genteel', makes a disturbing statement about the possibility of knowing much about one's fellows in the bleak world of the Victorian city.

Before he retreats into the group he makes ready use of the 'you' form. It implies a specific, precisely visualised Reader about whom much can be assumed. Such a person knows London well, as collusive topographical references make clear. The Narrator takes for granted the Reader's familiarity with the areas around Charing

Cross, Aldgate, Drury Lane, Long-acre with its posts, and Camden Town canal. He takes for granted an urban sensibility, an urban way of responding to fleeting glimpses that has been brilliantly discussed by Raymond Williams as 'a way of seeing men and women that belongs to the street'.[19] The Reader notices urban types, such as 'a man lounging up Drury Lane, or leaning with his back against a post in Long-acre', but only in passing, uncomprehendingly. But he does not know as much about London as does the Narrator; indeed, the latter's knowledge of the urban environment contrasts revealingly with his failure to know even those whom he closely observes. The Narrator knows Holborn in the early morning, has been inside the Insolvent Debtors' Court and on 'Change, is familiar with the British Museum Reading Room in a way the Reader seems not to be. He knows more about those at whom the Reader has only glanced, knows, for example, who are genuine 'shabby-genteel' and who are simply public-house entertainers. The Narrator has even, on occasion, employed one of the breed and had brief glimpses of the way they live. And when the Narrator writes of 'a very poor man, "who has seen better days", as the phrase goes', the inverted commas and the final clause both suggest that the Narrator is far more conversant with city slang, even of this mild variety, than is his Reader.

The Reader, then, is a specific urban type. As the Narrator suggests, the Reader might be a philosopher or a political economist, though that is unlikely even though he is a man with sufficient means to pursue a retiring and cultured life. He has read Scott, is conversant with folios, is addressed in dignified language that presupposes the educated response. Very likely he has a tender heart: he is appealed to by the Narrator on behalf of poor people. He is, that is to say, essentially bourgeois. His world is safely distanced from that of the 'shabby-genteel' and from that of the Narrator. The latter's, as has been seen, is sufficiently removed from the shabby-genteel to make him uncertain about many of its aspects. The textual presence of the Narrator, Reader, and the 'shabby-genteel' person, in their distinct and differing characterisations, dramatises this short sketch's basic theme of social separation. The Narrator has only limited knowledge of what goes on further down the scale. His attempts to explore only emphasise his uncertainty. The Reader, on the other hand, is firmly visualised, socially placed and understood. His world is above and beyond that of the Narrator. The latter reports to his Reader like a missionary from a still-baffling foreign land. This visualising of Victorian society in terms of separated strata points to Dickens's profound pessimism and to the great social novels of his maturity. The structure of *Our Mutual Friend*, for example, though stressing sad connections, is similarly concerned to exhibit, in all its profound complexity, the tragic fragmentation of Victorian society.

(iii) Character and Ideas: Simon Tuggs in 'The Tuggses at Ramsgate'[20]

'The Tuggses at Ramsgate' is in much lighter vein than either 'A Parliamentary Sketch' or 'Shabby-Genteel People'. The well-known story of members of a grocer's family from the Surrey side of the Thames who inherit £20 000, give up their business and, whilst on holiday at Ramsgate, are deceived by confidence-tricksters who play on son Simon's romantic susceptibilities, is one of the most interesting and successful of Dickens's early pieces of fiction. Through Simon Tuggs's romantic feelings and self-indulgence Dickens mocks the snobbishness and gullibility of the socially aspiring *nouveau riche*. The basic structures of Simon's characterisation enact and demonstrate such themes, and provide an interesting early example of a character functioning as the vehicle for the writer's ideas.

The Tuggses are plump and amiable – apart from Simon, whose long, thin face and legs, plus his liking for a Hamlet-like black, are evidence 'of a great mind and romantic disposition'. This affecting of romanticism is basic to his character and is emphasised in the very first paragraph.

The first scene of the Sketch shows Simon's character in action. A lawyer arrives at the grocer's shop with the welcome but unexpected news that Mr Tuggs senior had been left twenty thousand pounds. Even before this is communicated, as the lawyer informs Joseph Tubbs that 'we have been successful',

> Mr Simon Tuggs rose from the tub of weekly Dorset, opened his eyes very wide, gasped for breath, made a figure of eight in the air with his pen, and finally fell into the arms of his anxious mother, and fainted away without the slightest ostensible cause or pretence.

In this opening sequence is the fundamental pattern of the characterisation: Simon reacts to a new situation with extreme and inappropriate behaviour, in this instance romantic gesturing that expresses a fundamental romantic egotism.

The Tuggses are now rich and Simon responds by changing his name to 'Cymon', an ambiguous move given the unchanged pronunciation; no one apart from Cymon and those few who might see his signature can know that anything has changed. Here is a second basic point: the discrepancy between Cymon's view of himself and how others see him. For the latter do not perceive a romantic hero but an easily exploitable grocer's son lately come into money.

The grocery business is given up and venues for holidays considered. Cymon is against Brighton, nervously fearing a carriage accident, following numerous recent reports. The rejection is small but significant in being another example of a concern for self that rebounds upon him: the rejection of Brighton leads to the choice of Ramsgate and so to Cymon's romantic problems. That choice ends the first part of the tale in which susceptible Cymon's basic characteristics have been established.

The second part introduces Captain Waters and his wife Belinda, who meet the Tuggses on the 'City of London Ramsgate steamer'. The Captain quickly discovers Cymon's naive pretensions to being a Nature-lover and discomfits him with questions about foreign travel. A similar sequence follows: the romantic Cymon finds himself staring at the Captain's beautiful young wife only to hear her complain to her husband about similar behaviour from other young men. The Captain simulates fearsome anger and Cymon, though he seems not to have been noticed, nervously and prudently looks elsewhere. In both cases Cymon's expressed romantic egotism is at odds with the real world. His behaviour continues to lack precise appropriateness: a pompous attempt to restrain the Captain from exacting vengeance on the staring young men – '"Do, [be calm] sir," interposed Mr Cymon Tuggs. "They ain't worth your notice."' – exposes the basic vulgarity of his diction, doubly ironic for someone only too ready to correct his father's pronunciation. Again, having eagerly involved himself in conversation with the Captain, Mrs Waters discomforts him by flatteringly comparing him to 'the Marquis Carriwini'. Cymon may be inwardly gratified but is outwardly reduced to extreme embarrassment. Each instance enacts the Sketch's main theme of the relationship between romantic pretension and harsh, because hostile, reality.

At Ramsgate Captain and Mrs Waters take temporary leave of the Tuggses. Cymon feels 'alone in a heartless world'. But, when back in the family circle and away from the worldly-wise, he reestablishes himself as the arbiter of correct social behaviour and, particularly, as a romantic figure. The first evening in their Ramsgate lodgings ends with a jocular reminder from Mr Tuggs to the adoring Cymon that Mrs Waters is a married woman. This jocularity triggers romantic anguish:

> 'Why,' exclaimed Cymon, starting up with an ebullition of fury as unexpected as alarming, 'why am I to be reminded of that blight of my happiness, and ruin of my hopes? Why am I to be taunted with the miseries which are heaped upon my head?' . . . He stalked dramatically to bed. . . .

Extreme affectation is, again, the keynote. Cymon's basic character having thus been reestablished, to restate the theme of romantic aspirations thwarted by a hostile reality, preparations are made for the visit to Pegwell.

Cymon and the ladies travel by donkey. During the journey he begins an engaging conversation with Mrs Waters, to which she responds provocatively, only for his donkey to bolt before pitching its helpless rider through the doorway of the Pegwell Bay hotel. He is rescued by the waiters and joins the luncheon party in the hotel garden; that is followed by games on the lawn and an excursion to the beach that furthers his romance. That evening, at a concert in the Ramsgate library, the relationship continues to progress, as it does for the next six weeks of the same routine. Cymon's experiences on a donkey form the comic centre to the tale's second part. They illustrate, once more, how the romantic aspirations of, here, the would-be cavalier, are thwarted. But the second part does not simply repeat the points already made through Cymon's character in action in the opening sequences. A wider dimension is added: Cymon's discomfiture is no longer simply personal, a result only of faults of character, but also the result of external circumstances, hostile to romance, over which he has no control.

The third and final part of the sketch begins six weeks later. Captain Waters is away but will shortly return; Cymon and Mrs Waters sit alone in the moonlight on the Ramsgate cliffs. Cymon languishes; Mrs Waters expresses regret that 'even this gleam of happiness, innocent as it is . . . is now to be lost for ever!' As he returns Belinda to her lodgings the Captain and a fellow officer are heard. She hides Cymon behind a curtain where he is quickly discovered. Faced with an angry Captain, Cymon faints away. Threats of legal action are bought off by Mr Tuggs for £1500 'and there are not wanting some who affirm that three designing imposters never found more easy dupes'.

The fainting returns us to the tale's beginning, so that we end with Cymon once more trying to escape from harsh reality into romantic self-indulgence. In perceiving this we see also how carefully the tale has been structured: its three parts correspond to the characterisation's three-part development. In part one, Cymon's egotistic sense of self expressed through romantic affectation leads only to discomfiture. His strange name-change shows how mistaken he is in believing that the world will view him as he views himself. In part two, his personal flaws continue to disable his responses and he becomes, additionally, the victim of circumstances, particularly since Captain Waters and wife easily see through his self-projecting. Finally, circumstances overwhelm him as he is wholly duped by the three confidence-tricksters. From his first appearance in the text as a self-professed romantic to his recovery from his final fainting-fit, Cymon is incapable of learning from experience, as we see from the fact that each incident involving him has the same basic structure: a new situation, an extreme romantic reaction, discomfiture. What changes, of course, is the seriousness of the situations and the hostile pressure of external circumstances. The latter development is, thus, counterpointed against the series of repetitions.

The effect, despite the comedy, is, as so often in Dickens, ultimately serious and pessimistic. Cymon's imaginative flights and his romantic longing are not wholly to be deplored as reactions to the narrow world of the suburban grocer's shop. He may appear ridiculous but, as Charles Lamb once wrote of Malvolio, that ridiculousness is on a scale sufficient to be taken seriously, to have 'a kind of tragic interest'.[21] For Cymon's inability to escape from posturing into successful action, from affectation into a sincere engagement with a wider, deeper, emotional world, is a bleak assertion of the persisting power of his upbringing. In this, if in nothing else, he is an unexpected precursor of Arthur Clennam, and 'The Tuggses at Ramsgate' is a surprisingly early instance in miniature of the later dominant theme, in *Little Dorrit* and else-where, of the power of the personal past. In both early work and mature masterpiece this idea and the problems of personal dis-satisfaction and romantic longing common to both Cymon and Clennam, are clearly conveyed through the characterisation's structuring.

(iv) Character and Structure: Beadles in 'Our Parish'[22]

Seven chapters of *Sketches By Boz* explore 'Our Parish'. The approach is character-based, focusing on various parish officials and eccentrics as they are involved in parish elections, charitable societies, feuds with neighbours, and humanitarian gestures, or are simply down on their luck. The sequence begins with the Beadle, who dominates the opening pages. Chapter 2, almost wholly concerned with very different characters, begins with a reminder of that opening: 'We commenced our last chapter with the beadle of our parish, because we are deeply sensible of the importance and dignity of his office.' A further reminder comes, indirectly, at the chapter's end, in a reference to the 'half-pay captain's' constant opposition to 'the constituted authorities of the parish'. Chapter 4 is 'The Election for Beadle'; Chapter 5 is about the new one. The main subject of the penultimate chapter is 'The Ladies' Societies' and the new Beadle returns to the text when he appears before one and later talks about their procedures. He is not seen again.

The Beadle, then, is a point of reference throughout a sequence that ranges widely over members of the parish and across the tonal range. From the first he is a distinct textual presence, entering the text via the Narrator's heavily ironical account of the fate of a 'poor man, with small earnings, and a large family' who slides into irretrievable ruin. But, insists the Narrator, he can apply to his parish with its 'Excellent institutions, and gentle, kind-hearted men', the latter including Simmons, the parish Beadle. Simmons is given textual life through a few carefully selected details. Of his appearance little can be learned: he is dignified and pompously self-important, with 'a glare of the eye peculiar to beadles' and wearing a 'lace-trimmed ... state coat and cocked-hat, with a large-headed staff for show in his left hand, and a small cane for use in his right'. These are generalisations from which the individual hardly emerges. Neither does he as a result of the Cruik-shank illustration, 'The Parish Engine', which, in any case, did not appear until the Chapman and Hall edition in parts of 1837–9. For Cruikshank is not wholly faithful to the text – the Beadle has no staff and his coat and hat no lace trim – so that the picture blurs the text rather than enhances it. Simmons is almost wholly characterised through his actions on behalf of the parish authorities; we are allowed no glimpse of his private life or past history. He helps explain and administer the Poor Law regulations as interpreted by the parish authorities, checks on hard-luck stories, brings in the distressed or the unruly, and gives evidence in court. On Sundays he ensures the church attendance and good behaviour of the children in the parish's care, often taking a sadistic delight in using his cane to enforce order. Generally he is an efficient bully but, when in charge of the parish fire-engine, an incompetent fire-chief more concerned with rewards than with dousing flames.

Simmons, then, is the deindividualised agent of harsh parish authority, a negative standard in relation to whom the other officials and parishioners can be judged. This is clearly seen in Chapter 1 when the Narrator deals with other parish figures. The vestry clerk, though more briefly described, is given far more humanising detail through references to his 'pudgy' figure, ostentatious watch-chain, crumpled gloves and red book. The master of the workhouse is also brought to life through detail. He is a 'small tyrant . . . bullying to his inferiors, cringing to his superiors', who 'eyes you, as you pass his parlour window, as if he wished you were a pauper, just to give you a specimen of his power', a more vivid and cutting notion than a generalised reference to the Beadle's glaring eye. The 'Pauper Schoolmaster' is the product of an unfortunate past, recounted in detail, having come down in the world through bad luck and personal weakness. He is now old, 'meek, uncomplaining, and zealous', a broken man.

In relation to the Beadle's faceless and unchanging authority these other parish officials, whatever their personal qualities, emerge as individuals with foibles and varying pasts. Together they say much about the nature of public office and its ability to dehumanise the holder. Importantly, we grasp this through the contrast, established early in the sequence, between the Beadle and the rest. To put this another way, the Beadle's textual presence generates a pattern of comparisons and contrasts that structures and so unifies all seven chapters.

Chapter 2, 'The Curate. The Old Lady. The Half-Pay Captain', which, after the opening reminder of the Beadle, reaches into areas of parish affairs seemingly remote from beadledom, continues the same pattern, its reader able, constantly, to relate back to the first chapter. The Curate is young and handsome. He breaks hearts, and female rivalry makes him immensely popular. The arrival of another clergyman, not handsome but expressively romantic, 'a pale, thin, cadaverous man, with large black eyes, and long straggling black hair', demonstrates 'the inconstancy of public opinion': the Curate's congregation 'migrated one by one' to the new man's chapel-of-ease. The widowed Old Lady is surrounded by mementos of the past. She is pious, sociable and sincerely philanthropic. She lives quietly and calmly through her last years with 'everything to hope, and nothing to fear'. That quietness and calm is only disturbed by the Half-Pay Officer who lives next door. For he is 'bluff and unceremonious', demanding glasses of ale, and damaging the Old Lady's possessions through well-meaning but incompetent attempts to repair and renovate them. 'But all this is nothing to his seditious conduct in public life'. The Half-Pay Captain is an indefatigable attender of parish meetings and a thorn in the flesh of all constituted authorities. Yet, 'he is a charitable, open-hearted old fellow at bottom'.

As we read Chapter 2 with the Beadle in mind our sense of reprehensible authority is strongly reinforced. For Chapter 2 describes three worlds dominated by romantic, nostalgic, and anti-authoritarian feelings that are full of energy and, at times, creative life. The chapter is also about intrusions: clergymen into the parish, female parishioners into the clergymen's lives, the Old Lady into the lives of her pensioners, the Half-Pay Captain into that of the Old Lady. To be motivated by strong and attractive feelings, to seek to establish human relationships with figures of authority, to try to help, to refuse simply to accept what parish officials say and do, is to be very different from the Beadle and all he stands for. Chapter 2 points to areas of human concern and interaction not dreamt of in Beadle Simmons's philosophy.

Chapter 3 is 'The Four Sisters', a domestic vignette about the Miss Willises who 'seemed to have no separate existence, but to have made up their minds just to winter through life together'. The sisters call on others and attend church. One – it is uncertain which – marries a Mr Robinson and has a child. But little really *happens*; Chapter 3 is a textual backwater in which the characters behave as if in a fairy-tale, the dreamy, unreal atmosphere of which is sustained by the ritualistic quality of the sisters' lives, and the assumed naivety of the Narrator's response to even the most obvious occurrences. The episode is assimilated into the overall structure of the 'Our Parish' sequence through our apprehension of the difference between it and the world of philanthropic women and energetic half-pay captains, and its absolute contrast to the bustling and harassing action of the Beadle's authoritarian domain.

The idyll is abruptly destroyed by Chapter 4, 'The Election for Beadle', which sustains the structure and develops the theme. The death of Simmons gives rise to the election contested by Spruggins, 'a little thin man, in rusty black, with a long pale face, and a countenance expressive of care and fatigue...' and Bung, who wears 'a cast-off coat of the captain's – a blue coat with bright buttons' and has 'a serenity' in his 'open countenance'. The election decides whether the parish authorities 'should impose a vestry-elected beadle on the parish, to do their bidding and forward their views, or whether the parishioners, fearlessly asserting their undoubted rights, should elect an independent beadle of their own'. The parishioners' choice is Bung, who wins handsomely. In itself the win marks a shift to a more humane approach to parish affairs, for Bung is a cheerful, unpretentious man with a past, as a broker's man, lighted up with acts of kindness and humane feelings. We learn of these last in Chapter 5, during which he tells the story of his life and how much he was affected by the plight of the poor to whom the appearance of the broker's men to distrain property was invariably a prelude to complete financial ruin and family collapse. Bung is thus given a detailed, humanising context, a past, deep feelings, a sense of humour sometimes directed at himself, that was withheld from Simmons. Indeed, the contrast with Simmons is emphasised in 'Mr Bung's Narrative'. His work, like that of Simmons, requires him to enter the houses of the unfortunate. Unlike Simmons he reacts with compassion: he and his colleague allow a distressed lady to retain a gold-mounted miniature of her dead father, he himself gives his dinner to starving children. Bung emerges as the most fully-developed and sympathetic character in the 'Our Parish' sequence. Parish authority itself has discarded the cruel edge that marked Simmons's actions.

Chapter 6, 'The Ladies' Societies', can now be understood in relation to the new positive standard represented by Bung. Private,

middle-class charities, such as 'the ladies' soup distribution society, the ladies' coal distribution society, and the ladies' blanket
distribution society', are seen to be no more than expressions of the
self-importance of their founders, exploit those they are designed
to help in order to further rivalry between ladies with time on their
hands, and are sometimes supported as a means of personal
advancement, as when helping with the 'childbed linen monthly
loan society' can, in the opinion of some mothers, enhance a
daughter's marriage prospects. Mr Bung's occasional appearance
before society committees points up the contrast now much to the
advantage of the Beadle and the parish.

Chapter 7 begins with a short dissertation on door-knockers
followed by accounts of lodgers requiring eviction for unruly
behaviour or who disappear with the landlord's possessions. Such
front-door confrontations, notices to quit, and uneasy personal
relationships, recall the world of Simmons if not that of Bung. But
Chapter 7 provides its main effect and the emotional climax to the
sequence in the closing vignette of a widowed mother and her
dying son. This short account stresses their poverty, their pride
and their desperation. Their only income is what the boy can earn
as a copyist and translator. When that is lost through his illness,
the mother, who cannot bring herself to admit that her son is
dying, tries to scrape a living through needlework and embroidery.
The boy does not last long, hoping, on his deathbed, for a grave in
the countryside from which they so recently came.

Of course, the whole is a sentimental cliché that the young
Dickens cannot resist, but within the structure of 'Our Parish' even
this pathos-laden final scene succeeds in making a serious point.
The reader is now conditioned to making links, turning back to
Simmons and Bung as points of reference. This final scene is
untouched by any parish process or constitutional officer, harsh or
benevolent, so that we end with a clear sense of the limitations of
such power. To use Lamb's phrase once more, the widow and her
son have 'a kind of tragic interest'; faced with such matters of life
and death no beadle can helpfully intervene. Some matters are
beyond the scope of any parish vestry or its most well-meaning
officer. Even the sentimental handling fails to blur the final
implication that here is potentially tragic action unaffected by an
institution. No Beadle's aegis can apply here, no parish authority
can make a scrap of difference to the boy's fate. That we end 'Our
Parish' with a strong sense of the Beadle's ultimate irrelevance

where such matters of life and death are concerned puts constitutional authority in its place. This is a gesture at once optimistic, in that it reveals the limits of institutionalised authority, and pessimistic, in suggesting that there is much that is beyond any help. Certainly the Beadles' characterisations structure the sequence and, in so doing, at least begin to develop a powerful theme.

2
Modifying Summaries

1   THE FAT BOY IN *THE PICKWICK PAPERS*[1]

Two critics of *The Pickwick Papers* make interesting comments on the Fat Boy. For Barbara Hardy he is 'a kind of parody of Pickwick himself' and used by Dickens 'to bring out the proximity of sex and eating';[2] James R. Kincaid notes that, at Dingley Dell, 'in the midst of health and hearty conviviality is this slightly sadistic eating-machine . . . the divorce and separate embodiment of some of the darker aspects of the central impulse towards childhood'.[3] Both interpretations touch on aspects of the book even though, in being, respectively, a kind of comparison and a type of contrast, they disagree fundamentally. More importantly, both regard the single and comparatively minor character as embodying a central theme of the whole novel. To put this another way, both begin to view the character as a microcosm or summary of that whole, huge work.

Joe first appears at the military manoeuvres at Rochester and is prominent during the Pickwickians' first visit to Dingley Dell. He then disappears from the text for twenty chapters, over six serialised instalments, until the Pickwickians return to spend Christmas with Mr Wardle. A further twenty-three chapters, over seven instalments, pass before his final return during Mr Wardle's visit to London. Yet Joe's importance to the novel is more in proportion to his size than to the frequency of his appearances; we can see this not only through an awareness of his various activities but also by grasping the overall pattern of his characterisation.

When first met, at Rochester, Joe is unique, a '"natural curiosity"' (iv, 65); loving sleep more than food, he is lethargy personified, and he has nothing to say. He stands in simple contrast both to the scene, the energetic and noisy 'evolutions of the military' (iv, 66), and to Pickwickians and Wardles similarly engaged in parallel manoeuvres of eating, talking and flirting. Even the Fat Boy's interest in food, seemingly a link with the company, in context underlines his separateness: his amorous eating contrasts with communal flirtatiousness. The contrast is intensified by Mr Wardle's hostility; from him Joe receives continual violence, both verbal and physical: shouts, curses, punches, and blows with a stick. Despite Mr Wardle's pride in Joe's uniqueness, such violence not only keeps him awake and up to the mark, but *in* the Wardles' world. It is inflicted not only (or mainly) because Mr Wardle enjoys it, but also because Joe, awake, is relied upon: he is in charge of the food, the wine, the cutlery, the crockery, and helps Tom with the horses. His efficiency surprises us: he 'proceeded to unpack the hamper, with more expedition than could have been expected from his previous inactivity' (iv, 62).

At Dingley Dell, simple contrast no longer applies as Joe lines up with the old. Physical habits are similar: 'Isabella and Emily had strolled out with Mr Trundle; the deaf old lady had fallen asleep in her chair; the snoring of the fat boy, penetrated in a low and monotonous sound from the distant kitchen' (viii, 109). More important are shared aims: Joe aids Mr Wardle's mother in seeking to thwart Tupman's courtship of Rachael. In supporting the old against the elderly, his role becomes harder to define, a difficulty increased by his more varied practical activities. Thus Joe is still Mr Wardle's 'faithful attendant' (v, 77), relied upon as alarm-clock and retriever during the shooting-expedition, consulted about absentees, and the indefatigable arranger of social furniture. But his basic condition has changed: as the shooting-party gathers he 'did not appear to be more than three parts and a fraction asleep' (vii, 94); during the first arbour scene he is 'awake – wide awake – to what had been going forward' (viii, 114); during the second he speaks loudly and terrifyingly. The change points to his own new authoritativeness and exertion of a kind of power: on his own initiative, 'with peculiar sagacity, and to prevent the possibility of any mistake' (vii, 95), he awakens (ironically, given his own initial somnolence) all three Pickwickians for early-morning shooting. He takes charge when the inebriates return from their cricket dinner at Muggleton: '[Mr Winkle] was borne to his apartment by two young giants under the personal superintendence of the fat boy, to whose protecting care Mr Snodgrass shortly after confided his own person' (viii, 117). He dominates the arbour scenes, disconcerting and deceiving Tupman and Rachael, and frightening the old lady. Joe's attitude in the arbour scenes provides a further complication: though, in one sense, he has geriatric leanings, yet in wanting mildly sadistic pleasure ('I wants to make your flesh creep' (viii,

119)) he differs from the old with their decorous disapproval. In being willing to obtain such pleasures from the old lady's fears he shows himself opposed to the old whilst seemingly on their side.

Our sense of Joe not 'belonging', and of his uneasy relationship with *all* generations, is deepened when Rachael elopes. Young Mr Jingle has taken advantage of him, old Mr Wardle thinks him a bribed deceiver and tries to attack him. The 'natural curiosity' has become a 'villain' (ix, 127) and both young and old rise against him: 'the fat boy was scratched, and pulled, and pushed from the room by all the females congregated therein' (ix, 127). Joe's first appearances in *Pickwick* end in violent expulsion.

In Chapter 28 he returns, reestablished as 'Mr Wardle's favourite page' (xxviii, 413), reliable and appropriately responsible: he takes charge of the Pickwickians' luggage in Muggleton, continues as wine-waiter and as the provider of vital information on the whereabouts of skates and the depth of the frozen pond. He is, once again, generally somnolent, invariably voracious. But this is not to say he has now been restored to a permanent and suitable (and suitably capacious) niche in the novel's world; whereas, during his first appearances, Joe's role as lethargically dominant servant was accompanied by a complicated, uneasy, and, ultimately, disastrous relationship with the old, now, on his return, that role merges into what we later see to be similarly-developing connections with the young. And here we are concerned not with such random and mild vindictiveness as that of Benjamin Allen at breakfast ('he takes a aim vith the shells at young dropsy, who's a settin' down fast asleep, in the chimbley corner' (xxx, 446), even though this incident reinforces our sense of 'the young *versus* Joe', but with Joe's rivalry with Sam Weller.

From the moment they meet, Sam and the Fat Boy are constantly juxtaposed. They are left together at Muggleton to load the luggage-cart, offer contrasting responses to Mr Pickwick's wedding-speech, meet below stairs, unite to sweep snow off the ice and then to slide. At first Joe dominates: as the Pickwickians' luggage is stowed away, 'the fat boy stood quietly by, and seemed to think it a very interesting sort of thing to see Mr Weller working by himself'. Sam buys Joe a drink and then:

> 'Can you drive?' said the fat boy.
> 'I should rayther think so,' replied Sam.
> 'There, then,' said the fat boy, putting the reins in his hand,

and pointing up a lane, 'It's as straight as you can go; you can't miss it.'

With these words, the fat boy laid himself affectionately down by the side of the cod-fish, and placing an oyster-barrel under his head for a pillow, fell asleep instantaneously.

(xxviii, 413–14)

Joe's self-indulgence contrasts unfavourably with Sam's tolerant open-heartedness, a contrast further emphasised by the response to Mr Pickwick's speech at the wedding of Trundle and Bella: Sam is carried away 'in the excitement of his feelings'. Joe is simply sorry for himself, bursts 'forth into stentorian blubberings' (xxviii, 420–21), and has to be removed. But we not only recognise Sam's moral superiority, we also see his clever speech and physical skill counter Joe's dominance. The clever speaking includes the ridiculing of Joe's grotesqueness: Sam calls him '"young twenty stun . . . a prize boy"', '"young dropsy"' well supplied with '"elastic fixtures"' (xxviii, 413) and tells stories that point the penalties of obesity; he makes Joe's flesh creep as Joe did that of the old lady. Physical counters follow, as Sam hauls Joe out of the wedding reception and, even though Joe is surprisingly good on the ice, outdoes the striving boy with a display of fancy-skating that includes the figure '"knocking at the cobbler's door"' (xxx, 452). Joe's efforts to establish himself in Sam's world are as unsuccessful as his previous overtures to the geriatrics and his essential predicament is underlined by Hablot Browne's famous plate of 'Christmas Eve at Mr Wardle's' (xxviii, opp. 426): the company in happily animated groups or couples, except Joe, who sits alone, an isolated muncher ignored by all.

The hammering on Perker's door that marks Joe's return not only recalls Sam's fancy skating and thus the two servants' rivalry, but also suggests Joe's continuing disruptive role. Reappearing only briefly as a reliable sleeper he becomes involved in urban arbour scenes by inadvertently bursting in upon Emily and Snodgrass in the Adelphi hotel-room. But the young lovers are more aggressive and more resourceful than were their elderly counterparts, Rachael and Tupman. Snodgrass's hostility terrifies the boy, and the four schemers, Snodgrass, Emily, Arabella, and Mary, prevent disclosure by drawing Joe into the conspiracy by giving him money and a meal with Mary. Thus, for the first time, Joe ceases to be an outsider; for the first time the opposite sex treats

him with kindness. The effect is devastating: Joe is in league with
the young and seeks with ruthless foolishness to deepen and
confirm the connection. Complicity brings out the worst in him:
his 'cannibal' (liv, 834) advances to Mary, his 'smirking, grinning,
and winking, with redoubled assiduity' (liv, 839) at Emily and
Arabella during dinner are expressions of uncontrolled self-
gratification. He then encounters the desperate Snodgrass, trapped
in Mr Wardle's hotel bedroom as Wardle and company eat in the
next room. Snodgrass begs Joe to find someone to extricate him,
and Joe, asked to be responsibly rather than selfishly loyal, panics.
Joe seeks help from the young, but Mary, his most likely ally, has
left. With difficulty and in the end violently he tries to appeal to old
but sympathetic Mr Pickwick. Mr Wardle thinks him to be
'"drunk"' and '"vicious"' (liv, 841–2) and calls for his expulsion
from the room just as Snodgrass enters in confusion from the
bedroom.

One scene remains. As the penultimate chapter closes Sam
meets Joe in the court of the George and Vulture:

> 'I say,' said Joe, who was unusually loquacious, 'what a pretty
> girl Mary is, isn't she? I am *so* fond of her, I am!'
>   Mr Weller made no verbal remark in reply; but, eyeing the fat
> boy for a moment, quite transfixed at his presumption, led him
> by the collar to the corner, and dismissed him with a harmless
> but ceremonious kick. After which, he walked home, whistling.
>   (lvi, 869–70)

The key word is 'presumption': here, as throughout the novel, the
stress is on Joe's lack of a role acceptable to others. And it is a final
stress; Sam's disposal of his rival, the young dispatching the
younger, is our last sight of the Fat Boy. He is not mentioned again,
even in Dickens's closing summary.

The above account points to the partial accuracy but essential
inadequacy of Hardy's and Kincaid's separate interpretations.
Combined, they illuminate a central function of the characterisation: though Joe is not wholly reprehensible he is, in important
ways, one of the novel's negative standards and one able to offer a
point of reference at once essentially comparative *and* contrasting
in significant respects.

This dual function can be seen in terms of Joe's most distinctive
characteristics, his fatness and his somnolence. The novel is

obsessed with the former and uses it as an indication of human deceptiveness rather than demonstrating a comfortable relationship between size and good nature. Mr Pickwick, Tupman, Mr Weller, and Mr Wardle are fat and virtuous; Doctor Slammer, Doctor Payne, Mrs Sanders, Mrs Weller, and Serjeant Buzfuz, are fat and morally variable; Dodson is 'plump, portly' (xx, 293), and disreputable. But, of all the stout parties, Joe's appearance is the most deceptive, for Joe is the only fat character whose appearance, of well-fed contentment, is wholly at odds with his real nature, which is a surprising efficiency and shrewdness, a slightly sinister, mildly sadistic, but essentially ruthless concern for self-gratification.

The somnolence makes a similar point in a novel much concerned with sleep. The Pickwickians sleep to live: Mr Pickwick bursts 'like another sun from his slumbers' (ii, 7) and, at Dingley Dell, 'like an ardent warrior from his tent-bedstead' (vii, 93); after the cricket dinner Mr Winkle drunkenly insists that he '"won't go to bed"'. Only excess living forces sleep upon them. This is, after all, a novel about awakening to life's realities and then staying awake. On the other hand, Joe mainly lives to sleep, and even when an unusual alertness seems to reverse this role we see that he still contrasts with the Pickwickians and others by awakening to selfish possibilities rather than to the improving effects of experience.

Joe as modifying summary – summarising much of the novel's thematic material whilst also modifying it through contrast – can be further illustrated with reference to three other themes. First, the novel is much preoccupied with relations between servants and masters. Sam Weller and Mr Pickwick illustrate mutual trust and loyalty, a benevolent hierarchy, a continuing, two-way, educative process. Lowten and Perker, Trotter and Jingle, Jackson and Dodson and Fogg, all reveal similar qualities, albeit displayed with less moral exactitude or as versions of villainy; whatever moral judgements are made on their conduct they exist as compatible pairs (Dodson and Fogg being considered together). Joe and Mr Wardle provide the negative and salutary extreme, a relationship based on suspicion, some vindictiveness, and, on the master's part, a satisfying sadism. Such a relationship is more that between a grotesque and its owner than of two human beings.

Second, the novel is full of storytellers who stop the narrative to tell tales or, like Sam Weller and Jingle, to embroider the fantastic

anecdote, or, like H. Walker, Betsy Martin, et al., to offer improb-
able accounts of conversions to temperance, or, like Buzfuz in
court, to fictionalise fact in aid of his clients. This is a novel full of
flesh-creepers and, again, Joe is the extreme example. Whereas,
invariably, given the accompanying harmless desire to make flesh
creep, stories are told to entertain, or to point morals, or to sustain
disguises, or for gain, or, as sometimes with Sam's, as the spon-
taneous expression of inventive high spirits, in Joe's case his tale of
Rachael and Tupman is told simply for self-gratification; his is a
uniquely selfish telling. Further, Joe's tale differs from those of all
other tellers in that it is true and it is not believed. In a novel much
concerned with ways in which appearance overcomes reality (as it
does, for example, in Jingle's early career, in Mr Pickwick's
encounter with Mrs Bardell, in Allen and Sawyer's apothecary's
shop, and, in terms of fictional persuasiveness, in most of the tales
and anecdotes), the fate of Joe's tale is, again, the unique and
cautionary example. It is not only an instance of truth's limited
efficacy but makes the further point that truth divorced from
benevolence of heart takes on the best-known attribute of the
boomerang.

Third, the novel explores the relationship between kindness and
its recipients. Mr Pickwick's generosity of spirit means a moral
education and marriage for Sam Weller, marriage for Mary, redemption for Jingle and Trotter, security for Sam's father, and a
reprieve and a lesson for Mrs Bardell. Such characters are in-
fluenced for good, enabled to live commendable lives and, in some
cases (Jingle's, Trotter's, Mrs Bardell's) are brought through kindness up to a kind of moral scratch. We see also, particularly in the
examples of Jingle, Trotter, and Mrs Bardell, that kindness confers
responsibility on the recipient, insists on the need to live up to the
standards of the gesture. Snodgrass, Emily, Arabella and Mary are
kind to Joe, but the demands this kindness makes upon him,
demands for loyalty and immediate aid, intensify his conceit before
devastating him with panic. Joe's reactions counter any suggestion
that the novel asserts a necessary connection between kindness
and beneficial effects, even though the need for kindness is always
stressed.

In such ways Joe's main activities relate to the rest of the novel.
Much the same could be said in relation to the latter's concern with
violence and the treatment of children. In addition, the whole
pattern of Joe's progress is equally functional. For example, the

novel contains a number of recurring characters, Mr Jingle and Mrs Bardell among them, who appear, disappear, and reappear throughout the narrative. Such recurrences not only help unify this huge, neo-picaresque work but also, in themselves, help express themes: they show the way in which the novel's movement from innocence to experience rejects easy evasions and requires the solving of persistent problems. Jingle and Mrs Bardell, in particular, keep turning up. Mr Pickwick has to come to terms with those who have deceived and exploited him, and redeems, through the strength of his heart's goodness, those who have grasped the errors of their ways, before he gains a final wise happiness. Joe is also a recurring character but his pattern of reappearances is no movement towards repentance and better things; rather, it is a consistent illustration of indulgence and self-regard. Significantly, Mr Pickwick can come to terms with Jingle and Mrs Bardell but Sam Weller can only dismiss with a kick the incorrigible boy.

The novel's progression from innocence to an experienced happiness involves, for the main developing characters, the discovery of appropriate roles and fitting conduct. That is, they cast aside feigned or unconsciously wrong behaviour and find ways of living that seem truer to their essentially commendable natures. For example, Tupman ceases to act the lover and becomes a likeable confirmed bachelor; Winkle forgets his sporting charlatanry to settle down as a 'civilized christian' (lvii, 875), married and back on good terms with his father; Jingle and Trotter 'go straight'; Mrs Bardell, after her materialistic affectations, now behaves herself. Several of the lesser figures, including Allen and Sawyer and the falsely fierce Dowler, make the same transition. So, preeminently, does Mr Pickwick, in 'metamorphosing from pompous amateur scientist to humble student, from gullible reporter to effective diplomat, from irascible and impetuous traveller to a more reflective and deliberate suburban gentleman.'[4] Very occasionally, as with Snodgrass and his continued poeticising, we discover a character really is what he always has appeared to be; generally, the main characters not only become true to themselves but, in so becoming, achieve a status that is exemplary either morally, as is that of Jingle and Trotter, and Mr Winkle and his father, or (/and) socially, as witness Mrs Bardell's place-keeping, Tupman's decorum, and the perfect master/man bond between Mr Pickwick and Sam Weller.

Further, in its concern with fitting conduct the novel includes an interest in that befitting a character's age: in one of the key scenes Tupman dresses as a bandit for Mrs Leo Hunter's fancy-dress breakfast, only to be criticised by Mr Pickwick, as '"too old"' and '"too fat"' (xv, 217) for such a costume. For a careful distinction is made between a Mr Pickwick who, though elderly, finds proper expression of talents and energies in curious travel and an abiding concern for '"the happiness of young people"' (lvii, 871), and a Tupman who affects youthful behaviour and so is ridiculed by 'being ignominiously compared to a dismounted Bacchus' (ii, 22), as a youth only in the eyes of elderly spinsters, and by being called 'a young fellow' (xviii, 265) by a satirical Mr Wardle. The comic attack on the pretensions of the elderly is mainly directed at Tupman but is given added thematic importance by being extended to include a Rachael flirtatious even '"at her time of life"' (viii, 120), Angelo Cyrus Bantam, Esquire, M.C. at Bath, described as 'a charming young man of not much more than fifty' (xxxv, 542), and the spitefully false Bath world in which all pretend that '"nobody's fat or old"' (xxxv, 548), this last being a general exemplification of the wish-fulfilment shown by Tupman-as-bandit.

This stress on Tupman, for much of the novel a kind of Fat Boy, brings us back to the ubiquitous Joe, for he, too, relates to the work's concern with role-finding and fitting conduct. He plays various roles and has the chance to exhibit exemplary action: Joe is good servant and scapegoat and wielder of some authority and power *and*, because of Snodgrass's predicament, has at least the opportunity to emerge as responsible and loyal. Further, Joe takes part in various relationships with various age-groups: he joins the old against the elderly and the young against the old; he seeks to dominate the old and take advantage of the young; he is deceived by the young and threatened by the old; the whole company rises to expel him and Sam Weller finally dismisses him.

Once again the resemblance to the novel's other characters suggested by such shared concerns is accompanied by our sense of Joe's uniqueness. He is an uneasily subservient servant, a victimised scapegoat, a vulnerable power-wielder. A suitable role always escapes him. When he is responsible he is not believed and his loyalty is undermined by fear, so that of all the novel's role-seekers Joe alone fails to become truly exemplary. And he cannot sustain conduct proper to his own age or acceptable to any generation. Joe is unique in failing to find a way of behaving that will allow him permanent escape from his essential isolation, from his recurring state of rejection. Even Dodson has his Fogg, Mrs Bardell her Mrs Sanders, the Reverend Stiggins his young ladies and Mrs Weller. The Fat Boy has no one and, even though his isolation is sometimes forced upon him, all too often it seems not to be wholly undesirable because linked to his particular kind of self-gratification. For the villains, whether crooked lawyers, aggrieved landlady, tipsy minister, or Jingle and Trotter, have in common a concern for audience, a public conceit, a liking to be thought 'the sharpest of the sharp' (lvii, 876), a desire for conduct to be approved of and supported by friends, a penchant for snook-cocking during the abduction of a spinster with prospects. But the Fat Boy has a monstrous solipsism; invariably he cares for no one's opinion and lives within his own selfishness.

Garrett Stewart writes of the relationship of the part to the whole of a Dickens novel: 'points of focal concentration in Dickens are acts of *symbolic synecdoche*, the part standing for and even amplifying the whole. To locate these moments in a given novel is often to take its deepest pulse, to find not only clues to meaning, but compacted versions of it. [Such] nerve centres of Dickens's prose frequently collapse into a single disclosure the largest themes of their books'.[5] Stewart is much concerned with the synecdoche-like roles of dialogue and description but characters and characterisations certainly have a similar function. Joe summarises the novel's important thematic material but, in offering variations upon it, demonstrates that the part-to-whole relationship can be more complex than Stewart indicates. Certainly a further complexity stems from Joe's existence as a seriously humorous character who supports our notion of *The Pickwick Papers* as a novel in which misunderstanding is the main cause of laughter. For, again, Joe is a special case: in *always* misunderstanding and being *completely* misunderstood he remains apart as a clearly-defined negative standard. The language through which he is created, in the main a satirically elevated and circumlocutionary style, preserves him as a distanced humorous object and reinforces our sense of his isolation. His relationship to the novel becomes essentially paradoxical, the isolated figure as an important unifying and organising force, as a modifying summary.

2   YOUNG BAILEY IN *MARTIN CHUZZLEWIT*[6]

In Chapter 8 of the very different and more ambitious *Martin Chuzzlewit* we meet Young Bailey. Pecksniff and his two daughters, Charity and Mercy, begin a visit to London by seeking lodgings at the 'Commercial Boarding-House', near the Monument, kept by Pecksniff's acquaintance, Mrs Todgers. They are admitted by the 'boots', the young boy named Bailey. He is confident and loquacious beyond his years, so much so that when he whistles and fools whilst laying the fire in the Pecksniffs' room an irritated Mrs Todgers boxes his ears. The boy helps show Charity and Mercy over the boarding-house. The oppressive urban view from the roof and the noise that rises from the busy streets make the two girls so bewildered and giddy that, they tell Mrs Todgers, they were in danger of throwing themselves off. The 'youthful porter' (ix, 132), however, walks daringly on the parapet.

Until the Pecksniffs leave for home, Bailey has a developing relationship with the two sisters. He entertains them with horse-play. As the boarding-house kitchens prepare the Sunday dinner at which Pecksniff and daughters are guests of honour he keeps the latter up-to-date about the food they can expect. Towards the end of their stay it is he who admits Jonas Chuzzlewit to see Charity and, verbally and through facetious miming, ridicules Jonas's romantic intentions so that Charity 'could not help smiling. . . . There was always some ground of probability and likelihood mingled with his absurd behaviour' (xi, 171). He takes a constant and fiendish delight in the sisters' quarrelling.

As they prepare to leave, Bailey never loses a chance to mock their pretensions: he offers his own version of the previous night's serenading of the sisters by the tipsy guests, by howling like a dog. Nonetheless he seems to regret their departure and tells them he is thinking of leaving Todgers's, perhaps for the army. They tip him handsomely, which makes him treat the Pecksniffs' luggage with damaging enthusiasm.

All the while he has to carry out his duties for Mrs Todgers. When he tries to play in the street with local lads he is 'pursued and brought back by the hair of his head, or the lobe of his ear' (ix, 143); she keeps him in line with frequent threats and a liking for the 'manual compliment' (ix, 144). Despite this he is a boy 'whom nothing disconcerted or put out of his way' (ix, 147). His manner is always engagingly careless of social form: at the Sunday dinner-party he appears in a suit of cast-offs far too big for him and acts so much more like a guest than a servant that Gander, one of the commercials, even proposes his health in a 'convulsing speech' (ix, 149).

The novel's action moves from Todgers's, and Bailey does not return to the text until Chapter 26, in a chance encounter with an old acquaintance, Poll Sweedlepipe, the bird-seller and barber. He now works for Tigg Montague in London's west-end, and smart livery has replaced the cast-offs. He remains irrepressibly confident, with a marvellous patronising manner, acting the part of a flashy, rakish, horsey man-about-town which, given his size and age – he is hardly into his 'teens – is 'in defiance of all natural laws' (xxvi, 420). Poll is overwhelmed; even Mrs Gamp is impressed, to such an extent that Bailey begins to believe she has taken a fancy to him.

He has become Tigg's 'tiger', the groom who accompanies his master's carriage to look after the horses. The boy also answers Tigg's door, admits guests, and sometimes drives them home. He admires Tigg, but is treated no better than at Todgers's. In Chapter 28 Jonas Chuzzlewit calls on Tigg at the start of their fateful association. Bailey admits him and then has to wait up until 3 a.m. to drive the drunken Jonas back home to his wife Mercy. For the first time he is much affected by what he witnesses: Mercy's deep despair and Jonas's brutal treatment of her. Though he continues to play his old precocious role in front of Poll and still impresses Mrs Gamp with flattering repartee, knowledge of Mercy's predicament and Jonas's evil nature now troubles him sufficiently to curb his tongue when Mrs Gamp questions him about Mercy's life with her husband.

At the end of Chapter 41 Tigg roughly insists, despite Jonas's objections, that Bailey will accompany them on their overnight carriage-ride to Salisbury to entice Pecksniff to invest in the fraudulent Anglo-Bengalee Disinterested Loan and Life Assurance Company. The boy sits in the rumble, the open seat at the rear of the carriage, and is drenched by persistent heavy rain. Tigg is concerned; Jonas is not and refuses to allow 'damp boys' (xlii, 644) inside. Similarly, when the carriage crashes only Tigg thinks of Bailey. He is found, unconscious, in a field and taken to Salisbury, seemingly near death. Poll believes he *is* dead and is greatly upset, then overcome with delight when Bailey reappears – bandaged, giddy, but still alive – to claim centre-stage in the great scene at the close of Chapter 52 in which Old Martin punishes Pecksniff and dismisses Mrs Gamp. The latter is escorted from the text by Poll and by a Bailey still confused by the effects of the crash.

Even such a brief summary illustrates Young Bailey's paradoxical function in the novel. He is a minor character in that he appears infrequently, is not essential to the plot and, in a work much concerned with manipulation, has no power. Yet he has a starring role in that important late scene. As Pratt comments: 'It is rather as if *Dombey and Son* ended with Mr. Toots in center stage'.[7] Dickens wants us to remember Young Bailey, and we do.

Certainly we need to, though how he should be remembered has been a matter for disagreement. Marcus and Stewart, to take two well-known examples, consider Bailey to be, respectively, almost wholly, and wholly extraneous to their influential interpretations of *Martin Chuzzlewit*.[8] Others are too overwhelmed – presumably by the young man's personality – to offer much more than appreciative impressionism. Thus Dyson includes him in a group of characters about whom a 'radiance ... plays',[9] and Kincaid asserts, more lyrically than helpfully, that Bailey and Poll give to the novel 'the pure exuberance and soaring joy it must have'.[10] A rare critical note is sounded by Barbara Hardy, who uses Bailey as an example of Dickens's failure to create consistent characters: 'the comic boy of Todgers ... bears no resemblance to the pathetic boy who is merely a silent dummy used to arouse pity and fear'.[11] But a few, perceiving that the character participates in central themes, treat Bailey more thoughtfully and precisely. Miller[11a] links Bailey to the work's concern with changing identity, Daleski[11b] to the importance of appearances. Barickman, in a suggestive interpretation of *Chuzzlewit* as a study of 'the systematic corruption of the family', stresses the importance of Bailey's relationship with Poll: it is one of several that 'seem to be groping toward some substitute relationship that is less sterile and emotionally crippling than erotic pairings'.[12]

The fullest treatment of the character comes from the appropriately named Branwen Bailey Pratt, who studies him in relation to the theme of freedom: Bailey, argues Pratt, shows 'the possibility of individual freedom'. In *Martin Chuzzlewit* he is unique in that his *joie de vivre*, his mythic suggestiveness – such as his links with Pan and Puck – are reminders of life's basic and unrestrained impulses. Bailey is 'the wise fool', the 'free man as fool', who acts out the reader's suppressed desire for liberty.[13] Though Pratt's is the fullest, Furbank's is, perhaps, the most perceptive and suggestive treatment of the character. He insists on its complexity and centrality: Bailey stands not only for imaginative force and power (Pratt's freedom) but also for the dangers of unrestrained fantasising. Furbank follows Miller in regarding Bailey as important to the novel's major theme of personal identity and the pressures upon it. He goes further than Miller in stressing Bailey's structural functions: 'So many links are forged and cross-lights thrown by this one incidental comic character, and so subtly does Dickens use him to direct our sympathies, that you can sense the whole novel flowing through him'.[14]

Generally, critics who accept Bailey's importance in the novel explore one central character-function: the extent to which he is a positive counter to the novel's thematic thrusts. Only Furbank is much concerned with Bailey's structural importance and, in an introduction to an edition, that concern is necessarily perfunctory. Not even Furbank explores, in relation to Young Bailey, the full implications of Dickens's own feeling, expressed in his preface to the first edition of *Martin Chuzzlewit*, that the nature of his fiction was changing: 'I have endeavoured in the progress of this Tale, to resist the temptation of the current Monthly Number, and to keep a steadier eye upon the general purpose and design. With this object in view, I have put a strong constraint upon myself from time to time, in many places' (p. lxix). It could be argued from the evidence of the Fat Boy in Dickens's first novel that the novelist's eye had always been fairly steady and that his remark is a case of belated realisation of what he had long been doing. Certainly the distinct relationship between part and whole obtaining in all Dickens's novels extends the applicability of Marcus's observation that

> in any one of Dickens's mature novels scarcely a page goes by which does not in some way further the central course of development; no detail is too small or by-the-way for it not to be discovered as elaborating some larger organic theme.[15]

Both comments – Dickens's as well as Marcus's – remind us that Bailey has never received adequate detailed attention.

This last can first be given to his name: readers of *Martin Chuzzlewit* remember him as 'Bailey' or 'Young Bailey'. In Chapters 8 and 9 he is nameless and referred to as 'a small boy', 'the boy', 'the youth', and, as has been noted, 'the youthful porter' (viii, 125; ix, 132); only in Chapter 9 is a name offered and that tentatively: 'Benjamin was supposed to be the real name of this young retainer.' If, indeed, this had once been the case it had long since been replaced by satirical tags, some of which associate him with unfortunate or delinquent apprentices: 'Uncle Ben . . . Uncle . . . Barnwell . . . Mr Pitt, Young Brownrigg', and the like. At the period of which we write, 'he was generally known among the gentlemen as Bailey junior; a name bestowed upon him in contradistinction, perhaps, to Old Bailey' (ix, 144–5).

The terms, as distinct from names, applied to the boy in Chapter 8 and never wholly relinquished thereafter (see, for example, the 'young retainer' description in Chapter 9) control the reader's changing impressions of a person whose manner makes his age problematic. That is to say, the absence of a certain name and some uncertainty about age force the reader to respond, as it were, to 'pure' personality that, with all its absurdity, is attractive and compelling, particularly during the early textual appearances. This initial response is then undermined by the eventual naming. For Dickens insists on the link with 'Old Bailey' and on the latter's significance. As young Martin in America retorts to Elijah Pogram:

> 'Are bloody duels, brutal combats, savage assaults, shootings down and stabbings in the street, your Institutions! Why, I shall hear next, that Dishonor and Fraud are among the Institutions of the great republic! . . . But the greater part of these things are one Institution with us, and we call it by the generic term of Old Bailey!' (xxxiv, 534)

Mrs Todgers believes the boy to be well on his way there for to her he is a 'vicious boy', the 'most dreadful child . . . I ever had to deal with. . . . I'm afraid nothing but hanging will ever do him any good' (ix, 144). Her response is, of course, an exaggerated one, but the ever-present association of 'Bailey junior' with the Old Bailey and all it represents changes the reader's perception of him by introducing the possibility of viciousness. *Martin Chuzzlewit* is much concerned with this last quality and the way it lurks behind deceptive façades, such as Pecksniff's beguiling inventiveness, or Mrs Gamp's anecdotal liveliness and professions of public concern. Indeed, such qualities come to be seen as reflections of incipient vice. Similarly, Dickens's presentation of Bailey links compelling surface qualities and latent moral turpitude. The minor characterisation embodies a major theme.

Before being named he is seen in action answering Todgers's front door to Pecksniff and his daughters. In this way his import-ance is quickly established for, in 'Town and Todgers's', the subject to which Chapters 8 and 9 are mainly devoted, doors are an important motif. They are symbols of deception, as Dickens's irony acknowledges in his description of the accommodation hastily arranged for Pecksniff's daughters: 'The sleeping apartment de-signed for the young ladies was approached from this chamber by a mightily convenient little door, which would only open when fallen against by a strong person' (viii, 128). Again, in the narrow streets around the boarding house

> there lingered, here and there, an ancient doorway of carved oak, from which, of old, the sounds of revelry and feasting often came; but now these mansions, only used for storehouses, were dark and dull, and, being filled with wool, and cotton, and the like . . . had an air of palpable deadness about them.

And

> the grand mystery of Todgers's was the cellarage, approachable only by a little back-door and a rusty grating . . . and was reported to be full of wealth . . . whether in silver, brass, or gold, or butts of wine, or casks of gunpowder.
>
> (ix, 130–31)

In both extracts the point is the same: visitors to Todgers's – it is a cliché of Dickens criticism – are overwhelmed by the seemingly animate hostile confusion of the urban world partly generated by the discrepancy between appearance and reality.

The use of door symbolism to dramatise this discrepancy in the Todgers's sequence is only one instance of a recurring pattern of such symbolism throughout the novel. As early as Chapter 2, for example, Pecksniff is knocked flat by his front door swinging in the wind – a victory, it can be remarked in passing, of natural force over affectation that anticipates the novel's conclusion – and this early incident is a comic yet serious and significant pointer to the misleading nature of the world. Seven chapters later is a more substantial and subtle example: the Pecksniffs and Mrs Todgers visit Ruth Pinch in her employer's mansion at Camberwell. The house is described as 'so big and fierce that its mere outside, like the outside of a giant's castle, struck terror into vulgar minds and made bold persons quail', thus presenting Ruth as a prisoner in a fairy-tale. The visitors negotiate the 'ceremonies' of entrance at the 'great hall-door' tended by a 'great footman' (ix, 135), but rather than bringing comfort or release for the prisoner, they compound her unhappiness by allying themselves with her gaoler-like employers. Much of the effect of this sequence is achieved through the fairy-tale elements disappointing the reader's expectations. Certainly the door is, once again, an instrument of deception.

At the close of Chapter 20 'a loud knocking was heard at the hall-door' (xx, 340) of Pecksniff's house. It announces the arrival of Old Martin at a time when Jonas, the nephew he detests, is visiting and so throws Pecksniff into a panic. At the beginning of Chapter 21 Dickens uses that noise to effect a deliberately clumsy and non-sequential humorous shift to young Martin Chuzzlewit and Mark Tapley's American progress. Chapter 21 is the first of three chapters set in America during which Old Martin's arrival is held in Sterne-like suspense until Chapter 24 and Jonas's comment that the knocking was '"loud enough to wake the ... Seven Sleepers"' (xxiv, 383). The panic seems unnecessary, for Old Martin is strangely subdued and comparatively easy to deal with. But, as we learn later, his appearance at Pecksniff's front door begins the masquerade that has such dire consequences for the man he visits. Here again Pecksniff's expectations, and the reader's on a first reading, are mistaken. The knocking on the door begins another sequence demonstrating the characters' difficulty in understanding their world.

This works both ways; that is, the unexpected is not always a hostile force. Thus, though Tom Pinch knocks timidly on John Westlock's door and is uncertain about entering, his unexpected appearance delights his friend. Again, like Pecksniff and Mrs Todgers, he negotiates both door and door-keeper to surprise Ruth in her prison; unlike them, and even more surprisingly, he rescues her from her employer's oppression. Further, John Westlock reports to Tom: 'As I was sitting at breakfast this morning, there comes a knock at my door' (xxxix, 605). It is the strange Mr Fips who enters to astound Westlock with a lucrative proposition for Tom. Mr Fips works in Austin Friars, behind 'a little blear-eyed glass door' (xxxix, 609) against which all visitors trip and so warn

him of their presence. That unprepossessing door is itself deceptive in being, for Tom, the first gateway to comparative prosperity.
The second is, of course, the shabby, paint-smeared, and hard-to-
open door to Tom's office that becomes the entrance to delight:
'[Tom] rubbed his hands in the pleasant anticipation of a task so
congenial to his taste' (xxxix, 612) as that of shelving and catalo-
guing the mounds of books heaped within the room.

In *Martin Chuzzlewit* doors invariably open upon or admit the
unexpected. They acquire histories or – with knocks that wake the
dead, or with Seven Sleepers behind them – take on a mythical
resonance. Such recurring symbolism helps fuel the power of two
crucial scenes. The first follows the carriage crash that almost kills
Bailey. Tigg lies in his hotel bed and suspects that Jonas had tried
to kill him in the aftermath of the crash. This suspicion and the
effect on his mind of the shock of the crash make him obsessed
with a strange door in his room:

> His fears or evil conscience reproduced this door in all his
> dreams. He dreamed that a dreadful secret was connected with
> it: a secret which he knew, and yet did not know. . . . Incoherent-
> ly entwined with this dream was another, which represented it
> as the hiding-place of an enemy, a shadow, a phantom; and
> made it the business of his life to keep the terrible creature closed
> up, and prevent it from forcing its way in upon him.

The dream is of Jonas pursuing him. When a frightened Tigg
awakes the next morning he finds 'Jonas standing at his bedside
watching him' (xlii, 651).

The second is after Jonas has murdered Tigg. On his way home
he cannot stop thinking of 'the closed-up room' to which he is
returning,

> the possibility of their knocking on the door . . . of their bursting
> it open; of their finding the room empty; of their fastening the
> door into the court, and rendering it impossible for him to get
> into the house without showing himself in the garb he wore. . . .

In his head, as he travels back, he hears the knocking 'like a
warning echo of the dread reality he had conjured up. As he could
not sit and hear it, he paid for his beer and walked on again.' When
he reaches home he locks the door and waits, fearfully, for 'that

knocking that should bring the news' (xlvii, 723–5).

In Chapter 31 the Narrator apostrophises on the need to prevent crime rather than to punish it: men had a 'duty to discharge in barring up the hundred open gates that wooed him to the felon's dock, and throwing but ajar the portals to a decent life!' (xxxi, 495). Tigg and Jonas fail in the first and are incapable of the second.

In *Martin Chuzzlewit*, then, doors, knocks and entrances contribute centrally to the novel's sense of the unexpected, confusing and flickering discrepancy between appearance and reality. To Tigg and Jonas such objects, sounds and appearances come to represent the fragile façade behind which they try to shelter from the force of conscience and from society's retribution. Certainly, after murdering Tigg, Jonas's conscience racks and undermines him. As he sits in the country ale-house waiting for the coach back to London, Jonas's nervous speech, sudden questions and horror of a knocking somewhere outside the inn that reverberates through his mind as he hurries from his beer to walk on down the country road, remind us that in the subtext of this novel are many reminders of *Macbeth*, the play that haunts so many of Dickens's texts. It is certainly present in Dickens's imaginative reconstruction of Jonas's thoughts following the murder.

The 'knocking' motif reminds us of Macbeth's Porter and so brings us back to Bailey. As 'the youthful porter' (viii, 128) he exists in a complex relationship to his Shakespearian counterpart. Macbeth's Porter admits Lennox and Macduff into the evil castle; their entry, we learn, begins the slow fight-back of an outside world that remains essentially good. Bailey, when at Todgers's, is responsible for admitting Pecksniff and his daughters; left to herself, Mrs Todgers, her house full, would simply not have answered the door. As Tigg's doorman, he admits Jonas to see Mercy Pecksniff, encourages him and takes a fiendish delight in the relationship. In each case he furthers the fates of those admitted: Todgers's feeds Pecksniff's self-esteem and so hastens his downfall, whilst the visit affects for the worse the daughters' amatory lives; Mercy, as Mrs Jonas Chuzzlewit, is reduced and abused. As for Tigg: the results of Bailey admitting Jonas into his room and life are, of course, fatal. That is to say, Bailey's is the opposite function to that of Macbeth's Porter: he admits intruding and ultimately evil forces. Further, he delights in this activity so that, for most of the novel, he is a disturbingly amoral figure.

But he and Macbeth's Porter are alike in their ready speech. In

Bailey's first words, his response to Pecksniff at Todgers's door, is prefigured his basic conversational mode:

> 'Still a-bed, my man?' asked Mr Pecksniff.
> 'Still a-bed!' replied the boy. 'I wish they wos still a-bed. They're very noisy a-bed; all calling for their boots at once. I thought you wos the Paper, and wondered why you didn't shove yourself through the grating as usual. What do you want?'
>
> (viii, 125)

The boy repeats Pecksniff's query and then responds to it by performing both parts of a dialogue, as he does for the Pecksniff sisters as dinner is prepared: '"I say", he whispered ... "young ladies, there's soup tomorrow. She's a-making it now. An't she a-putting in the water? Oh! not at all neither!"' (ix, 143). Again, when Bailey protests to Mercy Pecksniff that Mrs Todgers vents her fury on him when her lodgers eat too much, and Mercy wonders whether all really think he is always to blame, he retorts, '"Don't they though? ... No. Yes. Ah! Oh! No one mayn't say it is; but some one knows it is"' (xi, 189). He offers replies and reactions to his own question. When Poll encounters him in his new role as Tigg's 'tiger' there is a similar response, Bailey even creating his own alter ego:

> 'Why, it an't you, sure!' cried Poll. 'It can't be you!'
> 'No. It an't me,' returned the youth. 'It's my son, my eldest one. He's a credit to his father, ain't he, Polly?'
>
> (xxvi, 417)

Such self-consciousness and performing of 'dialogue' that, at times, consists almost wholly of private references and meanings ('No. Yes. Ah! Oh!', and so on) and almost always of question-and-answer routines, generate powerful links with other more important characters. The use of the creative interrogative as the prelude to performing both sides of a dialogue is, of course, a characteristic of Pecksniff's conversation ('"What are we?" said Mr Pecksniff, "but coaches? Some of us are slow coaches"' (viii, 119)). The frequent use of the exclamation mark is another link between Pecksniff and Bailey, as is, of course, the general liveliness and inventiveness of both characters' speech. The dialogue with Poll introducing Bailey's imaginary 'son' bears embryonic resemblance

to Mrs Gamp's frenzied exchanges with Mrs Harris. A rich cluster
of the novel's main themes is thus embodied in the textual life of
this minor character: language as mask, language as isolator
pointing to the essential loneliness, conceived of as a function of
arrogance, of so many characters in this novel, are ideas central to
this characterisation. But, as always, we are not perceiving simple
repetition. As a 'Junior Gamp' and 'Junior Pecksniff' Bailey reminds us of earlier versions of those mature grasping hypocrites;
we are reminded that spirited assertiveness, dramatising a concern
for self, is invariably, in this novel, a cover for vicious potential.

An account of the language used by Bailey must lead to a
consideration of the language used by Dickens to describe him.
Here it is necessary to disagree with the otherwise perceptive
Branwen Bailey Pratt. She states that Dickens describes Bailey 'in
matter-of-fact language which implies that his behaviour is entirely
reasonable',[16] so that we are persuaded that it is Bailey who is wise.
But the language describing Bailey is neither homogeneous nor
simple. Its style is always self-consciously foregrounded. For
instance, Dickens's treatment of Bailey is never without satirical
edge: 'Considering his years, which were tender, the youth may be
said to have preferred this question sternly, and in something of a
defiant manner' (viii, 125), is how Dickens describes him asking
Pecksniff his business at Todgers's door. That edge is never
blunted and, as the characterisation develops, is presented in
terms of special kinds of language. Firstly, there is the language of
law-enforcement and the courts. Thus, Bailey, 'being afterwards
taken by that lady in the fact, was dismissed with a box on his ears'
(viii, 128), and, a second example, 'Bailey junior, testifying great
excitement, appeared in a complete suit of cast-off clothes several
times too large for him, and in particular, mounted a clean shirt of
such extraordinary magnitude . . .' (ix, 145). As, respectively,
apprehended criminal or as witness on the stand the legal imagery
makes his relations with others essentially impersonal, professional rather than friendly. Secondly, the legal suggestiveness of
'appeared' and 'mounted' (the witness appearing and mounting
the stand) are also theatrical (the actors appearing, the production
mounted), the latter found again during Bailey's last encounter
with the Pecksniff sisters before they leave Todgers's: his 'vocal
offering . . . an imitation of the voice of a young dog, in trying
circumstances', his 'facetious pantomime' of grateful gestures
when the sisters tip him liberally, the heightened emotional

language, even 'ardently' (xi, 188–9) hauling down the luggage, all stress the element of performance, of theatricality, in the way Bailey presents himself to the world. In being a performer, using mime as well as language, Bailey embodies yet another of the novel's central themes.

Again, there is the following exemplary passage from the Todgers's sequence:

> Bailey junior, at the jocund time of noon, presented himself before Miss Charity Pecksniff, then sitting with her sister in the banquet chamber . . . and having expressed a hope, preliminary and pious, that he might be blest, gave her, in his pleasant way to understand that a visitor attended to pay his respects to her. (xi, 170–71)

This language is not only satiric but also archaic; it doesn't properly belong to the 'present' of the novel. Chapter 27 introduces Bailey as Tigg's 'tiger':

> Mr Bailey, Junior – for the sporting character, whilom of general utility at Todgers's, had now regularly set up in life under that name, without troubling himself to obtain from the legislature a direct licence in the form of a Private Bill, which of all kinds and classes of bills is without exception the most unreasonable in its charges – Mr Bailey, Junior, just tall enough to be seen by an enquiring eye, gazing indolently at society from beneath the apron of his master's cab, drove slowly up and down Pall Mall about the hour of noon, in waiting for his 'Governor'. (xxvii, 425–6)

The archaic touches, small counters to any suggestion that the character changes too abruptly, remind us of that earlier Bailey. The periodic sentence, in itself accumulating an impression out of all proportion to the boy's size, and in its language and complexity hinting at the legalistic, enacts the boy's way of behaving: the style mirrors the pretentious dignity of the toff, the arrival of verbs jerks him into life. In the sections dealing with Bailey as 'tiger' the tone of the language applied to is more insistent and aggressive than in the Todgers's chapters, even more suggestive of a performer concerned to ram his impression down his audience's throat. This is an inevitable development given that the boy's façade is now desperately thicker but, paradoxically, more fragile because of the greater sustaining effort now required. The Shakespearean analogy and other Shakespearian echoes – Bailey as 'an abstract of all the stable-knowledge of the time', for example – confer a spurious dignity. Scientific imagery, as in references to the 'highly condensed', the 'high pressure' (xxvi, 419–20) nature of his personality and his work for Tigg, helps convey the unnaturalness of his behaviour. The insistent, pretentious style persists until Bailey drives the drunk and violent Jonas home to his frightened wife, Mercy. Then, depressed and chastened by what he learns of Mercy's domestic predicament, he sheds his toff's veneer and shows that he is still only a boy.

'It may have been the restless remembrance of what he had seen and heard over-night, or it may have been no deeper mental operation than the discovery that he had nothing to do' (xxviii, 457), is how the Narrator continues in explanation of Bailey's visit to Poll Sweedlepipe and the shaving of his youthfully-smooth chin. Such fantasising, part of the projection of himself in this scene as a rakish, sporty man-about-town, is his last assertive fling. From this point onwards the performer becomes victim.

Poll Sweedlepipe is a strange bachelor, 'a little elderly man, with a clammy cold right hand' (xxvi, 416). He is not only a barber but also a bird-seller. Mrs Gamp lives above his shop and, when Pecksniff calls for her, the birds are described. The goldfinch in his toy suburban villa 'mutely' desires death; his companions in their separate cages dance a 'little ballet of despair' (xix, 311). Poll's business is to imprison the naturally and, at times, beautifully wild, rabbits as well as birds. He does to them what, in *Great Expectations*, Mr Pumblechook does to seeds. He himself has 'something of the bird in his nature' (xxvi, 416), sparrow-like, dove-like, magpie-like in his walk. His name is Paul but he is known as Poll, reminding us of the wig he wears, the red-polls he sells and, importantly in a later scene, a parrot. He hardly thinks about the birds and animals he imprisons, or of shaving on Sundays, or of much else. He is cheerfully and thoughtlessly amoral and so a fit acquaintance for Bailey.

The boy buys birds from him and so, as bird-owner and Poll's friend, exemplifies another important structural pattern. At the opening of Chapter 2, the story's real beginning, in the sudden reminder of summer on a late autumn day, 'the birds began to chirp and twitter . . . as though the hopeful creatures half believed that winter had gone by, and spring had come already' (ii, 7). The birds, so to say, are optimistic but deceived; they become despondently silent as the sun goes down. As the text unfolds, the link between birds and deception is insisted upon: Mercy Pecksniff is a 'playful warbler' (ii, 14); the Blue Dragon's bedroom where Old Martin lies ill is a 'dull, leaden, drowsy place' with 'no round-eyed birds upon the curtains, disgustingly wide awake, and insufferably prying' (iii, 27); Pecksniff is compared to a dove; Mercy has such 'gay simplicity . . . that . . . the robin-redbreasts might have covered her with leaves against her will, believing her to be one of the sweet children in the wood' (iv, 52–3). Birds contribute, directly or indirectly, to ultimately deceptive suggestions of innocence and helplessness.

The Pecksniffs are strongly associated with bird-imagery – drunken Pecksniff at Todgers's is seen 'to flutter on the top landing' (ix, 153), and his daughters are almost always birds to him – though never more significantly than when Seth Pecksniff walks through the countryside *en route* to propose to Mary Graham; the Narrator comments, 'The birds, so many Pecksniff consciences, sang gaily upon every branch' (xxx, 479). Such associations extend outward from the Pecksniffs: Jonas is a cuckoo, Elijah Pogram a raven, Americans have magpie-like honesty, peacock-like vanity, ostrich-like evasiveness and, concludes Martin not altogether convincingly, Phoenix-like powers of renewal. Some birds sing outside Tom's office window, or should be skylarks as Ruth Pinch crosses Fountain Court; Jonas, travelling to murder Tigg, is unaffected by the dawn-chorus.

Ornithological reminders of natural goodness demonstrate the ramifications of the imagery but heighten through contrast the main function of the bird-motif, to highlight the world's deceptive surface and the attack on the natural. We are returned to Bailey: his ownership of birds is a further link with Pecksniff, who keeps a caged and mutilated sparrow. Bailey's birds, plus his friendship with Sweedlepipe the supplier, serve as emblems of his own unnaturalness, the youth imitating the seedy behaviour of his urban elders.

The distancing effect of the style, the exuberance masking vicious potential and callous amorality, the suggestions of unnaturalness, might well make us sympathise with Mrs Todgers's treatment of her servant, the 'manual compliments' already described. He receives more of the same during his work for

Montague Tigg, not from Tigg himself who, though hardly con-
siderate, is not violent towards him, but from Tigg's henchman
Jonas:

> [Jonas] walked back into the hall . . . conducting Mr Bailey with
> him, by the collar.
>   'You are not a going to take this monkey of a boy, are you?'
>   'Yes', said Montague, 'I am.'
> He gave the boy a shake, and threw him roughly aside.
>
> (xli, 641)

Significantly, as an indication of the force of Jonas's terrorising
malevolence, though Bailey preserves his aggressive defiance
against Mrs Todgers's onslaughts he makes no protest at Jonas's
rough handling of him. In the end, ironically, much greater
violence is done to him, in a sense accidentally, via the carriage-
crash that leaves him for dead, a representative instance of the dire
indirect effect upon those associated with the Anglo-Bengalee.

Mrs Todgers's 'manual compliments' are instinctive reactions to
Bailey's indiscipline. Martin's attack on Pecksniff when the latter
dismisses him, Tom Pinch's exchange of blows with the insulting
Jonas, Old Martin's striking-down of Pecksniff in the penultimate
chapter, all are instances of equally instinctive violence. This kind
of violence is very different from the premeditated mayhem
mainly, but not exclusively, associated with Jonas Chuzzlewit.
When he strikes Mercy, the act expresses long-suppressed hatred;
the murder of Tigg has been carefully planned. In the novel's
treatment of violence Bailey's role as recipient is crucial as a
counter to any suggestion that instinctive violence is in some way
'better' than the premeditated: Mrs Todgers may chastise him for
indiscipline and neglect of duty but she, like Jonas Chuzzlewit, is
also attacking the boy's sense of fun, his imaginative inventiveness, his very boyishness. All violence is reprehensible, as Bailey's
role makes clear.

Two further points: when Bailey becomes Tigg's 'tiger' he
exchanges the cast-off clothes of Todgers's boarding-house for a
resplendent livery of top-boots, white cord breeches, a '"grass-
green frock-coat . . . bound with gold! and a cockade in your hat"'
(xxvi, 418), such magnificence matching that of Montague. He thus
contributes to the theme of clothing as façade and disguise, here
linked to the sustaining of the Anglo-Bengalee's public image. But

he also modifies the theme by remaining detectable, behind the fine attire, as the young boy at Todgers's who wished to play in the street.

Bailey's final appearance, in the resolution-scene, summarises and resolves other important themes. He began as door-keeper, now he makes an entrance. 'Is there anybody here that knows him?' (lii, 808), Poll parrots again and again as the injured and disorientated boy staggers in. Nobody there does know him. He has no past, precise social place or certain name. In a novel about gaining self-knowledge and asserting the real known self, the disengaging of characters from the roles they have clung to, Bailey is the exception. He remains mysterious as Poll prepares a new life for him that continues aspects of the old. Bailey will become his partner, cries Poll, and will handle the sporting side of the bird business. He becomes one of Poll's 'two patients' (liii, 810), the other being the swooning Mrs Gamp who is linked by Old Martin to the Old Bailey as she is dismissed from the text. Bailey goes with her, a final and pessimistic modification of the idea that self-knowledge and the capacity for change are available to all.

3   GAFFER HEXAM IN *OUR MUTUAL FRIEND*[17]

Gaffer Hexam dominates the opening chapters of *Our Mutual Friend*. Despite this his textual life is a short one. The novel begins with him working at his gruesome trade of searching for and finding bodies in the Thames, the first chapter describing not only his skilful handling of boat and body but also the important relationships with his daughter Lizzie and his former partner, Rogue Riderhood. The body found in Chapter 1 is wrongly believed to be that of John Harmon and when the two young lawyers, Eugene Wrayburn and Mortimer Lightwood, investigate the discovery, they visit the riverside district and Gaffer's home; he takes the lawyers to the nearby police-station, where the body is viewed. His next stop is the pub, and the narrative moves from him to his two children at home, whose conversation provides insights into Gaffer's parental role, his tenderness towards Lizzie and, in particular, his prejudice against education.

He returns to the text in Chapter 6 when he is discussed by Rogue Riderhood and the publican Miss Abbey Potterson. Riderhood falsely insists that Gaffer not only finds bodies and so claims rewards but often provides the bodies himself. Miss Abbey, in whose pub, The Six Jolly Fellowship Porters, Gaffer is a regular, is sufficiently convinced by Riderhood that Gaffer may be a murderer to send for Lizzie, to tell her that her father is banned from the pub, and to urge her to leave him. The chapter ends with Gaffer's return home, his anger at learning that his son Charlie has left to work as a teacher, Lizzie fainting with fear at seeing her father so disturbed, and his consequent tenderness towards her. In Chapter 12, in Lightwood's office, Riderhood repeats his accusations; in particular, that Gaffer Hexam murdered John Harmon before claiming the reward for his body, and had confessed as much to him. Led by Riderhood the two lawyers return to the riverside to tell the police. The latter, having decided to arrest Hexam, search for him through a cold, stormy night on the river. He is found at dawn, dead, having fallen into the river and been strangled by his own tow-rope.

Gaffer Hexam is last seen alive at the end of Book 1, Chapter 6. His body is recovered from the river in Book 1, Chapter 13. As has been noted, to him belongs much of the vivid and crucially important opening chapters and this in itself helps keep him in the reader's memory as the whole text is read. His surviving children ensure the continuing textual life of his surname, and daughter Lizzie, in particular, often recalls how things were when father was alive and brother Charlie still at home. The action frequently turns back to the riverside and Gaffer's haunts in Limehouse Hole. In addition, a vast array of reminders, recurring motifs, and stylistic details, too many to list in full, ensures that his presence infiltrates almost every part of the text. A number of these devices are well-known: the wind, for instance, that in so much of later Dickens is a symbol of psychological as well as environmental hostility, and which blows on Gaffer in life and death and in most of *Our Mutual Friend*'s textual corners; the 'bird of prey' imagery, used to suggest Gaffer's predatory instincts and applied in later chapters to, for example, Eugene Wrayburn, Silas Wegg, the Veneerings, the Lammles, and Fledgeby; the recurring fishing motif, the first example of which is, of course, Gaffer's watery work. These last two motifs have been described and analysed.[18] Reminders of boating also abound, as when Eugene and Mortimer 'float with the stream through the summer' (I, xii, 191), little Johnny plays with his Noah's ark, Jenny Wren stows her key so that, as she says, it will 'trim the ship' (III, ii, 493), George

Sampson, attempting to converse with the Wilfers, perceives 'his frail bark to be labouring among shoals and breakers' until, 'with admirable seamanship he got his bark into deep water' (III, xvi, 677), or when Mrs Podsnap is 'brought to anchor' (III, xvii, 691) on the left of her host at the Veneerings' party; Bradley Headstone dresses as a bargeman; finally, Lizzie, in the scene that, above all others, recalls the novel's opening pages, uses her old skills to rescue the half-dead Eugene from the river. Images of drowning, whether applied, for example, to parts of London or to the Veneerings, reinforce the connection, as do recurring 'pastoral' motifs: Gaffer's 'windmill' home begins a sequence that includes Boffin's bower, the ironically idyllic Plashwater Weir scenes, the 'bower' of Jenny Wren's hair, and young Johnny's angling.

Such examples – and they are *only* examples – are supported by a host of smaller links that also preserve Gaffer as a ghostly presence in the text. A few connections must again suffice: the egg in Twemlow's hair and the dead Hexam's hair clotted with hail; placards advertising the discovery of Harmon's body on Hexam's living-room wall and on Rokesmith's desk when Boffin's secretary; the secretary's own dexterity with knots as he parcels up documents; the barge tow-ropes slackening and tightening, noticed by the wandering Betty Higden, and Gaffer's slip-knot fastening fatally upon him. The turned-out pockets of all Gaffer's corpses, mute witnesses to one source of his income, are recalled in Jenny Wren's insistence that her father, Mr Dolls, should 'Turn all your pockets inside out, and leave 'em so' (II, ii, 293), and in the naming of Veneering's constituency as 'Pocket-Breaches'.

Such details in themselves, of course, effect links between Gaffer and other characters unconnected or, at best, remotely connected with the rough waterman. There are many others: the cold wind links Gaffer and Wegg, illiteracy Gaffer and Boffin. The smallest of textual details furthers the latter connection: Gaffer's 'ragged grizzled hair' and 'eager look-out' of the novel's first page are echoed in Boffin's 'eager' eyes and 'ragged' eyebrows (I, v, 90); we also recall Pleasant Riderhood's 'ragged' (II, xii, 407) hair. An even smaller detail ensures Gaffer's subtextual presence even at the Veneerings' dinner-party: the guests 'lunged at Mrs Podsnap and retreated' (I, xi, 181) as the corpse 'lunged' at Gaffer's boat as he towed it home at the close of Chapter 1.

A more dominant stylistic mode, the negative description of Gaffer in Book 1, Chapter 1 – 'He had no net, hook, or line, and he could not be a fisherman . . .' – is echoed six chapters later when Venus is introduced – 'His eyes are like the over-tried eyes of an engraver, but he is not that; his expression and stoop are like those of a shoemaker, but he is not that' (I, vii, 122) – and, less directly, in Book 1, Chapter 11, in the negative-filled conversation of the put-upon Miss Podsnap. Wrayburn and Lightwood's discussion of '"moral influences"' (II, vi, 337) on their tedious lives, Mrs Wilfer's attitude to her wedding anniversary ('It was kept morally, rather as a Fast than a Feast' (iii, iv, 509)) and the ironical reference to the 'magnanimous morality' (II, xii, 406) of the inhabitants of Lime-house Hole, keep in subtext and mind Gaffer's assertion of 'the high moralities' in his opening exchange with Riderhood on the impropriety of robbing the dead. The reader can even link Mr Dolls, his fellow-drunks in Covent Garden, all of whom have clothes indistinguishable from the vegetable matter around them, and Gaffer's boat, seemingly connected to the river bottom by its covering of 'slime and ooze' (I, i, 43).

Gaffer's often posthumous but still potent presence in almost every textual interstice is carefully ensured by Dickens because of the character's powerful summarising function. We can begin to appreciate this last by studying the novel's opening:

> In these times of ours, though concerning the exact year there is no need to be precise, a boat of dirty and disreputable appear-ance, with two figures in it, floated on the Thames, between Southwark Bridge which is of iron, and London Bridge which is of stone, as an autumn evening was closing in.

This paragraph, a long and complex single sentence, begins and ends with the same word. But whereas, in that first phrase, the 'in' contributes to an initial sense of a common bond, that same word, in the final phrase, suggests oppression, hunting-down. That progression (or regression) from a sense of relationship to hostile encounters is of central importance in this novel: Headstone, Riderhood, Wrayburn, Charlie Hexam, the Lammles and Silas Wegg, come readily to mind as characters involved in such a shift. And Gaffer Hexam, as we shall see. This first paragraph offers a second effect, a strong contrast between the boat with its occu-pants – described in terms of two generalising adjectives and a vague and slightly dehumanising noun – and the setting, which is precisely located and strongly described through the heavily stressed 'iron' and 'stone'. The domination of the urban environment over its inhabitants is a fundamental Dickensian theme here redramatised at the start with compelling economy. Again, the first paragraph ends as darkness comes; Gaffer Hexam is a creature of the night. Indeed, natural light does not return during the whole of the first instalment of a novel in which darkness dominates. Light fades, darkness comes: this opening contrast is profoundly pessimistic. But all such contrasts – the two uses of 'in', the boat with figures and its setting, the light and the dark – are united in the single party of that long and complex sentence comprising paragraph one. The tension thus set up between connection and contrast is the main structural principle of the novel, and a representation of the way in which the novel presents Victorian society as a number of social groups seemingly wholly separate and indifferent to each other but bound, indissolubly, by several despairing concerns, such as a susceptibility to the power of a hostile past and a dehumanising materialism that, itself, is one aspect of an ubiquitous Podsnappery. In his very first appearance, before he is even named, Gaffer brings together central themes.

They are all negative ones: so many of Gaffer's relationships – with his former 'pardner', Rogue Riderhood, with his son Charlie, with Abbey Potterson, with the general run of his acquaintances – deteriorate into estrangements and hostilities. The man who cries 'Is there summ'at deadly sticking to my clothes? What's let loose upon us? Who loosed it?' (I, vi, 121), is a man at odds with a hostile world. That hostility is not only generated by estranged relationships but also by specific perceived social and mental threats. One such is education, which is to fuel his son Charlie's social and economic advancement. Hexam's stubborn opposition to his son's ambitions culminates in his anger when Charlie leaves home: '"His own father ain't good enough for him. He's disowned his own father. His own father therefore, disowns him for ever and ever, as a unnat'ral young beggar"' (I, vi, 120). The anger reflects a fierce acquiescence in the prevailing rigid class-structure, a clear and disturbing instance of Podsnappery in action. And in a novel of strange and unsatisfactory parent–child relationships – R. Wilfer and Bella, Jenny Wren and Mr Dolls, Podsnap and Georgiana – Hexam's with his son (and possibly with his daughter also, given that she retains her place in his home only because she satisfies his expectations of her) has a close resemblance to the Podsnap duo in that both fathers desire and seek to create the child as parental clone. Attitudes to the children are exploitive in that they are designed to sustain parental positions and notions of the world.

The work done by Hexam is also essentially exploitive: he preys upon the dead, robbing bodies and claiming rewards, tasks that seem to suit a man sometimes presented as 'half savage' (I, i, 44). Garrett Stewart, in his brilliant discussion of this novel, considers that Gaffer's work is so horrible that 'he must expel fancies in order to fend off neuroses'.[19] This may be so; what is certain is that Gaffer, who 'was no neophyte and had no fancies' (I, i, 47), is a negative standard in the novel's exploration and endorsement of the worth of the imagination; he is a Podsnappic counter to, for example, all the good that is implied in Lizzie's fire-gazing and Jenny Wren's Blakean reveries. This lack of imagination, particularly of the sympathetic kind, fuels his frustration, as when, learning of Charlie's defection, he strikes the air with his knife so terribly that Lizzie faints with fear. Hexam's capacity for violence, here and on the river when he threatens Riderhood to '"chop you over the fingers with the stretcher, or take a pick at your head with the boat-hook"' (I, i, 47), introduces us to his violent world in which such men as Riderhood are prominent and out of which comes the murderous Headstone. The world of darkness entered by Gaffer Hexam as the novel opens is an oppressive and dangerous prison.

But Hexam's negativity is only one part of his character. The rest is best approached through the scene in Book 1, Chapter 6, that transforms his textual life. Abbey Potterson, with Gaffer at work on the river, has told Lizzie of the suspicions about Gaffer that will exclude him from the Six Jolly Fellowship Porters. When he returns home the following morning his landing is described:

> The white face of the winter day came sluggishly on, veiled in a frosty mist; and the shadowy ships in the river slowly changed to black substances; and the sun, blood-red on the eastern marshes behind dark masts and yards, seemed filled with the ruins of a forest it had set on fire. Lizzie, looking for her father, saw him coming, and stood upon the causeway that he might see her.
>
> He had nothing with him but his boat, and came on apace. A knot of those amphibious human-creatures who appear to have some mysterious power of extracting a subsistence out of tidal water by looking at it, were gathered together about the causeway. As her father's boat grounded, they became contemplative

of the mud, and dispersed themselves. She saw that the mute avoidance had begun.

Gaffer saw it, too, in so far as that he was moved when he set foot on shore, to stare around him. But, he promptly set to work to haul up his boat, and make her fast, and take the sculls and rudder and rope out of her. Carrying these with Lizzie's aid, he passed up to his dwelling.

'Sit close to the fire, father, dear, while I cook your breakfast. It's all ready for cooking, and only been waiting for you. You must be frozen.'

'Well, Lizzie, I ain't of a glow; that's certain. And my hands seem nailed through to the sculls. See how dead they are!' Something suggestive in their colour, and perhaps in her face, struck him as he held them up; he turned his shoulder and held them down to the fire.

(I, vi, 118)

The passage is crucial and turns on two details. Firstly: 'Lizzie, looking for her father, saw him coming, and stood upon the causeway that he might see her.' The sentence, in echoing the rhythms of the Authorized Version, points us towards the imaginative source for this Thames-side scene, those familiar Gospel scenes of Christ disembarking from Galilean boats, when, as Luke, for example, tells us: 'when Jesus was returned, the people gladly received him: for they were all waiting for him' (9:40). Such direct use of the New Testament is not, of course, unknown in Dickens: in *Great Expectations*, Jaggers moving through the Little Britain crowd that includes garment-hem-kissing Jews, is a well-known example. The second detail is the vivid image of nailing used by Gaffer about his frozen hands. This 'Crucifixion' image combines with the earlier rhythmic suggestion to evoke powerful but bitterly ironic links between Christ and Gaffer Hexam. The links are those of contrast, for whereas Christ came ashore to acclaiming multitudes, Gaffer's return, in the early morning cold, with hints of Armageddon in the flaming sky, the fierce independence but essential isolation of the man as the riverside loiterers turn away from him, his links with death and, in the minds of many, as Lizzie knows only too well, with murderous violence, the bitterly sinister way in which Gaffer, too, is a 'fisher of men', all constitute a reversal of our sense of Christ at Galilee. Shortly after this, Gaffer becomes literally the hanged man, caught fatally in his own line, 'baptized unto Death' (I, xiv, 222) in the river which he seemed to have mastered.

The passage changes the nature of Gaffer's characterisation by encouraging us to view him as encapsulating in his career the central spiritual predicament of mid-Victorian England. Gaffer is a Christ for his time in being, in several ways, an inverted Christ-figure. But it is too glib to say that he is simply this; the effect of linking Gaffer to the religious leader who, above all others, was an attractive and positive figure, is also to his advantage. For though Gaffer Hexam is destroyed by what he does, and though the textual sequence that characterises him is a movement to a death that in its similarities to those of Riderhood and Headstone is given a negative class meaning as well as a negative moral one, the links with Christ, if only through association, suggest Gaffer's attractive and positive side.

He may be at odds with the world but this can be another way of saying that he asserts himself against it. Thus, in the second paragraph of the novel, though the negatives strip away civilised contexts to leave Gaffer half-savage, primitive, dirty, an extension, almost, of the river's ooze, yet this is not the whole story or his complete character. For much of that second paragraph presents him attractively: he is 'eager', with an 'intent and searching gaze . . . there was business-like usage in his steady gaze'. In a novel in which so many characters – the Veneerings, Podsnap, Wrayburn, Lightwood – have no more than the 'fiction of an occupation' (I, viii, 131) performed by Mortimer Lightwood's clerk, and though others – Fledgeby, Wegg, even Riah – have work of which they might well be ashamed, Gaffer Hexam is a skilled waterman and a competent handler of the bodies he so cleverly finds. The horrible nature of his trade does not prevent Dickens from responding to his positive qualities as, to some extent, Gaffer preserves himself through what he does.

Again, though we can see how Gaffer is another bad parent, his role is again crucial for a full understanding of parent–child relationships. The novel not only opens with a man working but with him working with his daughter and even though she detests the work and feels natural repugnance towards the bodies they find it is a fine tribute towards Gaffer's fatherly qualities that she still loves him: when he vehemently reminds her of the benefits they derive from the river she 'took her right hand from the scull it held, and touched her lips with it, and for a moment held it out lovingly towards him' (I, i, 46). Thereafter tenderness is never wholly absent from the scenes they share. As for Gaffer and his son Charlie: though, of course, we cannot support the father's opposition to his son's educational and social progress, we have to recognise, in the extreme fierceness with which he responds to news of Charlie's departure, the strength of his feelings – irrational, confused, wrong, but still truly parental – for the son who has gone. When he strikes the table with his knife, crying, '"Now I see why them men yonder held aloof from me. They says to one another, 'Here comes the man as ain't good enough for his own son'"' (I, vi, 120), we recognise that such a terrible expression of inadequacy proceeds out of love. It proceeds also, of course, out of Gaffer's adherence to Podsnappic principles, that rigid view of the social structure that denies ambition and imagination. We can condemn that but can still see Gaffer to be motivated by admirable familial feelings: he wishes to keep his family together in harmonious accord. That at least we can respect and possibly admire.

Gaffer is a man of principle. In Chapter 1 he rejects Riderhood because the latter was accused of robbing 'a live man'. When Riderhood retorts that Gaffer robs the dead he gets an indignant reply: '"How can money be a corpse's? Can a corpse own it, want it, spend it, claim it, miss it? Don't try to go confounding the rights and wrongs of things in that way."' (I, i, 47). Gaffer's moral position may be shaky but he certainly does not deserve the Narrator's ironically contemptuous description of him as 'one who had asserted the high moralities and taken an unassailable position' (I, i, 47). Gaffer's 'philosophy' is preferable to Rogue Riderhood's cynical amorality; at least it is a *kind* of morality. The violence with which Gaffer threatens Riderhood, like that expressed against Charlie's departure from home, proceeds, we feel, from genuine principles designed to order his working life and preserve the family group.

We are always able to sympathise with Gaffer Hexam's behaviour, paradoxically even when we also condemn it. We are always able to see that he is not a wholly negative character. His characterisation embodies major themes but he does not merely illustrate them. He is one of the foremost exemplars of Podsnappery in the novel but, invariably, offers Podsnappery with a human face. He is a good worker, a devoted parent, a principled man, and such qualities survive our strong sense of the horrible nature of his work, his blinkered ambitions for his children and the dubious

morality of his 'philosophical' reasoning. Above all, in his embodiment and demonstration of the novel's concern with the spiritual
barrenness of mid-Victorian England, in the way in which we are
made to think, momentarily, of Gaffer Hexam as an inverted
Christ-figure, we see the main point of the characterisation: it
reminds us that there are few Dickensian characters who fail to
preserve an essential goodness, a divine spark glowing amidst the
most unpropitious circumstances. The world conspires against
Gaffer: not only the dreadful social forces lined up against the
Victorian poor, put his own class in the shape of Riderhood, who
hates Gaffer's principles in action, the suspicious Abbey Potterson,
and, he feels, his own upwardly mobile son. Even the essentially
benevolent river traps him and kills him. Yet, in life, nothing
touches the basic goodness mourned by his daughter and pre-
served in the text by proliferating echoes that, often, more directly
suggest the opposite. Thus Gaffer is always an exception. He
prevents easy condemnatory responses to the novel's main thematic assertions about the evils of Victorian life.

The Fat Boy in *The Pickwick Papers* and Young Bailey in *Martin
Chuzzlewit* provide negative similarity, reminders that a too-
optimistic view of human affairs is to some extent modified by the
thematic summaries they provide. Gaffer Hexam, in what must
surely be Dickens's darkest novel, is a *positive* modifier of *Our
Mutual Friend*'s darkest concerns. The Gaffer Hexam characterisation is a potent warning against any unthinking assumption that
Dickens's was simply a steadily-darkening vision.

3

Narrators

1 SOME EPISTOLARY PERSONAE[1]

Compared to, say, Keats or the Carlyles, Dickens was not a great letter-writer; where in Dickens's correspondence, we might ask, are phrases to rival the former and pen-portraits the latter? But, though there may be questions about quality, there can be none about quantity: over 13 000 of his letters have survived, a total that few great novelists can match. More than any other form of writing the letter is shaped to fit the needs of its reader; it is at once the most personal, self-conscious and readerly kind of literature. Letter-writing on the Dickensian scale ensured that authorial role-playing, the main consequence of acute reader-awareness, was a daily activity, an influential adjunct to the writing of fiction.

The constant assumption of varying personae is seen clearly in the letters Dickens wrote during May 1837, following the death of his sister-in-law, Mary Hogarth. The circumstances are well-known: she had lived with Dickens and his wife Catherine since their marriage in 1836 and on the evening of the day of her death Dickens wrote to his publisher, Edward Chapman:

> We are in deep and severe distress. Miss Hogarth after accompanying Mrs. Dickens & myself to the Theatre last night, was suddenly taken severely ill, and despite our best endeavours to save her, expired in my arms at two O'Clock this afternoon.
>
> (I, 256)

Dickens had a mainly professional relationship with Chapman. The letter's tone, controlled and slightly distant, reflects this. So, too, does its composition: the short, heavily-stressed, opening statement is followed by a longer sentence the precise balancing of which restricts Dickens's emotional excitement to no more than a hint. Only the careless echoing of 'severe' in 'severely' provides a more direct indication of the extent of Dickens's emotional reaction to his sister-in-law's fatal illness.

The following day Dickens wrote to George Thomson, his wife's grandfather:

> It is my painful and melancholy duty to inform you, that poor Mary died here at three oClock yesterday afternoon. She had been with us to the Theatre the evening before; was taken suddenly ill in the night; and breathed her last in my arms at the time I have mentioned. . . .
>
> You cannot conceive the misery in which this dreadful event has plunged us. Since our marriage she has been the grace and life of our home – the admired of all, for her beauty and excellence – I could have better spared a much nearer relation or an older friend, for she has been to us what we can never replace, and has left a blank which no one who ever know (*sic*) her can have the faintest hope of seeing supplied. (I, 256–7)

This familial letter seems, on a first reading, to be more emotional than the short note to Edward Chapman. The objectives are very different: to convey something of the harrowing quality of the event, to suggest the initial effect on those who witnessed it, and to praise the dead girl. But we swiftly recognise an important similarity between the two communications. In the letter to Thomson the careful pairing of adjectives, such as 'painful and melancholy', 'grace and life', the juxtaposing of concentrated statements with accumulating periodic effects, the care taken over the latter (the precise use of semi-colons and of developing chronology – 'the evening before . . . in the night . . . the time I have mentioned' – makes the second sentence the most obvious example), the Shakespearian echo ('I could have better spar'd a better man', says Prince Hal of Falstaff [*Henry IV, Part I*, 5, iv, 1041), for Dickens, here, either a slightly incongruous or oddly revealing reference), the final emphatic alliteration of 'seeing supplied', all point to a literary production as controlled and selective as that to Chapman. Dickens presents himself, implicitly, through structure and tone, as heartsick but valiantly self-controlled. As a letter to a man old enough (Thomson was in his eightieth year) to be at least partly insulated against the effect of young death, it is essentially ingratiating.

On the same day Dickens also wrote to his close friend at that time, the novelist William Harrison Ainsworth:

It is my melancholy task to inform you that Mrs Dickens' sister whom you saw here, and at the dinner on Wednesday, died in my arms yesterday afternoon. She had accompanied us to the Theatre the night before apparently in the best health; was taken ill in the night, and lies here a corpse. She has been our constant companion since our marriage; the grace and life of our home. — Judge how deeply we feel this fearfully sudden deprivation.

(I, 257)

The language and tone have changed. To a writer whose stories – *Jack Sheppard* and *Rookwood* amongst them – were *grand-guignol* melodramas Dickens presents the incident as a series of sudden shocks, of abrupt and affecting emotional effects. 'Died' has replaced the gentler 'expired' and 'breathed her last'; sentence one ends with the dying embrace, two with the heavily stressed 'corpse', three with lyrical remembrance, and four with dreadful realisation in which the reader is imperatively involved. The concern to emphasise the shocking suddenness of the death by means of description verging on the melodramatic exhibits the letter-writer – now more accurately called the Narrator – as a character hardly out-of-place in an Ainsworth tale. Importantly, the Narrator begins to cast himself and surviving family as pathetic victims.

In these examples, as in Dickens's other surviving letters on Mary's death, though the persona changes one fact remains constant: Mary Hogarth died in the narrator's arms. If clinching evidence is sought for Dickens's abiding awareness of his addressees and so the deliberate arrangement of his material to allow them a controlled view of his narrator-constructs, this fact provides it. Even as late as 8 June 1837 an unknown correspondent was told that Mary

died in such a calm and gentle sleep, that although I had held her in my arms for some time before, when she was certainly living (for she swallowed a little brandy from my hand) I continued to support her lifeless form, long after her soul had fled to Heaven. (I, 268)

Distance and restraint have largely been replaced by an ever-strengthening sense of how the Narrator wishes to be regarded: he is the sad, bereaved survivor commanding the world's pity for his part in a neo-tragic drama. As for Mary herself: one is tempted to say that at the moment of her death she is embraced by so many different personae as almost to put at risk her lifetime's reputation for purity. That aside, the whole sequence conveniently demonstrates the range and crucial importance of narrator-constructs in Dickens's letters.

In the letters of 1840–41, to choose a period not dominated by correspondence, such as that from America and Italy, written with a view to future publication, and during which Dickens wrote to many different correspondents, that range is further extended. Thus to young Mary Talfourd, before Dickens left for America:

> I should be delighted to come and dine with you on your birthday, and to be as merry as I wish you to be always; but as I am going, within a very few days afterwards, a very long distance from home, and shall not see any of my children for six long months, I have made up my mind to pass all that week at home for their sakes – just as you would like your Papa and Mamma to spend all the time they could possibly spare, with you, if they were about to make a dreary voyage to America; which is what I am going to do myself. (II, 446)

The Narrator, of course, is not childlike but an adult who understands and empathises with children: the diction, the calculated repetition of 'very', the long, accumulative sentence, together spread out simple thoughts with apparent spontaneity, temper hinted excitement with slight apprehension, *and* preserve a sense of adult authority and superior wisdom.

Letters to women adopt a different style and so reflect yet another persona. Thus to Mrs Macready, wife of the great actor and so a close friend:

> Now is there not *one* other day, early in next week, when we could meet for this delightful purpose? *Do* cast about in your mind for a snug, happy, undisposed-of evening, and say it shall be then. I am going out on no day but Thursday, and shall have no peace of mind until you write again. Therefore, pray relieve me soon from a despondency which is already stealing over my spirits, and unfitting me for Clock work. . . .
>
> I have got *such* a cold! I have been crying all day, and upon my word I believe that my nose is an inch shorter than it was last

Tuesday, from constant friction. (II, 150)

Dickens was never the feminist's friend and this letter is unfortunately similar in its narrative stance to that to the young Mary Talfourd: the Narrator is given generic characteristics thought to be possessed by the recipient, in this instance such stereotyped 'feminine' ones as socially-motivated sentimental over-emphasis, a tendency to gush, as well as adopting attitudes that, to judge from the instructive tone, overstated flattery, and childish yet explained joke, patronise Mrs Macready whilst expecting her automatic admiration.

To Mary Hogarth's mother, when her son also died, he wrote, linking both deaths:

> Try – do try – to think that they have but preceded you to happiness, and will meet you with joy in Heaven. There *is* consolation in the knowledge that you have treasure there, and that while you live on earth, there are creatures among the Angels, who owed their being to you. (II, 408)

The mawkish, morbid sentimentality was not a characteristic solely of Dickens's letters to women; examples of it can be found in letters to Forster, particularly when Little Nell's fictional death recalled the emotions of Mary's passing. But in the correspondence with female friends or relations, the instructive tone, the invariable assumption of superior wisdom and the consequent relegation of those females to a 'delightful' but trivial corner, are unique elements. In letters to children and to women, those two oppressed Victorian groups, the Narrator's invariable propensity to identify, invariably patronisingly, with the recipient can be most clearly seen. But this kind of negative capability can also be seen in Dickens's letters to men. He wrote to Landor, who was off to Paris to meet his son travelling from Italy:

> I am in fearfully low spirits tonight – bilious, behind-hand in my work in consequence, blue devil haunted and miserable. Thank God there are no real causes for this (saving, I suppose, some slight disorder in the system) and it's no great matter to me and less to you, except as an explanation of this poor note – for which reason I mention it.
> Four months! I don't believe a word of it. If you're away from

Bath four whole months consecutively, I'll write four novels for
fourpence. . . .

Don't talk of such rash acts. Don't think of them. Come to
London. Go to Paris. But return to Bath at short intervals
wherever you go. How can a man live without sun, light,
heat—How are you to be inspired—How are you to go on
writing (as I know you do)—How are you to go on at all? It
cannot be done. Or if it can, it must be by some frozen-hearted,
slow-blooded, torpid wretch; and you are not the man to do it.

If you do, I renounce you. I hold the Landor faith no more, and
publicly recant. (II, 251)

Here Dickens anticipates Boythorn, the character in *Bleak House*
closely modelled on Landor. Boythorn (and Landor) is always
inclined to 'some great volley of superlatives' (ix, 168),[2] to language
extreme in its vehemence, force and stentorian tone. He enters the
text late for dinner with Jarndyce and exclaims to the waiting
company:

'We have been misdirected, Jarndyce, by a most abandoned
ruffian, who told us to take the turning to the right instead of to
the left. He is the most intolerable scoundrel on the face of the
earth. His father must have been a most consummate villain,
ever to have such a son. I would have had that fellow shot
without the least remorse!' (ix, 166–7)

Dickens's essentially parodic letter is a tactful because understated
version of the Boythorn/Landor manner.

The same can be said of a letter to Leigh Hunt, the model for
'Skimpole' in *Bleak House*. In thanking Hunt for manuscript copies
of his new poems, 'The Walk' and 'The Dinner', Dickens not only
refers directly to lines in the poems – 'The sun is in my eyes, the
hum of the fields in my ears, the dust upon my feet' – but also,
more subtly, through poetically rhythmic gestures in the letter's
text that recall the movement of Hunt's verse, such as the hint in
the phrase 'the jingling wire more noisy than the bell' of, for
example, 'Heart enter thee, nor any sigh remember' in the opening
apostrophe to 'The Dinner',[3] – and, generally, in a genial parody of
Leigh Hunt's prose style. When Dickens's Narrator writes:

A crowd of thanks, treading on each others' heels and tripping one another up most pleasantly – a crowd of thanks, I say, for that Rustic Walk which I have just taken with you, and for the dinner. . . .

Good God how well I know that room! Don't you remember a queer, cool, odd kind of smell it has, suggestive of porter and even pipes at an enormous distance? (II, 66–7)

he recalls the sentimental sweetness of Hunt's essays, particularly evident in such lines as 'Good God! I could cry like one of the Children in the Wood', or 'I think I have them in a sort of sidelong mind's eye' from 'My Books'.[4] Again, the postscript to the letter of 10 July 1840 reads:

I fancied there was the slightest possible peculiarity in your speech last night – just an elaborate show of distinctness – a remarkably correct delivery – an exquisite appreciation of the beauty of the language, with the faintest smack of wine running through it – This was mere fancy, I suppose? (II, 99)

The precious and precise aesthetic evasiveness of this passage catches perfectly the essence of Hunt-as-Skimpole.

Elsewhere the narrative stance effects literary self-parody:

Post just going – compression of sentiments required – Bust received – likeness *amazing* – recognizable instantly if encountered on the summit of the Great Pyramid – Scotch anecdote most striking and most distressing – dreamed of it – babbies well – wife ditto – yours the same, I hope? (II, 271)

This, in 1840, was to Basil Hall, a fervent admirer of Dickens's works; the Narrator, of course, is a latter-day Jingle.

To Edward Chapman, about to be married, he is, facetiously, a misogynistic monster:

'Farewell! If you did but know – and would pause, even at this late period – better an action for breach than – but we buy experience. Excuse my agitation. I scarcely know what I write. – To see a fellow creature – and one who has so long withstood – still if – Will *nothing* warn you – (II, 384)

Early in 1840, at the time of Queen Victoria's marriage, he wrote to a number of men-friends in the character of her hopeless, distracted and unrequited lover, able only to 'wander up and down with vague and dismal thoughts of running away to some uninhabited island with a maid of honor' or possessed by thoughts 'of turning Chartist, of heading some bloody assault upon the palace and saving Her by my single hand' (II, 23–4). In June of the same year, writing to Maclise, he parodied Thomas Moore and local guidebooks to suggest an uncritical and enthusiastic tourist in Broadstairs (II, 79). During the following year he praised *George Cruikshank's Omnibus* in the style of a voluble cockney: 'It is wery light, wery easy on the springs, well horsed, driv in a slap up style, and altogether an uncommon spicy con-sarn' . . . (II, 276).

There are as many different narrators as there are letters; Dickens moves effortlessly, chameleon-like, from one to the next. A comic *tour-de-force* can be followed by the most serious and businesslike of notes, as, for example, when humorous letters to T.J. Thompson and Daniel Maclise about the Narrator's devotion to Queen Victoria were written on the same day as correspondence to Thomas Mitton regarding Dickens's contractual dispute with Richard Bentley the publisher (II, 25–30). Given the common authorship, we see what Bakhtin, writing of Dostoevsky, has described as a 'plurality of independent and unmerged voices and consciousnesses'[5] creating the 'polyphonic' novel that enables some critics, for example Flint, to find a graspable narrating consciousness in the major novels. If sufficient letters are read, distinct recurring attitudes – for example, to the dead Mary Hogarth, to women in general, to money, to literary affairs – can be discerned, hinting at the notion of a Supra-narrator possessing a character of some complexity and whose attitudes to his letters' recipients are invariably prejudices. This construct is, however, unable to counter the presence in each letter of each individual Narrator sufficiently to undermine the notion of difference implicit in the Bakhtin definition. Our main impression is of a series of comparatively simple narrative personae but it is true to say that the relationship between these and the Supra-narrator who writes *all* the letters offers a clear and usefully simplified paradigm of a narrative strategy that remains similar in kind but increases in complexity as Dickens's fiction-writing moves towards and through its last great period. Each Narrator, characterised by each letter-text, controls the narrative's effect on the reader. As we move from letters to the great novels the various personae are replaced, in the longer works, by the varying aspects of the text which combine to create an increasingly complex narrator-characterisation, the equivalent of the Supra-narrator of the letters but, now, a successful unifier even of the most tonally diversified novels. This 'polyphonic narrator' filters the fictional experience through its consciousness and so helps establish its meaning.

2   THE TROUBLED TRAVELLER IN *PICTURES FROM ITALY*[6]

In moving to the increasingly complex the natural progression is from letters to a volume of non-fictional prose, here *Pictures from Italy* of 1846. This was the eventual result of Dickens's decision, as he told Forster in 1843, to live abroad for a year in 'some place which I know beforehand to be CHEAP and in a delightful climate'.[7] Though Dickens insisted that he went mainly to increase 'his store of recollections and improvement',[8] in reality other pressures, including those of writing itself, begging letters, accumulating social engagements, disappointing *Martin Chuzzlewit* sales, forced his hand. Though his publishers, Bradbury and Evans, gave him an unconditional advance of £2800 he went as a worried man, needing a rest in a quiet and cheap place, seeking it in July 1844, and finding it in Genoa, staying abroad until July 1845. During the year he wrote and published *The Chimes* and the series of letters to Forster and others on which *Pictures from Italy* is based. Since, by Dickens's standards, this was idleness, the stay in Italy constituted 'an unprecedented pause in his writing life'.[9]

Most writers on Dickens regard *Pictures from Italy* as a mine of autobiographical information. The few who look for more rarely find much: Praz discusses Dickens's interest in Rome as that of a romantic artist;[10] Carey writes of Dickens's fascination with rotting Italian villas that connects with memories of Warren's Blacking warehouse;[11] Angus Wilson notes views on Italian history and religion, and Dickens's delight in marionette theatres and foreign absurdities;[12] Burgam, in relating the book to the Italian scenes in *Little Dorrit*, explores notions of oblivion,[13] Kaplan Dickens's obsession with dreams, including the opposition between dream-like Venice and London's reality.[14]

There is, then, virtually no extended analysis of *Pictures from Italy* as a literary text even though there is much evidence that the finished work was carefully crafted. It began as a series of letters mainly to Forster and a number of 'travelling letters' in the *Daily News* that, revised and extended, became the basis of the book. Textual analysis can usefully proceed from awareness of the biographical background, in particular of the fact that the year abroad was not perceived wholly positively by Dickens; to a great extent it was a forced response to the first real crisis of his writing life and not a result, simply or mainly, of a bright-eyed spirit of adventure.

With this in mind the first paragraph of *Pictures from Italy* is what might be expected:

> On a fine Sunday morning in the Midsummer time and weather of eighteen hundred and forty-four, it was, my good friend, when – don't be alarmed; not when two travellers might have been observed slowly making their way over that picturesque and broken ground by which the first chapter of a 'Middle Aged' novel is usually attained – but when an English travelling-carriage of considerable proportions, fresh from the shady halls of the Pantechnicon near Belgrave Square, London, was observed (by a very small French soldier; for I saw him look at it) to issue from the gate of the Hôtel Meurice in the Rue Rivoli at Paris. (39)

The single, complex, nervously-tense sentence has its developing narrative drive arrested by the two insistent parentheses, so that any sense of forcefully and confidently setting-out is greatly undermined. The first parenthesis, in making satirical and negative use of literary analogy, is a significant early example of a frequently encountered motif.

Examples of literary analogy abound. In the fifth paragraph of 'The Reader's Passport', the book is described as 'a series of faint reflections – mere shadows in the water – of places to which the imaginations of most people are attracted' (36), later recalled by the words 'whose name was writ in water', the inscription on Keats's tomb in Rome, a visit to which is one of the book's final incidents (201–2). The countryside between Paris and Châlons is, suggests the Narrator, best described by taking 'any pastoral poem, or picture, and [imagining] to yourself whatever is most exquisitely and widely unlike the descriptions therein contained' (43). The inhabitants of the Rhône valley are 'Lilliputian' (51); pictures in Avignon Cathedral recall the painter 'of the Primrose family, [who] had not been sparing of his colours' (53), in *The Vicar of Wakefield*; the Narrator and a Genoese cowman are 'like Robinson Crusoe and Friday reversed' (67); the Jesuit priest with disordered stockings in the coach to Piacenza resembles 'Hamlet in Ophelia's closet' (100); the courier carrying fuel 'looks like Birnam Wood taking a winter walk' (101–2); the attendant at Bologna cemetery, resplendent in 'cocked hat ... and dazzling buttons' (111), is like Gulliver in Brobdingnag. In Venice the Narrator imagines Shylock on a bridge, Desdemona leaning through a latticed window, and Shakespeare's spirit 'stealing through the city' (126). Verona, predictably, is dominated by Romeo and Juliet. When the Narrator is shown what purports to be Juliet's tomb he is not convinced of its authenticity and thinks it better that her real resting-place is forgotten and so 'out of the track of tourists' (129), unlike Yorick's Ghost, who wished 'to hear the feet upon the pavement overhead, and, twenty times a day, the repetition of his name' (129). Mrs Primrose returns in Milan to help the Narrator convey warm feelings about a saint. In Rome the mood changes: the 'hideous' (185) pictures of Christian martyrdom in the church of St Stefano Rotondo in Rome recall the bloodiest moments in *Macbeth*.

Shakespeare's darker writings comprise a recurring motif-within-a-motif, as do two other groups of literary references. The first is to Grimm-like fairy-tales: the 'ghostly, goblin inn' (158) at Radicofani; the roadside inns during the journey from Naples back to Rome are 'such hobgoblin places, that they are infinitely more attractive and amusing than the best hotels in Paris' (237). In particular, similar references dominate parts of the extended treatment of the Narrator's tour of the Palace of the Popes at Avignon. There the *concierge* is a 'She-Goblin' who escorts the Narrator through the prison cells once used by the Inquisition:

I am gazing round me, with the horror that the place inspires, when Goblin clutches me by the wrist, and lays, not her skinny finger, but the handle of a key, upon her lip. She invites me, with a jerk, to follow her. I do so. She leads me out into a room adjoining. ... She folds her arms, leers hideously, and stares. I ask again. She ... throws up her arms, and yells out, like a fiend, 'La Salle de la Question!'
The Chamber of Torture! ... (55–6)

Second, and most important of all, are a series of analogies with the Arabian Nights. Avignon, with its heat, flowers, narrow streets, and awnings, is 'all very like one of the descriptions in the "Arabian Nights"' (52); the Palazzo Peschiere in Genoa is 'more like an enchanted Palace in an Eastern story than a grave and sober lodging' (91); the 'brown, decayed, old town' of Piacenza is 'deserted, solitary', with a 'mysterious and solemn Palace, guarded by two colossal statues, twin Genii of the place' and 'a king with the marble legs, who flourished in the time of the thousand and one Nights' (103–4); the valley at Carrera is like 'the deep glen (just the same sort of glen) where the Roc left Sinbad the Sailor' (149).

For us, reading with hindsight, there is one further intertextual effect: when Dickens describes the hot, dusty countryside around Marseilles, Venice dreamlike on its lagoon, or the glories of Alpine scenery, we feel as much within the world of *Little Dorrit* as among the landscapes of nineteenth-century France and Italy. And a similar effect, of wandering through literary history, is created by the lurking Italianate presence of dead romantic poets, whether recalled through a waiter obsessed with Byron, or through allusions to and descriptions of the Roman graves of Keats and Shelley.

To the literary motif can be linked the theatrical: a sense of the latter is endemic to the book and evident from the first page as the pantechnicon trundles away in front of a Parisian backdrop. Indeed, a sense of the 'staged' opening is increased by the second parenthesis of that opening paragraph in which the small soldier plays a slightly comical part. Further south are 'Queer old towns, draw-bridged and walled: with odd little towers at the angles, like grotesque faces, as if the wall had put a mask on, and were staring, down into the moat' (42). Châlons market-place, full of country people and colourful stalls, 'looks as if it were the stage of some great theatre, and the curtain had just run up, for a picturesque ballet' (48). In the coach is an 'immeasurably-polite Chevalier, with a dirty scrap of red ribbon . . . as if he had tied it there, to remind him of something; as Tom Noddy in the farce ties knots in his pocket-handkerchief' (51). A woman unable to open her carriage doors is hauled through a window 'like a harlequin' (66). There is a lengthy critical description of theatre in Genoa with its 'uncommonly hard and cruel' (87) audience and indifferent acting. The 'Theatre of Puppets, or Marionetti' is very different: 'exquisitely ridiculous . . . the triumph of art . . . unspeakably ludicrous' (87–90). When visiting Italian cities the Narrator always notices things theatrical. In Parma he visits an old derelict theatre in the Farnese Palace: 'If ever Ghosts act plays, they act them on this ghostly stage' (107). A visiting equestrian company brings life and vigour into the streets of stagnant Modena. Another – perhaps the same – troupe was in Verona, leading the Narrator to imagine a long tradition of street-theatre in a city in which he also found a 'very pretty modern theatre' (131). As for Rome: St Peter's, decorated for a 'Festa', looked like 'one of the opening scenes in a very lavish pantomime' (163); the Pope's High Mass took place, thought the Narrator, in a 'kind of theatre', with Swiss guards like 'theatrical supernumeraries' and spectators in boxes 'shaped like those at the Italian Opera in England' (165–6). Even though parts of Catholic ritual, in particular the chanting in St Peter's and elsewhere, were 'monotonous, heartless, drowsy' (183), elements of theatre, of performance, were always present, if only when the sacristan rattled his box for money 'much as Punch rattles the cracked bell' (184). Outside, in secular Rome, the Coliseum still inspired memories of its spectacular history, shop-fronts at Carnival time were filled with people 'like boxes at a shining theatre' (171).

The Roman experience is the prelude to 'A Rapid Diorama', the theatrical metaphor of this subtitle underpinning the book's final section. It begins with the 'pantomime' (218) gestures of Naples, enters melodrama in the overnight ascent of Vesuvius, and returns to Naples 'airing its Harlequin suit in the sunshine' (231), thus ending the work with dramatic scenic diversions.

So to art, one of the great attractions of Italy for the Victorian traveller and another narratorial obsession. *En route* through France the Narrator has reservations about what he sees: frescos in Avignon cathedral seem 'very roughly and comically got up: most likely by poor sign-painters' (53). In Italy he is even more hostile: though there were some beautiful pictures in Genoese churches they were 'almost universally set, side by side, with sprawling effigies of maudlin monks, and the veriest trash and tinsel ever seen' (85); in Parma cathedral the paintings were 'decayed and mutilated; in the Cupola Correggio's 'rotting' frescoes were 'a labyrinth of arms and legs: such heaps of foreshortened limbs, entangled and involved and jumbled together: no operative surgeon, gone mad, could imagine in his wildest delirium' (105–6). The Vatican arouses the Narrator's deepest prejudices: too many travellers admire because it is expected of them whereas, insists the Narrator,

I cannot leave my natural perception of what is natural and true, at a palace-door, in Italy or elsewhere ... I cannot forget that there are certain expressions of face, natural to certain passions ... I cannot dismiss ... such common-place facts as the ordinary proportions of men's arms, and legs, and heads. ...

Therefore, I freely acknowledge that when I see a Jolly young Waterman representing a cherubim, or a Barclay and Perkin's Drayman depicted as an Evangelist, I see nothing to commend or admire in the performance, however great its reputed Painter. (194–5)

Even Michelangelo's 'Last Judgement' and Raphael's Vatican painting of Leo IV are not exempt from criticism: '[He] ... who will say that he admires them both ... must, as I think, be wanting in his powers of perception' (195–6), is the Narrator's strong opinion. The sculptures of Bernini and his disciples were 'intolerable abortions' (197), the influence of 'monks and priests' (196) found everywhere. Though he was able to admire the 'amazing beauty of Titian's great picture of the Assumption of the Virgin at Venice' (195) and 'the exquisite grace and beauty of Canova's statues' (196) in Rome, the Narrator invariably engages with the question of realism. For he has no sympathy with or understanding of historical artistic convention or appropriate style; all is judged in terms of resemblance to real life and from a simple Protestant standpoint and so most Italian paintings are found wanting. As for beautiful buildings: the response is all too often in terms of their poor physical condition and resulting atmosphere. Ferrara was 'grim' (114), Modena's colonnades 'sombre' (107), Mantua 'stagnant' (132). Parts of Pisa are praised for their beauty but the leaning tower disappointed because 'too small' (151) and beggars seemed 'to embody all the trade and enterprise' (154) of the place. As for Venice: here was 'such surpassing beauty, and such grandeur, that all the rest was poor and faded, in comparison with its absorbing loveliness' (121), yet 'decayed and rotten' (126) elements could also be found, together with persisting mementos of its cruel past. Despite its beauty it became a sinister place and about it 'crept the water always. Noiseless and watchful: coiled round and round it, in its many folds, like an old serpent' (127).

Such views on continental art and architecture dominate the book and their most important effect is on the title. The warm, glowing and glamorous connotations of 'Pictures from Italy' are deconstructed, when the reader turns back to it, by underlying narratorial antipathy. The pictures are 'penned in the fulness of the subject, and with the liveliest impressions of novelty and fresh-ness' (36), but as the book is read even the title has a subtext suggesting instinctive dislike.

This deconstructive urge surfaces in metaphor that is often distasteful. Examples include the rope harness 'embossed' (41) by the excrement of pigeons, the Diligence 'nodding and shaking, like an idiot's head' (43), poplars near Châlons that 'look in the distance like so many combs with broken teeth' (49), or, a fourth example, houses in Genoa 'afflicted with a cutaneous disorder' (69), whilst against 'the old Senate House, round about any large building, little shops stick close, like parasite vermin to the great carcase' (77). The urge surfaces again, less directly but no less effectively, in the basic negativity of numerous passages. Thus:

> The Villa Bagnerello: or the Pink Jail, a far more expressive name for the mansion: is in one of the most splendid situations imaginable. The noble bay of Genoa, with the deep blue Mediterranean, lie stretched out near at hand; monstrous old desolate houses and palaces are dotted all about; lofty hills, with their tops often hidden in the clouds, and with strong forts perched high up on their craggy sides, are close upon the left; and in front, stretching from the walls of the house, down to a ruined chapel which stands upon the bold and picturesque rocks on the sea-shore, are green vineyards, where you may wander all day long in partial shade, through interminable vistas of grapes, trained on a rough trellis work across the narrow paths. (65)

The initial attractive impression created by that first sentence, together with the impressive moments that lurk throughout the paragraph, are greatly undermined by the negative effect of 'monstrous', 'desolate', 'hidden', 'ruined', 'partial', 'interminable', and 'rough'. The Narrator turns instinctively to words that reflect his true feelings about his environmental predicament.

The same reductive, limiting negativity characterises the de-scription of Genoa's 'Streets of Palaces': 'its narrow perspective of immense mansions, reduced to a tapering and most precious strip of brightness, looking down upon the heavy shade below! ... great, heavy, stone balconies ... dreary, dreaming, echoing vaulted chambers . . .' (74–5). It is found, again, in the account of Festa-days and the custom of placing lighted torches outside churches:

> This part of the ceremony is prettier and more singular a little way in the country, where you can trace the illuminated cottages all the way up a steep hill side; and where you pass festoons of tapers, wasting away in the starlight night, before some lonely little house upon the road. (81)

Even the initial praise is grudging, saying only that the ceremony is done better in the country and then the realistic 'steep' counters suggestions of the picturesque. 'Wasting away' hints at criticism of Roman Catholicism in relation to its deprived society; 'lonely' undermines the effect of 'illuminated' and shifts the passage's tone towards the desolate; 'little' is hardly positive. Further, descending the Alps into Switzerland,

> passing under everlasting glaciers, by means of arched galleries, hung with clusters of dripping icicles; . . . through caverns over whose arched roofs the avalanches slide, in spring, and bury themselves in the unknown gulf beneath . . . lofty bridges . . . horrible ravines: a little shifting speck in the vast desolation of ice and snow, and monstrous granite rocks . . . deafened by the torrent plunging madly down. . . . (142–3)

the effect is strangely mixed. The Narrator is responsive to natural grandeur but for that grandeur he also feels a fundamental distaste.

A final example:

> The excursions in the neighbourhood of Rome are charming, and would be full of interest were it only for the changing views they afford, of the wild Campagna. But, every inch of ground, in every direction, is rich in associations, and in natural beauties. There is Albano, with its lovely lake and wooded shore, and with its wine, that certainly has not improved since the days of Horace . . . There is squalid Tivoli . . . minor waterfalls . . . one good cavern yawning darkly, where the river takes a fearful plunge and shoots on, low down under beetling rocks. There, too, is the Villa d'Este, deserted and decaying among groves of melancholy pine and cypress-trees. . . . (198–9)

The point hardly needs stressing: the Narrator, despite an impulse to praise, finds words, such as 'squalid', 'minor', 'yawning', 'low down', and 'deserted', that once again betray his fundamental alienation.

To the recurring references to literature and to the theatre, the obsessive, essentially dismissive reaction to Italian painting and architecture, the latent negativity undercutting ostensible admiration, the 'dream motif' can be added. So many descriptions have an unreal, dreamlike tone as the 'fancy' is indulged: Rhône 'villages and small towns hanging in mid-air ... and clouds moving slowly on' (51), Avignon with its 'quiet sleepy courtyards, having stately old houses within, as silent as tombs' (52); the Narrator at the Palais des Papes 'in a sort of dream' (59). In the hall of the Palazzo Peschiere, the Dickens family home for most of their stay in Genoa, the Narrator recalls staring at the view from the hall (it is a rare positive moment) 'in a perfect dream of happiness' (91). Impressions of Italy during travel 'came back like half-formed dreams' (118); Siena is 'very dreamy and fantastic' (156).

Predictably, the dream-like at times shades into more menacing night-thoughts:

I wonder why the head coppersmith in an Italian town always lives next door to the Hotel, or opposite: making the visitor feel as if the beating hammers were his own heart, palpitating with a deadly energy! I wonder why jealous corridors surround the bedroom on all sides, and fill it with unnecessary doors that can't be shut, and will not open, and abut on pitchy darkness! I wonder why it is not enough that these distrustful genii stand agape at one's dreams all night. . . . (114)

The interior of the Palazzo Tè in Mantua is decorated by Giulio Romano with 'unaccountable nightmares' (135) full of Giants that, the Narrator imagines, still stalk through the mists that surround the palace.

Such references, obsessions, latencies and motifs, are crucial structural elements. In particular, the theatre references and the recurring reminders of dreams move towards episodes that emphasise and confirm the pervasive thematic influence of each sequence. Thus the book ends in Rome, first at Carnival time, the great city becomes unreal and anarchically theatrical, and then during Holy Week when the Catholic Church, on public view at St Peter's, is presented as a tawdry impresario offering Papal Masses in the description of which the key word is 'performance'. Dreams culminate in 'An Italian Dream', the description of Venice as ghostly, strange, beautiful and sinister, the narrator reflecting upon 'this strange Dream upon the water: half-wondering if it lie there yet, and if its name be VENICE' (127). As for the literary references: these culminate in *Pictures from Italy* itself, in which the Narrator's France and Italy become a literary artifact.

This last reminds us that these countries are *created* as the expression of the Narrator's basic feelings about his travelling and his destinations, and so returns us to characterisation and its function. The Narrator emerges as a complex, unhappy and confused figure. The man who wants his pictures to be realistic transforms the continental experience into the insubstantial and unreal. For in the experience itself he finds little to like; he constantly discovers that even initial attractiveness quickly dissolves. What he wrote when first journeying to Genoa via the Cornice – 'Much of the romance of the beautiful towns and villages on this beautiful road, disappears when they are entered, for many of them are very miserable' (98) – is applicable to most of his travelling. His reservations about France and Italy, his reluctance to face them directly and consequent readiness to escape into analogy, obsession, metaphor, and negativity and his fervent final hope that the country might alter 'and a noble people may be, one day, raised up from these ashes' (242), the final image evoking Italy as a desert in which he had been condemned to wander, are all reactions to his own predicament.

Though it helpfully alerts the reader to know that the Narrator and Dickens may well be one and the same, though it is useful to grasp the biographical context of this excursion, *Pictures from Italy* is a self-contained monologue in which experience is filtered through and organised by the monologist's inadvertently revealing explorations of self. Attempts to praise and to engage sympathetically with new lands quickly give way to the expression of a dark, troubled and alienated psyche. The discrepancy thus shown between initial appearance and overwhelming psychological reality tells us much about the *Narrator*'s France and Italy. That is, *Pictures from Italy* has to be read as travel fiction in which the Narrator-character is the main source of interest and determines how the book can be read.

3 THE SENTIMENTAL PATERNALIST IN
A CHRISTMAS CAROL[15]

The concept of the fictional-work-as-monologue is also central to understanding *A Christmas Carol* but my discussion of the tale begins with the famous illustrations and their relationship to the text. This link is not a simple one, for though some pictures, such as the opening embodiment of benevolent paternalism in 'Mr Fezziwig's Ball', the chained phantoms sharing Marley's fate, or Scrooge attempting to extinguish the light of Christmas Past, are simple visual renderings of textual points, others are not.[16] For example, the Scrooge of the text is 'a squeezing, wrenching, grasping, scraping, clutching, covetous old sinner! Hard and sharp as flint. . . . The cold within him froze his old features, nipped his pointed nose, shrivelled his cheek, stiffened his gait . . .' (46). This is not the person seen in 'Marley's Ghost', nor in 'Scrooge's third Visitor'. The Scrooge we see there is old, vulnerable and full of amiable curiosity. In 'Scrooge's third Visitor', he is fascinated and attracted by the vibrant presence of the Ghost and the food and drink heaped around him. Further, in the plate of 'Marley's Ghost' the colours are unexpected. Scrooge's living-room, described in the text as part of a 'gloomy suite of rooms' (54), glows, in the illustration, with rich purple, blue, yellow and brown, the colours of life and growth. The foot-stool waits to enable a more indulgent Scrooge to escape the draught. The two illustrations suggest the human potential, the latent goodness, in both the man and his surroundings.

Stave III ends with Scrooge's confrontation with Ignorance and Want, arguably the most powerful and moving part of the text:

> From the foldings of its robe, it brought two children; wretched, abject, frightful, hideous, miserable. They knelt down at its feet, and clung upon the outside of its garment.
>
> 'Oh, Man! look here. Look, look, down here!' exclaimed the Ghost.
>
> They were a boy and girl. Yellow, meagre, ragged, scowling, wolfish; but prostrate, too, in their humility. Where graceful youth should have filled their features out, and touched them with its freshest tints, a stale and shrivelled hand, like that of age, had pinched, and twisted them, and pulled them into shreds. Where angels might have sat enthroned, devils lurked;

and glared out menacing. No change, no degradation, no perversion of humanity, in any grade, through all the mysteries of wonderful creation, has monsters half so horrible and dread. . . .

'Spirit! are they yours?' Scrooge could say no more.

'They are Man's,' said the Spirit, looking down upon them. 'And they cling to me, appealing from their fathers. This boy is Ignorance. This girl is Want. Beware them both, and all of their degree, but most of all beware this boy, for on his brow I see that written which is Doom, unless the writing be erased. Deny it!' cried the Spirit, stretching out its hand towards the city. 'Slander those who tell it ye! Admit it for your factious purposes, and make it worse. And bide the end!' (108)

The Spirit, in referring to Scrooge as 'Man' and the children as 'Man's' and in 'stretching out its hand towards the city' suggests that the existence of ignorance and want is the fault of Scrooge and those like him, wealthy individuals whose money is not put to proper use. The scene, like the story, is an argument for benevolent paternalism. But in the illustration the confrontation takes place against a background of Victorian factory-buildings with their smoking stacks. The point is a different one: the 'yellow, meagre, ragged, scowling, wolfish' children of the text, the existence of ignorance and want, are the dreadful products of unrestrained industrialism, of which the nineteenth-century factory system, in particular its use of child labour, is a dreadful manifestation.

The book's final pages are much concerned with the changed relationship between the converted Scrooge and Bob Cratchit, the jovial boss assuring his astonished clerk, 'I'll raise your salary, and endeavour to assist your struggling family, and we will discuss your affairs this very afternoon, over a Christmas bowl of smoking bishop' (133). On the venue for that discussion the text is silent but the final illustration shows Scrooge, foot comfortably on foot-stool, in his seasonally decorated living-room, ladling out punch for an eager Bob. The text asserts improved working relationships between master and man, the illustration socialising, benevolent to the extent that the worker is invited to the boss's home. That said, the illustration makes Bob childlike: his feet hardly touch the floor, his umbrella is as long as he is, Scrooge is fatherly towards him. Paternalism remains the keynote and the picture extends its scope.

The illustrations, then, are an integral part of *A Christmas Carol*.

They expose the limitations of the purely textual exploration of Scrooge's characterisation and Victorian social ills. In that the illustrations and text *combined* exhibit the complete work's wide-ranging insight into social conditions, the text alone necessarily indicates the Narrator's limitations. His is not the complete picture.

The story's opening is well-known:

Marley was dead: to begin with. There is no doubt whatever about that. . . . Old Marley was as dead as a door-nail.
Mind! I don't mean to say that I know, of my own knowledge, what there is particularly dead about a door-nail. . . . (14)

The bluff, insistent, buttonholing manner reminds us of similar openings but in a different *genre*:

No more wine? then we'll push back chairs and talk.
A final glass for me, though . . .

or

I am poor brother Lippo, by your leave!
You need not clap your torches to my face.

or

You know, we French stormed Ratisbon:
A mile or so away . . .

These lines from, respectively, 'Bishop Blougram's Apology', 'Fra Lippo Lippi', and 'Incident of the French Camp',[17] remind us that the age of Dickens was also that of Robert Browning and that the dramatic monologue was a ubiquitous form that has been precisely described:

[It] should include a first-person speaker who is not the poet and whose character is unwittingly revealed, an auditor whose influence is felt in the poem, a specific time and place, colloquial language, some sympathetic involvement with the speaker, and an ironic discrepancy between the speaker's view of himself and a larger judgment which the poet implies and the reader must develop.[18]

The relevance of this definition to a prose work like *A Christmas Carol* is immediately apparent. Indeed, Dickens himself realised his tale's monologising qualities: *A Christmas Carol* was a natural choice for the first public reading that he gave and, during the reading tours, the one he usually chose for important performances. This discussion will return to notions of sympathy and ironic discrepancy; here, the palpable presence of an auditor can first be stressed. He is, for instance, the person to whose queries the Narrator responds: 'Scrooge knew he was dead?' echoes the latter, 'Of course he did. How could it be otherwise?' (45). In Stave II the Narrator observes that Scrooge was as close to the Ghost of Christmas Past 'as I am now to you, and I am standing in the spirit at your elbow' (68), the moment above all others in which the Narrator's as well as the listener/reader's separate characterisation can be clearly discerned.

So far as the Narrator's characterisation is concerned very few critics have much to say. Indeed, some famous discussions of the tale fail to make any proper distinction between Narrator and Author. Chesterton, for example, though noting that the tale's 'festive and popular'[19] style counters ostensibly bleak events and scenes, thus implicitly recognising the importance of narrative tone, assumes the style to be Dickens's own and leaves it at that. Edgar Johnson, in his influential study of Scrooge as 'the personification of "economic man"',[20] also makes no distinction between Narrator and Author.

Later, more critically-aware analyses include Deborah Thomas on the relevance of the dramatic monologue term to many of Dickens's short pieces and his use of the 'first-person narrative as a tool for revealing mental processes'.[21] Michael Slater argues shrewdly that, in *A Christmas Carol* we receive 'an overwhelming impression of the story-teller's physical proximity' (xii) and the story-teller is understood as 'a jolly, kind-hearted bachelor uncle' (xi), generally joking and festive, occasionally sharp about the state of the country, momentarily grim in Stave III, when treating Scrooge's confrontation with Ignorance and Want. Graham Holderness, in a perceptive interpretation of the tale as Scrooge's rejection of materialism and cultivation of the sympathetic imagination, includes an important discussion of the Narrator's character. He argues that the Narrator embodies 'the power of imagination', expressed via the qualities of 'energy and vitality, humour and imagination'[22] so evident in most of the narrative, that eventually shapes and educates Scrooge. Holderness, though, is forced to conclude that, because we are so impressed by the Narrator's qualities, the final section of the tale disappoints: the prose loses its imaginative life and the Narrator declines into a sentimental conclusion.

Slater and Holderness can be persuasive. Both regard the Narrator as a positive and essentially simple character. Yet even the tale's opening suggests the inadequacy of these views. The narrative persona is hearty and emphatic, the bachelor uncle of Slater's account, but that it is also oddly self-conscious and insecure is evident in the way he scrutinises his own clichés: the statement that 'Old Marley was as dead as a door-nail' is followed by a paragraph discussing the appropriateness of the image. In the dismissive comment that ends that discussion – 'But the wisdom of our ancestors is in the simile; and my unhallowed hands shall not disturb it, or the country's done for' (45) – is a jocular but contemptuous view of popular sentiment. Behind the heartiness is a defensively prickly personality.

Through the opening pages this defensiveness is evident in three aspects of the narrative. First, the insistence on its fictiveness, effected mainly through obvious patterning that emphasises the Narrator as maker as well as teller. We see this in a small way as Marley's Ghost departs: 'at every step it took, the window raised itself a little' (64). The scene is manifestly contrived, here to retain distancing humour. More centrally, as a number of critics have pointed out, there is an enhanced concern for form and structure seen in the tale's precise divisions, and careful linking of parts evident, for example, in Scrooge's remarks on prisons and death being thrown back at him by the second spirit, in the philanthropic gentlemen in Stave I reappearing in the final stave to show Scrooge's new attitudes, in the careful contrasting of the chronological progression of the Spirit-scenes with the tale's timeless present, and the equally careful concern not only with the course of Scrooge's life but with its consequences. Small, early details have the same effect: the reader, insists the Narrator, must understand that Marley was dead, otherwise 'nothing wonderful can come of the story I am going to relate' (45). Having emphasised the importance of fictional conventions he begins the action proper with a deliberate 'Once upon a time' (47).

Second, a development of the first, is the Narrator's over-insistence on the facts, evident throughout and obvious even in the first two sentences: 'Marley was dead: to begin with. There is no doubt whatever about that.' That the Narrator too often protests too much counters any initial sense of this power through knowledge.

Third, the Narrator distances himself from the tale's events, and refuses to empathise. This he achieves by undermining seriousness. The first description of Scrooge is deprived of much of its force by its own verve and energy – 'Oh! but he was a tight-fisted hand at the grindstone, Scrooge! a squeezing, wrenching, grasping, scraping, clutching, covetous old sinner!' (46) – and by its jokey references to the weather. London fog seems less cold, bleak and polluted, indeed, can seem almost attractive when compared to steam from brewers' chimneys. In the scenes between Scrooge and his nephew, and Scrooge and the philanthropic gentlemen, even though Scrooge's superb diatribes attract us and have more life and force than the sincere platitudes of his visitors, his emotional force is partly neutralised by the way even the dialogue is imbued with some humour: 'At the ominous word "liberality", Scrooge frowned, and shook his head' and

'"You wish to be anonymous?"
"I wish to be left alone," said Scrooge.' (50–51)

Even one of the tale's serious concerns, the existence of free will, of moral choice, implicit in Marley informing Scrooge that the latter continues to labour on the chain that still frustrates him, is not free from facetiousness: following Marley's words 'Scrooge glanced about him on the floor, in the expectation of finding himself surrounded by some fifty or sixty fathoms of iron cable: but he could see nothing' (61). The shocking attitudes towards the poor and unfortunate ('"If they would rather die," said Scrooge, "they had better do it, and decrease the surplus population'"' become less so when Scrooge's delight in his own repartee allows us to be amused: '[he] resumed his labours with an improved opinion of himself, and in a more facetious temper than was usual with him' (51–2). Even in the grimmest passage, the encounter with Ignorance and Want, when the Narrator himself is moved by the youthful apparitions, his treatment of Scrooge hardly maximises pathos: 'Scrooge started back, appalled. Having them shown to him in this way, he tried to say they were fine children, but the words choked themselves, rather than be parties to a lie of such enormous magnitude' (108). The personifying of 'words' allows a hint of facetiousness even into this dark passage.

Humour is rarely absent from the text; its often fanciful presence, whether in the chattering teeth of a chiming clock, the 'misanthropic ice' (52), Scrooge's house when young 'playing at hide-and-seek with other houses' (54), the knocker in the shape of Marley's face glowing 'like a bad lobster in a dark cellar' (54), prevents full emotional involvement on the Narrator's part as well as on the reader's and mitigates the salutary effect of Scrooge's character and circumstances. All becomes, as the Narrator writes of poulterers and grocers, 'a splendid joke: a glorious pageant' (52).

These short phrases are examples of a further distancing effect, the use of the formally archaic, at times humorously effective language that increasingly replaces the heartily colloquial. For example: when the Ghost of Christmas Past materialises, the Narrator comments that because of its dissolving tendency 'no outline would be visible in the dense gloom wherein they melted away' (68). When Scrooge asks the Ghost to cover himself and is reprimanded, he

> reverently disclaimed all intention to offend ... He then made bold to inquire what business brought him there. ...
> 'Rise! and walk with me!'
> It would have been in vain for Scrooge to plead that the weather and the hour were not adapted to pedestrian purposes. ... (69)

During the remainder of the tale the Narrator often escapes from pleasurable engagement or emotional involvement into this highly-formal style. Two examples must suffice: neighbours shovelling snow hurl 'a facetious snowball – better-natured missile far than many a wordy jest' (89); the Ghost takes him through the city 'until besought by Scrooge to tarry for a moment' (123). The language mocks rather than dignifies; the narrative stance is one of patronising superiority. Certainly the readiness of the humour and the mock-elevation of the style suggest callousness. This last quality, always lurking, on occasion becomes troublingly overt.

To put this another way: the Narrator is all too willing to substitute for humane involvement a *bonhomie* that on occasion can be brutal:

Foggier yet, and colder! Piercing, searching, biting cold. If the good Saint Dunstan had but nipped the Evil Spirit's nose with a touch of such weather as that, instead of using his familiar weapons, then indeed he would have roared to lusty purpose. The owner of one scant young nose, gnawed and mumbled by the hungry cold as bones are gnawed by dogs, stooped down at Scrooge's keyhole to regale him with a Christmas carol: but at the first sound ... Scrooge seized the ruler with such energy of action, that the singer fled in terror. . . . (52–3)

The boisterous reference to Saint Dunstan who, in the legend, wielded red-hot pincers, in itself shows a cheerful delight in cruelty. The casual appearance in such a hearty paragraph of the savage simile describing the young carol-singer's nose betrays a disturbing lack of persisting compassion. Equally distasteful and cruel is the sketch of 'a red-faced gentleman with a pendulous excrescence on the end of his nose, that shook like the gills of a turkey-cock' (111). Such Swiftean fascination for the gross physical attribute is not indicative of warm fellow-feeling.

A lack of the latter is particularly evident in the treatment of the Cratchits. Bob, the family-man with scanty means and awesome responsibilities, is treated as a child who cheers simple Christmas sentiments, slides with the children, runs home 'as hard as he could pelt, to play at blindman's-buff' (53), and is too often described as 'Little Bob' (94). During Christmas dinner the family is patronised pedantically: the Narrator pokes fun at their pretence that the small pudding is sufficient and, when they draw around the hearth, corrects Bob's reference to the family 'circle, meaning half a one' (96). Revealingly, when the Ghost of Christmas Present stops to bless the Cratchits' home, 'Think of that!' cries the Narrator,

> Bob had but fifteen 'Bob' a-week himself; he pocketed on Saturdays but fifteen copies of his Christian name; and yet the Ghost of Christmas Present blessed his four-roomed house! (93)

In insisting that a man's income should not determine his just deserts he succeeds only in implying that it should.

As for the Cratchits' observance of Christmas: along with the knowingness and assumptions of pedantic superiority, the Narrator purveys the belief that even such a poor and unfortunate family can put out of its collective mind all but ideas of happiness and charity, to demonstrate that no circumstance, however hostile, can corrupt their innate Christian feelings. Further, their social compliance – admiration of the aristocracy, satisfaction that son will follow father into penury through clerking, absence of concern for domestic deficiencies – beggars belief as well as themselves. In stating that such a family is 'happy, grateful, pleased with one another, and contented with the time' (99) the Narrator withdraws from considered sympathy with decent but badly-treated folk into sentimental evasion.

Most disturbing of all is his treatment of Tiny Tim's death. A chair is set next to the child's body in the Cratchit bedroom:

> Poor Bob sat down in it, and when he had thought a little and composed himself, he kissed the little face. He was reconciled to what had happened, and went down again quite happy. (122)

The final sentence is breath-taking in its evasive manipulation in the interests of narratorial wish-fulfilment.

To the treatment of the Cratchits can be added another troubling and unexpected tendency: as the Ghost of Christmas Past leads Scrooge back through time, his 'grasp, though gentle as a woman's hand, was not to be resisted' (69). The simile is a small first indication of the Narrator's pronounced sensuality, evident again in his knowing excitement at the dancing at Fezziwig's and, particularly, as Scrooge and the Ghost observe Scrooge's nephew's family in their drawing-room on Christmas Eve. At first they watch the children play, before the nephew's beautiful young daughter

> soon beginning to mingle in the sports, got pillaged by the young brigands most ruthlessly. What would I not have given to be one of them! Though I never could have been so rude, no, no! I wouldn't for the wealth of all the world have crushed that braided hair, and torn it down; and for the precious little shoe, I wouldn't have plucked it off, God bless my soul! to save my life. As to measuring her waist in sport, as they did, bold young brood, I couldn't have done it; I should have expected my arm to have grown round it for a punishment, and never come straight again. And yet I should have dearly liked, I own, to have touched her lips; to have questioned her, that she might have opened them; to have looked upon the lashes of her downcast

eyes, and never raised a blush; to have let loose waves of hair, an
inch of which would be a keepsake beyond price: in short, I
should have liked, I do confess, to have had the lightest licence
of a child, and yet been man enough to know its value. (81–2)

The passage is intriguing and disturbing in that the imagery of
violence first applied to the children's innocent play is then used to
express the narrator's feelings for the beautiful daughter. She is
regarded as a gratifying object to be tousled, partially stripped and
then fondled; the irony and indirection – the cutting of hair
suggesting violation – may betray the Narrator's unease and
cannot hide his repressed sexuality. Such feelings recur briefly as
he describes Christmas festivities observed by Scrooge and the
Ghost of Christmas Present, in particular a 'group of handsome
girls' visiting a neighbour's house 'where, woe upon the single
man who saw them enter – artful witches: well they knew it – in a
glow!' (99), and, importantly, in a later scene in the nephew's
home. Now, the Narrator drools over Scrooge's niece –

a dimpled, surprised-looking, capital face; a ripe little mouth,
that seemed made to be kissed – as no doubt it was; all kinds of
good little dots about her chin, that melted into one another
when she laughed; and the sunniest pair of eyes you ever saw in
any little creature's head. Altogether she was what you would
have called provoking, you know; but satisfactory too. Oh,
perfectly satisfactory! (102)

– and savours, in Sternean fashion, Topper's performance at
blind-man's buff, his mock-attempts to identify the plump sister by
touching her headdress, ring and necklace. Topper's behaviour
was 'vile, monstrous! No doubt she told him her opinion of it,
when, another blind-man being in office, they were so very
confidential together, behind the curtains' (105). The Narrator
assumes a none-too-convincing knowledge of women that serves
only to remind us of his presumed bachelor status and repressed
sexuality.

The characterising of the Narrator is superbly consistent. His
readiness to withdraw from humane involvement, his patronising
superiority, make for an uneasy and imperceptive account of
Scrooge's career. His inability properly to empathise prevents him
from regarding those who feature in his tale as complex human

beings deserving consideration for what they actually are. Instead, too many of the characters – the Cratchits, the nephew's family – are manipulated into patterns of wish-fulfilment that include, so far as the latter are concerned, sensual-sexual fantasising.

Thus unlike Holderness, we should not be disappointed at the tale's ending. For Stave V describes a radical and fundamental change of character: the miser becomes the philanthropist. Stave V shows Scrooge expressing the latent benevolence and kindliness of the illustrations. But whereas, in the pictures, the point has positive force, in the text the effect is the opposite. This can be explained by reference to the language. The Narrator regains the heartiness and facetiousness of the tale's opening pages and takes them to the edges of hysteria. Thus, of Scrooge's laugh:

> Really, for a man who had been out of practice for so many years, it was a splendid laugh, a most illustrious laugh. The father of a long, long line of brilliant laughs! (128)

and

> Running to the window, he opened it, and put out his head. No fog, no mist; clear, bright, jovial, stirring, cold; cold, piping for the blood to dance to; Golden sunlight; Heavenly sky; sweet fresh air; merry bells. Oh, glorious. Glorious! (128)

The sense of strain is evident, as is the poverty of a language that seeks effects through exclamatory insistence. Whereas the illustrations contribute to a sense of man's innate goodness, Stave V illustrates the narrator's sentimentality evident in the imposition of a happy ending. Such manipulation and wish-fulfilment are exactly as expected.

To return to Holderness's criticisms of this last section: '[Dickens's] vision of a transformed life is far weaker, far narrower, far less *imaginative*, than his understanding of the world that needs to be transformed' and the resorting to 'abstract virtue', the 'thinness' of which 'can be measured by the unsureness of the prose', means that the story ends with a 'weary, unenthusiastic affirmation of "goodness"'.[23] The trouble with this statement, we now see, is that Holderness neglects the distinction between Author and Narrator. Once that distinction is made and the Narrator's character properly understood, Stave V has to be read differently as, on Dickens's part, a deliberately sentimental effusion proceeding from the Narrator's reactionary, because optimistically paternalistic, viewpoint. We can agree with Holderness that the final section demonstrates the Narrator's grave lack of a sympathetic imagination whilst recognising, as he does not, that this is the tale's essential point.

The Narrator is strongly characterised in all Dickens's writings. In this sense they are all monologues. *A Christmas Carol*, in particular, is properly understood only if it is recognised as such. As has been seen, the illustrations expose the limitations of the monologist's moral and imaginative insight into Scrooge's life and conversion. But whereas the pictures might be said to have a positively deconstructive effect on the text, the force of the Narrator's textual life, asserting his faulty vision, is a substantial subversion of the whole work's attempt at the optimistic gesture that offers understanding as a prelude to effective social action. The Narrator's misconceived and misdirected force and textual life put optimism firmly in its place.

4   EXTENDING THE INTERFACE: THE THIRD NARRATOR IN *BLEAK HOUSE*[24]

Dickens's first Christmas book is a minor masterpiece but the complexities of its short text do not, of course, compare to those of the major novels. *Bleak House*, in particular, poses difficult narratorial problems stemming from the novel's use of more than one Narrator. About this last there is considerable critical unease: several important discussions of the relationship between the third-person omniscient narrative and Esther Summerson's concern themselves with the extent to which each is produced by a consistent narrative persona. Grahame Smith, for example, describes the third-person Narrator as an 'urbane, witty, cultured'[25] and essentially decent character; Donovan,[26] however, asserts that a consistent third-person viewpoint is not sustained and, too often, cannot be clearly distinguished from Dickens himself; Flint, in agreeing implicitly with Donovan's first point, subscribes, as has already been noted, to Bakhtin's notion of the 'polyphonic' narrator, that series of voices that in their multiplicity deny, as Flint argues of *Bleak House*, that there can be an 'absolute organizing authority'.[27] As for Esther Summerson: though this young lady, once regarded as one of Dickens's failures, has been redeemed as a

Freudian heroine by those who recognise her psychologically warped character as a convincing, though not likeable, consequence of her unhappy and repressed upbringing, she has been subjected to reservations similar to those regarding the third-person Narrator. For even feminist interest in Esther Summerson as the heart-governed, subjective, domesticated Victorian woman can be accompanied by Bakhtin-inspired queries regarding her sustained and consistent separate existence. Flint's rejection of a single organising force has obvious application to Esther. Senf[28] argues that the third-person and first-person Narrators have limited perspectives on the novel's events; readers effect a synthesis to achieve a more complete because androgynous view. Her thinking, directed against the self-contained nature of the Narrator, has affinities with Flint's further argument that narrating characters in *Bleak House* do not exist exclusively, are not neatly juxtaposed. Rather, the male, near-omniscient, third-person Narrator 'invades'[29] Esther's first-person account. To put this another way, the reader becomes immediately and increasingly conscious of elements common to both narratives.

From the first there is a flow towards connection. The material is familiar: the opening Chancery scenes in the third-person sequence are experienced by Esther, in Chapter 3, as she is brought to Kenge and Carboys, to the Lord Chancellor and his court, and to her meeting with Miss Flite. Eleven chapters later Esther visits Miss Flite in her room above Krook's shop and reads the door-post bill advertising the now-vacant room where Nemo died, the description of that death being a vivid and moving part of the other sequence. Richard is distantly related to Sir Leicester Dedlock; 'Bleak House' adjoins the Chesney Wold estate. Those few early examples can suffice and to them can be added examples of characters who appear in both narratives: Esther herself, of course, and Woodcourt, Guppy, Sir Leicester and Lady Dedlock, Bucket, Mrs Chadband. Few characters of importance do not.

To such plot and structural connections can be added common uses of language, one of the most important being wit. Thus in the opening chapter of the third-person narrative, describing Chancery lawyers: 'Eighteen of Mr Tangle's learned friends ... bob up like eighteen hammers in a pianoforte, make eighteen bows, and drop into their eighteen places of obscurity' (i, 54). Lady Dedlock, we are later told, 'is perfectly well-bred. If she could be translated to Heaven to-morrow, she might be expected to ascend without any rapture' (ii, 58). Such moments are frequent; we come to expect them as this narrative continues and find wit and humour in abundance in the Snagsby, Smallweed and Bagnet sequences. The same sharp conceits occur throughout Esther's narrative: Mr Kenge 'casting his eyes over the dusty hearth-rug as if it were Mrs Jellyby's biography' (iv, 82); Mrs Jellyby's dress 'didn't nearly meet up the back . . . the open space was railed across with a lattice-work of stay-lace – like a summer-house' (iv, 85); as Mr Turveydrop 'bowed to me in that tight state, I almost believe I saw creases come into the whites of his eyes' (xiv, 244). And Esther's narrative also has its comic sequences involving Turveydrop, the Bayham Badgers, and Mrs Pardiggle 'applying benevolence . . . like a strait-waistcoat' (xxx, 479). Even though it might be argued that such material is too clever, too deliciously malicious to be at home in Esther's narrative, its prevalence in both narratives establishes an important stylistic point of reference.

Again, the third-person Narrator is a famous apostrophiser. A few examples must again serve: 'This is the Court of Chancery, which has its decaying houses and its blighted lands in every shire . . .' (i, 51), begins his powerful indictment of the Court. Equally powerful is his reaction to Joe's death: 'Dead, your Majesty. Dead, my lords and gentlemen. . . . And dying thus around us every day' (xlvii, 705). In Chapter 18, during Esther's narrative, she has her first glimpse of Chesney Wold:

> O, the solemn woods over which the light and shadow travelled swiftly, as if Heavenly wings were sweeping on benignant errands through the summer air; the smooth green slopes, the glittering water, the garden where the flowers were so symmetrically arranged in clusters of the richest colours, how beautiful they looked! (xviii, 300)

At the close of Chapter 35 Esther gives thanks that her face, now ravaged by smallpox, will not be seen by the departed Woodcourt, and that the relationship, as she believes, has not developed:

> O, it was so much better as it was! With a great pang mercifully spared me, I could take back to my heart my childish prayer to be all he had so brightly shown himself . . . and I could go, please God, my lowly way along the path of duty, and he could go his nobler way upon its broader road. . . . (xxxv, 557)

On all four occasions this most self-conscious of rhetorical tropes is used to express intense emotion. The third-person Narrator becomes the humane voice of society, using language as if addressing Parliament or writing a radical newspaper leader; Esther responds like a romantic nature poet and a thankful and impassioned pilgrim. The prominent foregrounding of apostrophes marks off the trope from its containing narrative to insist that such deep feelings are possible only when the parameters of the Narrators' characterisations are transcended. That is, each apostrophe indicates a third Narrator implied by and inferred from the third-person persona and Esther Summerson. The existence of this third Narrator is perceived via the elements common to both basic sequences, of which the flow towards connection, wit and apostrophising are the most important.

Most suggestive of all are effects at the interface, when, in each narrative, the reader is offered identical settings, similar scenes. Two examples follow, the first of scenes in the graveyard where Nemo is buried and to which Lady Dedlock eventually comes to die. The third-person Narrator describes the former:

Then the active and intelligent, who has got into the morning papers as such, comes with his pauper company to Mr Krook's, and bears off the body of our dear brother here departed, to a hemmed-in churchyard, pestiferous and obscene, whence malignant diseases are communicated to the bodies of our dear brothers and sisters who have not departed. . . . Into a beastly scrap of ground which a Turk would reject as a savage abomination, and a Caffre would shudder at, they bring our dear brother here departed, to receive Christian burial.

With houses looking on, on every side, save where a reeking little tunnel of a court gives access to the iron gate – with every villainy of life in action close on death, and every poisonous element of death in action close on life – here, they lower our dear brother down a foot or two: here, sow him in corruption, to be raised in corruption: an avenging ghost at many a sick bedside: a shameful testimony to future ages, how civilization and barbarism walked this boastful island together.

Come night, come darkness, for you cannot come to soon or stay too long, by such a place as this! Come, straggling lights into the windows of the ugly houses; and you who do iniquity therein, do it at least with this dread scene shut out! Come, flame of gas, burning so sullenly above the iron gate, on which the poisoned air deposits its witch-ointment slimy to the touch! It is well that you should call to every passer-by, 'Look here!'

With the night, comes a slouching figure through the tunnel-court, to the outside of the iron gate. It holds the gate with its hands, and looks in between the bars; stands looking in, for a little while.

It then, with an old broom it carries, softly sweeps the step, and makes the archway clean. It does so, very busily and trimly; looks in again, a little while; and so departs. (xi, 202–3)

Much later in the narrative Esther comes to the same place:

At last we stood under a dark and miserable covered way, where one lamp was burning over an iron gate, and where the morning faintly struggled in. The gate was closed. Beyond it, was a burial ground – a dreadful spot in which the night was very slowly stirring; but where I could dimly see heaps of dishonoured graves and stones, hemmed in by filthy houses, with a few dull lights in their windows, and on whose walls a thick humidity broke out like a disease. On the step at the gate, drenched in a fearful wet of such a place, which oozed and splashed down everything, I saw, with a cry of pity and horror, a woman lying ... with one arm creeping round the bar of the iron gate, and seeming to embrace it. . . .

I passed on to the gate, and stooped down. I lifted the heavy head, put the long dank hair aside, and turned the face. It was my mother, cold and dead. (lix, 867–9)

There are a number of features common to both passages. For example, they structure their descriptions similarly, focusing through the gloom and squalor on a single figure juxtaposed, prisoner-like, to the bars of the iron gate. The third-person passage has Joe, soon to die, Esther's her mother, Lady Dedlock, already dead. Each passage ends with a gesture of love. Words and phrases in common include 'hemmed in', 'disease'/'diseases', 'lights in the windows'/'lights in their windows', 'iron gate'; 'dread scenes'/'dreadful spot', and the similar 'straggling' and 'struggling'.

Of course there are differences. The 'reeking little tunnel' is, to Esther, 'a dark and miserable covered way'; 'ugly houses' are 'filthy houses'; the 'flame of gas, burning so sullenly above the iron gate' becomes, simply, 'one lamp was burning over an iron gate'. The 'churchyard', importantly, becomes 'a burial ground'; the former is 'pestiferous and obscene', the latter has 'heaps of dishonoured graves'. On the gate 'the poisoned air deposits its witch-ointment slimy to the touch', whilst Esther notes 'a thick humidity . . . like a disease' on the houses and, on the step at the gate, 'a fearful wet . . . oozed and splashed down everything'.

The third-person account uses rhetorical and literary effects that include echoes of *Macbeth* ('Come seeling night'),[30] and prose hinting at blank verse, to criticise fiercely the shocking indignities of pauper burial, the dangerous state of the graveyards as a source of contagious diseases, and the dreadful social complacency that allows such evils to exist. Though in Esther's account there is also a contriving literariness, evident in the dramatic alternation of long and short sentences, in the 'disease' simile, and in the movement to crescendo, concern is more directly moral than social as Esther emphasises man's distance from God and society's lack of reverence for the dead. Hence her replacement of 'churchyard' with 'graveyard' and her sense of the graves as 'dishonoured'. That said, her approach is less despairing: whereas the third-person Narrator calls for darkness, Esther notes that the morning 'faintly struggled in' as night was 'slowly stirring' among the graves.

Paradoxically, the differences support rather than counter the effect of the similarities. That is, the former also cause the reader to juxtapose the two passages and so foreground the *relationship* between them. The reader perceives the two passages to be linked and neatly complementary. That neatness suggests the need for a synthesis, which in turn infers the existence of a third narrative and Narrator.

Secondly:

On such an afternoon, if ever, the Lord High Chancellor ought to be sitting here – as here he is – with a foggy glory round his head, softly fenced in with crimson cloth and curtains, addressed by a large advocate with great whiskers, a little voice, and an interminable brief, and outwardly directing his contemplation to the lantern in the roof, where he can see nothing but fog. On such an afternoon, some score of members of the High Court of Chancery bar ought to be – as here they are – mistily engaged in one of the ten thousand stages of an endless cause, tripping one

another up on slippery precedents, groping knee-deep in tech-
nicalities, running their goat-hair and horsehair warded heads
against walls of words; and making a pretence of equity with
serious faces, as players might. On such an afternoon, the
various solicitors in the cause, some two or three of whom have
inherited it from their fathers, who made a fortune by it, ought to
be – as are they not? – ranged in a line, in a long matted well (but
you might look in vain for Truth at the bottom of it), between the
registrar's red table and the silk gowns, with bills, cross-bills,
answers, rejoinders, injunctions, affidavits, issues, references to
masters, masters' reports, mountains of costly nonsense, piled
before them. Well may the court be dim, with wasting candles
here and there; well may the fog hang heavy in it, as if it would
never get out; well may the stained-glass windows lose their
colour, and admit no light of day into the place; well may the
uninitiated from the streets, who peep in through the glass
panes in the door, be deterred from entrance by its owlish
aspect, and by the drawl languidly echoing to the roof from the
padded dais where the Lord High Chancellor looks into the
lantern that has no light in it, and where the attendant wigs are
all stuck in a fog-bank! This is the Court of Chancery; which has
its decaying houses and its blighted lands in every shire; which
has its worn-out lunatic in every madhouse, and its dead in
every churchyard; which has its ruined suitor, with his slipshod
heels and threadbare dress, borrowing and begging through the
round of every man's acquaintance; which gives to monied
might the means abundantly of wearying out the right; which so
exhausts finances, patience, courage, hope; so overthrows the
brain and breaks the heart; that there is not an honourable man
among its practitioners who would not give – who does not
often give – the warning, 'Suffer any wrong that can be done
you, rather than come here!' (i, 50–51)

Esther's visit is in Chapter 24:

When we came to the Court, there was the Lord Chancellor – the
same whom I had seen in his private room in Lincoln's Inn –
sitting in great state and gravity, on the bench; with the mace
and seals on a red table below him, and an immense flat
nosegay, like a little garden, which scented the whole court.
Below the table, again, was a long row of solicitors, with bundles

of papers on the matting at their feet; and then there were the gentlemen of the bar in wigs and gowns – some awake and some asleep, and one talking, and nobody paying very much attention to what he said. The Lord Chancellor leaned back in his very easy chair with his elbow on the cushioned arm, and his forehead resting on his hand; some of those who were present, dozed; some read the newspapers; some walked about, or whispered in groups: all seemed perfectly at their ease, by no means in a hurry, very unconcerned, and extremely comfortable.

To see everything going on so smoothly, and to think of the roughness of the suitors' lives and deaths; to see all that full dress and ceremony, and to think of the waste, and want, and beggared misery it represented; to consider that, while the sickness of hope deferred was raging in so many hearts, this polite show went calmly on from day to day, and year to year, in such good order and composure; to behold the Lord Chancellor, and the whole array of practitioners under him, looking at one another and at the spectators, as if nobody had ever heard that all over England the name in which they were assembled was a bitter jest: was held in universal horror, contempt, and indignation; was known for something so flagrant and bad, that little short of a miracle could bring any good out of it to any one: this was so curious and self-contradictory to me, who had no experience of it, that it was at first incredible, and I could not comprehend it. (xxiv, 399–400)

The differences between these two passages are similar to those between the two descriptions of the graveyard. The first account of the Court of Chancery is highly rhetorical, the third-person Narrator's anger spilling into repetitions that dramatise the Court's very procedure, into ridicule, and into extended conceits that reduce the humanity of those playing the legal parts. The passage insists upon itself, upon a fictiveness that heightens the Court's own artificiality, before moving into the huge, single-sentence crescendo that touches on the class-bias as well as the sheer evil of the Court before ending with an implied reflection on the honour of its lawyers. By contrast, Esther's is comparatively low-key, initially concerned with factual description.

The similarities are equally significant and begin with basic structure. Both passages focus first on the Lord Chancellor, move to counsel with their papers, then back to the Chancellor before commenting on the moral, human and social significance of the scene and its procedures. Such generalising comment from Esther is unusual and is expressed in, for her, language of unusual power, felt in such phrases as 'the roughness of the suitors' lives and deaths', 'beggared misery' and 'the sickness of hope deferred', this last with its Biblical echo.[31] Not only is such language reminiscent of the third-person sequence but Esther's closing sentence, in which clauses accumulate to an indignant crescendo, is startlingly similar to the close of the third-person account.

To repeat the point: the differences infer complementary roles and conscious juxtaposing, the similarities suggest more directly a further point of reference common to both narratives. In both cases the two narrating characters imply a third who is not so much androgynous as traditionally omniscient. He (and in a Victorian novel it is surely masculine, given such wide-ranging social access and knowledge of the world) understands, balances and, his main role, imposes order on experience. This order, proceeding as it does from a clear sense of purpose and power over circumstances, might be seen as dramatising a fundamental optimism about the possible course of human affairs. In practice it isolates the third Narrator in an impossible world of reasonable and complete apprehension and understanding so different from the mystery, misunderstanding, confusion, fear and struggle experienced by the action's participants. The reader's sense of the third Narrator as a source of the positively optimistic is undermined, certainly countered, by the essence of the story he oversees and manipulates.

5   THE MIDDLE-AGED BUSINESSMAN: THE NARRATOR OF *GREAT EXPECTATIONS*[32]

Tension between the Narrator's characterisation and the narrative's ostensible meaning is found again in *Great Expectations*. Though a move from the multiple narrative of *Bleak House* to a first-person account seems a shift from the complex to the simpler; in actuality, the shift is to the complexities of unreliability.

At the end of Chapter 56 Magwitch's death is followed by Pip's instinctive reflection: 'I knew there were no better words than I could say beside his bed, than "O Lord, be merciful to him, a sinner!"' (lvi, 470) The misquoting of the Biblical passage, the substitution of 'him' for 'me', has not escaped critical attention.

And though it might be argued that the replacing of the personal pronoun expresses Pip's new selflessness, greater weight must surely be given to the fact that Pip rejects the main force of Saint Luke's original passage and so reveals his own moral arrogance, possibly consequent upon a persisting lack of self-knowledge. His use of the passage – this is one example only – points to his unreliability and the reader's need for a clear understanding of the character who tells the tale.

Two critics see more clearly than most. Partlow writes: 'the narrator is neither Pip nor Mr Pip, but Mr Pirrip, a moderately successful, middle-aged businessman'.[33] Jordan makes the same point in much the same language: the Narrator is a 'moderately successful, middle-aged businessman'.[34] Both consider the implications of these statements: Mr Pirrip, argues Partlow, is a 'mature man, sober, industrious, saddened, aware of his own limitations, and possessed of a certain calm wisdom', and Jordan's Narrator is 'confident, secure, and powerful'. Both statements relate uneasily to Pip's use of the quotation from Saint Luke; both statements limit themselves to the consequences of middle-age and hardly begin to consider those of being a businessman.

Yet business is fundamental to Pip's life. He grows up in a world of small-businessmen. Apart from Mr Wopsle, who is 'the clerk at church', the guests at the Gargerys' Christmas dinner are the Hubbles, a wheelwright and wife, and Mr Pumblechook, the 'well-to-do corn-chandler' (iv, 55). Joe Gargery is, of course, a self-employed blacksmith for whom Mrs Joe doubtless kept the books. Mr Pumblechook's conversation with Pip 'consisted of nothing but arithmetic' (viii, 84) and though this is humorous it does contribute to our sense of an upbringing dominated by figures, buying and selling, profit and loss. Miss Havisham, though not connected with any *small* enterprise, is part of this world: she lives on the proceeds of a once-flourishing brewery business and applies capitalist thinking to her private life. She invests hatred in Estella in the expectation of a later, malicious return.

Pip becomes ashamed of his origins but cannot escape them. A key scene is that in Chapter 34 when Herbert and Pip, debts rising around them, combine to '"look into [their] affairs"'. They examine their papers, list their bills and calculate their financial positions:

I established with myself on these occasions, the reputation of a first-rate man of business – prompt, decisive, energetic, clear, cool-headed. When I had got all my responsibilities down upon my list, I compared each with the bill, and ticked it off. My self-approval when I ticked an entry was quite a luxurious sensation. When I had no more ticks to make, I folded all my bills up uniformly, docketed each on the back, and tied the whole into a symmetrical bundle. Then I did the same for Herbert (who modestly said he had not my administrative genius), and felt that I had brought his affairs into a focus for him. (xxxiv, 295–6)

Given Pip's belief that he is a gentleman, his pride in his own business acumen and clerical expertise is oddly misplaced. Bentley Drummle, for instance, a 'real' gentleman because of birth, would simply despise such qualities. They are those of the secretary and most Drummles would respond as Bella Wilfer does to John Harmon's similar exertions in *Our Mutual Friend*. On Pip's part we see memory in action, a lingering near-atavistic recollection of business virtues – orderly affairs, meticulously kept books, financial prudence – insistent during his childhood. In Victorian terms Pip will never be a 'real' gentleman, not only because he is far too conscious of money and cares what people think of him, but because he has always belonged to the world of small-businessmen. We see this again in Chapter 17, when he is greatly impressed by Biddy's powers of management, and later, when he wishes to help Herbert and thinks, instinctively, of furthering his friend's business career through secret financial sponsorship.

Throughout his life Pip practises the first rule of business, the need to provide what the customers want. In Chapter 9, after his first visit to Satis House, he satisfies his family circle's desire for class-and-wealth-based fantasies. He frequently and not unwillingly provides Estella with material for her practised sadism. And despite himself he provides Magwitch with what the latter considers to be evidence of gentlemanly behaviour.

Pip tries hard to be a gentleman but, instead, becomes the businessman whose thought-patterns have always controlled his thinking. When he sets down the account of his life he has spent much of it, most of his adult years, in the Eastern branch of Clarriker and Co. He has worked hard and in rising to 'third in the Firm' (lviii, 489), a partner with Herbert and Clarriker, has become Partlow's 'Mr Pirrip'. It is thus to be expected that Pip's retrospection is coloured by his travelling and commercial experiences. The effect of the former is evident in the imagery he sometimes uses. When harshly treated during his Christmas dinner he compares himself to 'an unfortunate little bull in a Spanish arena' (iv, 56–7); as he first walks across the derelict courtyard of Satis House the cold wind makes 'a shrill noise ... like the noise of wind in the rigging of a ship at sea' (viii, 85); Orlick's room, Pip notes, 'was not unlike the kind of place usually assigned to a gate-porter in Paris' (xxix, 255). These figures, suggestive as they are of shore visits, voyages out, and a land-haul home across France, are used during moments of tension or deep emotion. At such critical times Pip turns even more instinctively to the business life, conducted abroad, that became and remains the essence of his own.

In Pip's use of 'assigned' – a word loaded with commercial and legal meaning – in the description of Orlick's room, we glimpse the extent to which *Great Expectations* is a businessman's tale written in appropriate language that, again, so often surfaces during moments of great emotional pain. For example, when Pip, much frustrated by Estella during her stay at Richmond, accompanies her to Satis House, Miss Havisham

> seemed to pry into my heart and probe its wounds ... she extorted from [Estella], by dint of referring back to what Estella had told her in her regular letters, the names and conditions of the men whom she had fascinated. ...
>
> I saw in this, wretched though it made me, and bitter the sense of dependence and even of degradation that it awakened – I saw in this, that Estella was set to wreak Miss Havisham's revenge on men, and that she was not to be given to me until she had gratified it for a term. I saw in this, a reason for her being beforehand assigned to me. Sending her out to attract and torment and do mischief, Miss Havisham sent her with the malicious assurance that she was beyond the reach of all admirers, and that all who staked upon that cast were secured to lose. (xxxviii, 320–21)

In Mr Pirrip's account Miss Havisham treats Estella's letters like business correspondence, 'referring back' as if to a file. The older man recalls being sustained, despite everything, by the notion of 'transaction', of Estella, after a 'term', being 'assigned' to him, that had dangled before him the satisfying power of becoming the eventual owner of the woman he wanted. Even the final gambling image is mixed, oddly, with commercial suggestiveness in the use of the word 'secured'.

It is a word that recurs in the novel's key scene when Magwitch, the returned convict,

> surveyed me with an air of admiring proprietorship . . .
>
> It appeared to me that I could do no better than secure him some quiet lodging hard by, of which he might take possession when Herbert returned . . . [he] reserved his consent to Herbert's participation until he should have seen him. . . . This business transacted, I turned my face, on my own account, to Little Britain. (xl, 348–50)

As Pip hides Magwitch in his room he reflects that 'a ghost could not have been taken and hanged on my account, and the consideration that he could be, and the dread that he would be, were no small addition to my horrors' (xl, 353). Not only are actions fraught with human emotions represented, first and foremost, as 'business transacted', but the basis of Pip's vocabulary – 'proprietorship', 'secure', 'take possession', 'account', 'consideration', 'addition', and so forth – even when the text forces it to express other meanings, is drawn from the commercial world and never wholly free from commercial connotations.

Other scenes use commercial language more specifically. Pip's description, through Chapter 8 (83–94), of his first visit to Miss Havisham, is full of the lingering echoes of Victorian business-letters, as Pip, indeed, files his report of his past life: 'I entertained this speculation . . . I calculated . . . I took note . . . I regret to state . . .'. Even when he fights the young Herbert in Satis House garden and the latter butts him, he comments on Herbert's head: 'I had a right to consider it irrelevant when so obtruded on my attention' (xi, 119). Suddenly we are far from boys fighting and in a world of high desks, scratching pens and formal communications.

Again, Pip outlines to Wemmick his wish to help Herbert:

> Having thought of the matter with care, I approached my subject as if I had never hinted at it before. I informed Wemmick that I was anxious in behalf of Herbert Pocket, and I told him how we had first met, and how we had fought. I glanced at Herbert's home, and at his character, and at his having no means but such as he was dependent on his father for: those, uncertain and

unpunctual. I alluded to the advantages I had derived in my first rawness and ignorance from his society, and I confessed that I feared I had but ill repaid them, and that he might have done better without me and my expectations. Keeping Miss Havisham in the background at a great distance, I still hinted at the possibility of my having competed with him in his prospects, and at the certainty of his possessing a generous soul, and being far above any mean distrusts, retaliations, or designs. For all these reasons (I told Wemmick), and because he was my young companion and friend, and I had a great affection for him, I wished my own good fortune to reflect some rays upon him, and therefore I sought advice from Wemmick's experience and knowledge of men and affairs, how I could best try with my resources to help Herbert to some present income – say of a hundred a year, to keep him in good hope and heart – and gradually to buy him on to some small partnership. I begged Wemmick, in conclusion to understand that my help must always be rendered without Herbert's knowledge or suspicion, and that there was no one else in the world with whom I could advise. I wound up by laying my hand upon his shoulder, and saying, 'I can't help confiding in you, though I know it must be troublesome to you; but that is your fault, in having ever brought me here. (xxxvii, 313–14)

The passage has been quoted at length in order to illustrate two points. First, here is a key example of commercial language. Pip has certainly 'thought of the matter with care' for the paragraph is structured on the conventional outline of the business letter in all its Victorian formality and logic: 'I informed Wemmick I was anxious in behalf of Herbert ... I alluded to the advantages I had derived ... there I sought advice from Wemmick's experience ...' and, most revealingly, 'I begged Wemmick, in conclusion, to understand ...' with, in this final sentence, such distinct echoes of the formal subscription ('I beg to remain, Sir ...').

Second, the passage demonstrates what can only be called a commercial mentality. The sincerity of Pip's hopes for Herbert cannot be doubted but, in recollection, they are so organised and arranged that self-conscious restraint and contrivance prevent emotional involvement. It links with two other revealing moments:

My guardian then took me into his own room, and while he

lunched, standing, from a sandwich-box and a pocket flask of sherry . . . informed me what arrangements he had made for me. I was to go to 'Barnard's Inn', to young Mr Pocket's rooms, where a bed had been sent in for my accommodation; I was to remain with young Mr Pocket until Monday; on Monday I was to go with him to his father's house on a visit, that I might try how I liked it. Also, I was told what my allowance was to be – it was a very liberal one – and had handed to me from one of my guardian's drawers, the cards of certain tradesmen with whom I was to deal for all kinds of clothes, and such other things as I could in reason want. (xx, 194)

To be sure this listing of instructions – life reduced to a series of orders – tells us something of Jaggers's coldly methodical character but, equally significant, is the fact that this is how Pip recalls the occasion and instinctively reports it. Again, Chapter 21 opens with his description of Wemmick:

Casting my eyes on Mr Wemmick as we went along, to see what he was like in the light of day, I found him to be a dry man, rather short in stature, with a square wooden face . . . I judged him to be a bachelor from the frayed condition of his linen, and he appeared to have sustained a good many bereavements; for he wore at least four mourning rings . . . I noticed, too, that several rings and seals hung at his watch chain, as if he were quite laden with remembrances of departed friends. . . . (xxi, 195)

The listing – this time of Wemmick's features – is accompanied by deductions about his character and status. Here is a view from behind a desk, an ingrained habit of assessing.

The commercial language and commercial training combine to distance events and so prevent overwhelming emotional involvement. This text is, essentially, a cool account of fraught experience. The distancing, the coolness, help dramatise one of the novel's main themes, clearly expressed at the close of Chapter 51. Mike, one of Jaggers's regular clients, informs the lawyer and clerk that his daughter has been arrested for shoplifting. He weeps in the telling and Wemmick is indignant:

'A man can't help his feelings, Mr Wemmick,' pleaded Mike.

'His what?' demanded Wemmick, quite savagely. 'Say that again!'

'Now, look here my man,' said Mr Jaggers, advancing a step, and pointing to the door. 'Get out of this office. I'll have no feelings here. Get out.' (li, 427)

Wemmick, of course, solves his own personal problems consequent upon the need to exclude feelings from business by living a double life. Jaggers fails to effect such a separation and has no personal life outside his professional one. Pip is more complex and we become increasingly doubtful that he will respond to crises with appropriate feelings. For example, his attitude to Mrs Joe, his sister, is always uneasy: when the blow to her head damages her speech and she can communicate only by means of a slate Pip has little compassion and too much facetiousness: 'As she was (very bad handwriting apart) a more than indifferent speller, and as Joe was a more than indifferent reader, extraordinary complications arose between them' (xvi, 149). Mrs Joe's funeral inspires sentimental recollection, thoughts of his sister having 'a gentle tone' about them as 'the very breath of the beans and clover whispered to my heart that the day must come when it would be well for my memory that others walking in the sunshine should be softened as they thought of me' (xxxv, 298). It also inspires humour, mainly from descriptions of the undertaker's entourage and Joe in deep mourning. Further, Pip never wholly ceases to patronise Joe; when the latter looks after the convalescent young man and 'we talked as we used to talk', Pip comments that Joe was unchanged, 'just as simply faithful, and as simply right' (lvii, 477); the repeated adjective cannot wholly escape the disparaging connotation.

Pip has become a prisoner of the commercial mentality, the business outlook. To this extent he is similar to Jaggers. Both are incapable of a fully satisfying emotional life. Because of this and the lurches into sentimentality to which such flawed psyches are prone the often-criticised revised ending can be seen to be absolutely right. For the final scene is recalled in terms of popular sentiment and contrived emotionalism: 'The silvery mist was touched with the first rays of the moonlight, and the same rays touched the tears that dropped from her eyes' (lix, 492). What were once deep feelings are reduced in the remembrance to shallow reflections. Nowhere is Mr Pirrip's emotional predicament more apparent than in the final paragraph:

> I took her hand in mine, and we went out of the ruined place;
> and, as the morning mists had risen long ago when I first left the
> forge, so, the evening mists were rising now, and in all the broad
> expanse of tranquil light they showed to me, I saw no shadow of
> another parting from her. (lix, 493)

The contrivance apparent in the balance of 'morning mists' and
'evening mists', the measured overall tone, are pointers to Pip's
emotional restraint. The negative ambiguity of the last clause
allows the work to end with reserve, nervous restraint, lack of
commitment, the inability of Pip's heart to open to another, that
are the permanent and tragic consequences of his over-
commercialised career. The ostensible progress of the text towards
self-knowledge, principle, and happiness, is disturbingly undermined by the unfolding of the trapped Narrator's characterisation.

6   SEXISM AND CLASS BIAS: THE NARRATOR OF *OUR MUTUAL FRIEND*

Our Mutual Friend, Dickens's last completed novel, with its huge
and multi-styled text, seems so to deny the idea of a single
coherent narrative voice that the concept of the 'polyphonic
narrator' beckons seductively. The extent of that seeming denial
can be gauged from the first few chapters. Book the First, Chapter
1, is theatrical, the 'yellow moonlight' (I, i, 46) and red sunlight
playing on the intense emotional exchanges of the Hexams and
Riderhood on the river creating a scene from the period's popular
melodrama. The characters of Chapter 2, the Veneerings and their
circle, on the other hand, are given life through literary metaphor
mainly relating to furniture, the metaphoric mode continuing in
Chapter 3, particularly in the central sequence comparing the
dockside police-station to a medieval monastery. Chapter 4 introduces the Wilfers at home. Here the analogies are with painting, R.
Wilfer described as the 'conventional Cherub' (I, iv, 75) and his
formidable wife 'like some severe saint in a painting, or merely
human matron allegorically treated' (I, iv, 86), the humour becomes more whimsical with a mock-heroic element most evident in the
supper sequence 'as the firelight danced in the mellow halls of a

couple of full bottles on the table' (I, iv, 84). Wegg and the Boffins enter in Chapter 5 and the humour broadens, in the case of the Boffins becoming more affectionate. Despite such varying of styles and communicative modes, this present chapter argues that the reader *can* discern a coherent and all-pervading narrating characterisation.

This last is achieved through awareness of the patterns of language and recurring attitudes that structure the characterisation. One such pattern begins in the opening scene with the Narrator's reference to Gaffer Hexam's 'business-like usage' (I, i, 44) that might remind us of *Great Expectations. Our Mutual Friend* is another Dickens novel throughout which recurs the language of commerce. When Twemlow studies Veneering's guests he considers himself 'having profited by these studies'; then, 'having no lady assigned him' (I, ii, 51), he walks by himself into dinner. The meeting between the Milveys and the Boffins is conducted by the Narrator almost wholly in the language of business: Mrs Boffin,

> feeling it incumbent on her to take part in the conversation, and being charmed with the emphatic little wife and her ready interest, here offered her acknowledgements ... Mr Milvey referred the point to Mrs Boffin ... the kind, conscientious couple spoke, as if they kept some profitable orphan warehouse, and were personally patronized. . . . (I, ix, 150–51)

Commercial and financial imagery dominate the Boffins' procuring of orphan Johnny in Book the First, Chapter 16 ('A considerable capital of knee and elbow and wrist and ankle, had Sloppy, and he didn't know how to dispose of it to the best advantage, but was always investing it in wrong securities ...' (249) is one witty example), returns to characterise Bradley Headstone in Chapter 1 of Book the Second, particularly in the famous description of Headstone's fact-laden mind as a 'wholesale warehouse' (II, i, 266), Silas Wegg and Venus in Chapter 7 of Book the Third, when they negotiate a partnership as a prelude to attempting to ruin Boffin, and the account of John Harmon's career as Rokesmith the secretary.

More important than any recurring stylistic motif are recurring attitudes. One such is commercial, a natural consequence of the imagery already noted and which, through the link with *Great Expectations*, points to the existence of an Author, Dickens himself, whose polyphonic qualities as yet resist unification. As in the earlier novel, in *Our Mutual Friend* such attitudes impose their usual imaginative and social limitations. Another recurrence exhibits the Narrator's misogyny, an example being the contrasting treatment of Lady Tippins and Twemlow, Veneering's aristocratic acquaintances. Lady Tippins is treated viciously: 'an immense obtuse drab oblong face, like the face in a tablespoon, and a dyed Long Walk up the top of her head, as a convenient public approach to the bunch of false hair behind', with 'a certain yellow play in Lady Tippins's throat, like the legs of scratching poultry' (I, ii, 53–4). She becomes increasingly pitiful, 'a diurnal species of lobster – throwing off a shell every forenoon, and needing to keep in a retired spot until the new crust hardens' (II, xvi, 466). In the text's final chapter she orchestrates the chorus of snobbishness and rage. Twemlow, on the other hand, though sometimes ridiculous, as when he is discovered treating his hair with egg-yolk, is invariably presented as a man of fundamentally decent feelings who is, all too often, the bemused victim of circumstances. He is described as a peaceable man and credited, affectionately, with lingering romantic feelings:

> For, the poor little harmless gentleman once had his fancy, like the rest of us, and she didn't answer . . . Brooding over the fire, with his dried little head in his dried little hands . . . Twemlow is melancholy. (I, x, 164)

And he has the last word, disconcerting Podsnap and company, albeit temporarily, with his support of Eugene Wrayburn's marriage to Lizzie.

A similar contrast involves the Lammles. Though both, for much of the book and before conscience troubles Mrs Lammle, are equally villainous, their quarrels enable the Narrator to make additional sexist jibes. When her husband objects to being called 'disingenuousness' she replies:

> 'Pray, how dare you, sir, utter the word to me?'
> 'I never did.'
> As this happens to be true, Mrs Lammle is thrown on the feminine resource of saying, 'I don't care what you uttered or did not utter.'

She bursts into tears, threatens suicide, calls him names. 'Then she cries again. Then she is enraged again, and makes some mention of swindlers. Finally, she sits down crying on a block of stone, and is 'in all the known and unknown humours of her sex at once' (I, x, 169–71). Her husband, meanwhile, shows almost inhuman self-control.

Such stereotyping of women is seen again when Pleasant Riderhood, watching her father recover from the river, finds that her 'natural woman's aptitude soon renders her able to give a little help' (III, iii, 505). Miss Peecher, Bradley Headstone's teaching colleague, is a stereotype among stereotypes:

> Small, shining, neat, methodical, and buxom...; cherry-cheeked and tuneful of voice. A little pincushion, a little house-wife, a little book, a little workbox, a little set of tables and weights and measures, and a little woman, all in one. (II, i, 268)

Her romantic aspirations regarding Bradley Headstone are invari-ably mocked: he is far more than her 'simply arranged little work-box of thoughts, fitted with no gloomy and dark recesses, could hold' (III, xi, 609). Georgiana Podsnap, all too typical of Victorian daughters victimised by parents in the interests of ultra-respectability and social advancement, is treated comically rather than compassionately: she never wholly escapes the comic effect of the recurring conceit of her 'peering over the great apron of the custard-coloured phaeton, as if she had been ordered to expiate some childish misdemeanour by going to bed in the daylight' (IV, ii, 715). When Veneering runs for Parliament Mrs Veneering conducts herself 'in a distracted and devoted manner, compounded of Ophelia and any self-immolating female of anti-quity you may prefer' (II, iii, 295). Stereotyping, it seems, can also be diachronic.

Even seemingly positive female characters are beset with nar-ratorial reservations. Mrs Boffin, who acquires self-knowledge through her quest for an orphan and adds it to her inviolable goodness, is most memorable as 'a highflyer at fashion', appearing, at one point, 'in a walking dress of black velvet and feathers, like a mourning coach-horse' (I, ix, 144). Betty Higden is always patro-nised as essentially good but criminally foolish in her 'irrational, blind, and obstinate prejudices' (II, ix, 380). Jenny Wren, though she possesses a vibrant, Blakean imagination, is also 'a little quaint shrew; of the world, worldly; of the earth, earthy' (II, ii, 294). Lizzie

Hexam surmounts the problems of her upbringing and through her marriage to Eugene generates what, in this novel, passes for optimism, but also fails to escape the Narrator's stereotyping: her improper because slightly deceitful acceptance of Eugene's offer of instruction in reading is a consequence of being flattered by the attention of a man she likes. Initially, at least, her feelings are stronger than her sense of morality.

Most revealing of all is the Narrator's treatment of Bella Wilfer, whose decline from that rare Dickensian phenomenon, a woman whose lively-voiced dissatisfaction receives narratorial and authorial support, into a doll in a doll's house and John Harmon's 'Home Goddess' (II, xiii, 431), has often been discussed. Yet, even during her early textual days as the lively protester, stereotyping is not wholly absent: her signature, we are told in Chapter 4, 'was a bold one *for a woman*' (I, iv, 83, my emphasis). Such an attitude persists, as when, in working out her feelings for Sophronia Lammle she instinctively consults her looking-glass and the Narrator comments sourly that 'Perhaps if she had consulted some better oracle, the result might have been more satisfactory' (III, v, 533). And though her desire for money means she is, in any case, disadvantaged by John Harmon, this moral deficiency is frequently coupled with sexist criticism: for example, when John Harmon anticipates her attempt to fish for compliments, 'her colour deepened over the little piece of coquetry she was checked in' (III, ix, 582). Like Miss Peecher she is regarded as incapable of much deep thought and patronised accordingly:

> Bella met [John Harmon's] steady look for a moment with a wistful, musing little look of her own, and then, nodding her pretty head several times, like a dimpled philosopher (of the very best school) who was moralizing on Life, heaved a little sigh, and gave up things in general for a bad job. (III, ix, 585)

Even when she is transformed into a positive textual force and stands up for John Harmon against the miserly Boffin, the effect is undermined by references to her height and demeanour that make her seem no more than a spirited child: 'Very pretty she looked, though very angry, as she made herself as tall as she possibly could (which was not extremely tall), and utterly renounced her patron with a lofty toss of her rich brown head' (III, xv, 664). Her decline into marriage is almost total. Her role is to make home 'engaging';

she hardly knows what her husband does, makes only naive and childish attempts to talk to him of matters in the 'City', and can rise to no severer intellectual challenge than studying 'The Complete British Family Housewife' (IV, v, 748–9).

Bella Wilfer, like most of *Our Mutual Friend*'s female characters, is a recipient of the Narrator's mocking humour. Not all characters are. The direction and selectivity of his humour are key factors in establishing the pervading presence of his coherent persona. This we begin to see as early as Chapter 1, in which Gaffer Hexam is presented favourably until the final paragraph. Following the exchange with Riderhood as to whether a dead man could or should be robbed, from which, Gaffer considers, he emerged victorious, 'Lizzie's father, composing himself into the easy attitude of one who had asserted the high moralities and taken an unassailable position, slowly lighted a pipe, and smoked' (I, i, 47). The tone, so unexpected, as if the Narrator's real feelings have suddenly revealed themselves, is one of patronising irony. His attitude is partly explained two chapters on, when Mortimer and Eugene are taken by Charlie Hexam from the Veneerings' dining-room to the docks and riverside, 'down by where accumulated scum of humanity seemed to be washed from higher grounds, like so much moral sewage' (I, iii, 63). The whole sentence shocks. The lowest elements of society, *en masse*, are regarded fiercely, even viciously, with a total lack of compassion, and without humour. The same can be said of individual members of the riverside working class, such as Gaffer Hexam, Rogue Riderhood, Charlie Hexam, Pleasant Riderhood; they are rarely presented favourably and seem below humour. When we recall Riderhood, driven by his hatred of Gaffer Hexam, ploughing through the hailstones – 'He crushed through them, leaving marks in the fast-melting slush that were mere shapeless holes; one might have fancied, following, that the very fashion of humanity had departed from his feet' (I, xii, 204) – and the force of hatred in such words, we are as far from laughter as it is possible to be. The same can be said of Bradley Headstone who, though he has risen a few rungs above his origins is, in the scheme of things, destined never to escape them. His brooding presence, the extent of his violent obsessions, arrest and disturb but can hardly make us laugh. Lizzie Hexam, of course, is also a product of the riverbank; she is rarely criticised and never directly, nor does she even induce smiling. Betty Higden, with her 'minding school' and mangle, is slightly higher on the social scale;

the patronage to which she is unfailingly subjected by the Narrator is never mitigated by humour. Nor, indeed, is Jenny Wren's grotesqueness and Riah's strangeness. Riah, though outside mainstream Victorian society because of his Jewishness, is as much a victim as the lowliest mudlark.

The mitigating effect and its absence is central to this argument. The Narrator is obsessed by social class; where characters are situated, actually or, like Headstone, essentially, in the social hierarchy governs his attitude to them. Thus Silas Wegg, who can read and who does a more congenial job than fishing bodies out of rivers, even though he is morally inferior to, say, Gaffer Hexam, has the effect of his faults partly blunted by humorous conceits: for example, being described as 'a knotty man, and a close-grained, with a face carved out of very hard material, that had just as much play of expression as a watchman's rattle' (I, v, 89) points only indirectly to his ruthlessness. The Gibbon readings, his fantasies about the corner-house outside which he sets up his stall, the near-farcical sequences with Venus and the 'document', are sources of attractive fun that occasionally bring him close to being a likeable rogue. Mr Venus and the Boffins, a shopkeeper and a couple catapulted upwards by money, though morally far above Silas Wegg, are also rich sources of humour.

The Wilfers always provide humorous interludes in which, as has been seen, overt textual devices, including the mock-heroic and references to *Macbeth*, blur the human foibles of mother and younger daughter. The Veneerings, the Podsnaps, even the Lammles – remembering the husband's ubiquitous shirt-front – are often viewed through comic, though at times grimly comic metaphor. Mortimer Lightwood and Eugene Wrayburn, with sufficient means to idle away their lives, are wrapped in the Narrator's affectionate, sympathetic and often humorous prose. As is well known, Wrayburn wipes the floor with, in some ways, the more worthy Headstone, and eventually gets the girl. At the apex of the text's social range Lady Tippins and Twemlow are not approached with the directness accorded to, say, Riderhood or Charlie Hexam. Setting aside the differences in treatment already cited as examples of misogyny, they are sources of humour and this is so even of Twemlow at the close, when his effect is morally positive. Even there we see 'his wristbands bristling a little' (IV, xvii, 891) as indignation takes hold.

It is no accident that John Harmon/Rokesmith/Julius Handford is treated directly and in a style comparatively free of literary artifice. In that he has assumed a role and a false identity he is not properly part of the social hierarchy. For in *Our Mutual Friend* literary artifice is essentially ingratiating: the higher the social rank the more there is of it. It is as if the Narrator is only willing to criticise directly those at the bottom of the heap.

Both in his treatment of women and of the various social classes the Narrator shows himself to be rigidly prejudiced. To put this another way, his view of the world is essentially Podsnappic. In common with the social chorus he appears to learn nothing from a tale the central thrust of which is to demonstrate the evil inadequacy of social divisions in the face of man's deepest desires. As a pervading, coherent narrative voice, he is all too distinguishable. The concept of the 'polyphonic narrator' is not necessary to make sense of *Our Mutual Friend*'s narrative strategy and given that invariably Dickens's narrators are, to a degree, similar (to say the least they are flawed human beings, limited in their insight), the 'polyphonic *author*' may also be a concept readily jettisoned in favour of a single, all-embracing consciousness. It is one, however, that lies outside the scope of this chapter.

4

Two Re-readers

Like all the best writing about literature, reader-theory makes plain and compelling what we always seemed to know. What Booth[1] has helped do for the Narrator – established him as an identifiable character in all works of literature – Iser and Fish have helped do for what the former terms the 'implied'[2] and the latter the 'informed'[3] reader. But, in what is now a well-referenced concern with reader-involvement, insufficient attention has been paid to the relationship between reading and re-reading. This is not to say that texts are regarded as one-off experiences to which the reader never returns – such unsophistication is hardly a characteristic of the modern theorist – but that more could be said of second encounters with texts. In particular, more needs to be said of second encounters with Dickens's texts, if only because all his novels have mystery-solving plots. The re-read text stands in a very different relationship to the wiser Re-reader than does the text he or she first struggled to understand. Reader-response is important; informed reader-response doubly so, which is why this chapter concerns itself with what the reader does the second (or third, or fourth) time around. This Re-reader is not, strictly speaking, the construct postulated by Iser and Fish. Rather, he is an 'actual' Re-reader who in part resembles that construct and is to a great extent controlled and implied by the text with which he engages.

This chapter as a whole is about re-reading Dickens's last two novels: *Our Mutual Friend* and the unfinished *The Mystery of Edwin Drood*. Both pose unique problems the solving of which establishes the Re-reader as a distinct and coherent character. In *Our Mutual Friend* not only does Dickens at times depend for his effect on mysterious indirectness, on the slow release of information (a prime example being the sustaining of mystery during a first encounter with the first chapter), but he also deceives the new reader into believing that Boffin's money has corrupted him into miserliness. The undeceived Re-reader engages with a different text and so becomes a very different person.

In the opinion of some, that text is a lesser one and the reader's response problematic: Grahame Smith,[4] for example, argues that, once the reader knows the truth, the scenes in which Boffin acts the miser can never again be taken seriously; Angus Wilson considers that the devices used by Dickens to sustain Boffin's masquerade are at times 'overworked'.[5] This chapter rejects both comments, though accepts that Smith's argument, in particular, points to the book's unusual transformation. Though all books are changed by the Re-reader's hindsight, parts of *Our Mutual Friend* are exposed not as a confidence-trick but as a strategy to disturb. The Re-reader of the Boffin sequence is not so much deepening knowledge of the same text as coming to terms with a new one. *Edwin Drood*, of course, is incomplete but sufficient exists to encourage insistent speculation about the ending. Few readers of *Edwin Drood* can avoid or wish to avoid at least some of the mass of literary detection, whether extrapolating from known textual detail or proceeding from contemporary statements and documents that have firmly attached themselves to the text. Thus the account that follows also studies the way knowledge of the most important modern Droodiana changes the role and character of the Re-reader.

1 KNOWING WHAT HAPPENS IN *OUR MUTUAL FRIEND*

To re-read the opening chapter of *Our Mutual Friend* is, in one way, the same as re-reading Boffin's masquerade: both textual sequences, on a first reading, succeed through what they do not say, so that re-reading completes and changes them. In the novel's very first sentence the two figures are now known to be Gaffer Hexam and his daughter Lizzie. The Re-reader knows that Gaffer's work is finding bodies in the Thames to empty their pockets and to claim rewards, so knows what they are doing on this particular night on the river, what they find and tow behind the boat, what clinks in Gaffer's hand and why Lizzie is so horrified. The man in the second boat is known to be Rogue Riderhood; Gaffer is right to distrust him.

To some extent, of course, Dickens's rhetorical persuasiveness sustains a sense of mystery and tension in *every* encounter with this dark scene. But all else changes because the Re-reader now

knows the answers that the Narrator already knew; to this extent
Narrator and reader occupy the same superior position. The
Re-reader not only understands, more or less completely, what
goes on in the chapter, but also the ironic relationship between the
first chapter and the text that follows: the habitual activity, the
keen eye, the bravery, the Re-reader knows, will combine to kill the
expert practitioner.

This ability to make connections, this knowledgeable superiority, enable the Re-reader to impose upon, instead of being controlled by, the chapter's rhetorical strategies. For example:

> He had no net, hook, or line, and he could not be a fisherman;
> his boat had no cushion for a sitter, no paint, no inscription, no
> appliance beyond a rusty boathook and a coil of rope, and he
> could not be a waterman; his boat was too crazy and too small to
> take in cargo for delivery, and he could not be a lighterman or
> river-carrier. . . . (I, i, 43)

Gaffer Hexam's occupation being known, the rhetorical thrust of
the negative constructions towards imaginative inference no longer affects the reader. These negatives, rather than generating
mystery, become simply expendable alternatives to the known
positive. The Re-reader is freed from rhetorical influence because
he is in possession of the facts. So far as this extract is concerned,
on a first reading that influence was at its most potent at one
specific recurring moment at which the need to discover Hexam's
work imposed upon the reader, as a logical imperative, a sense of
the sentence as reading, 'He had no net, hook, or line, and [so] he
could not be a fisherman . . .'. Freed from the need to infer, the
Re-reader reacts to the dislocation, to the fact that the text actually
states, grammatically speaking, that the failure to possess 'net,
hook, or line' has nothing to do with not being a fisherman. The
momentary incoherence of the text is evidence of the Narrator's
struggle to sustain mystery through a first reading and so establishes his superiority as merely relative. The Re-reader becomes
aligned with the author and both look down on their narrating
intermediary.

In achieving this alignment the Re-reader has effected a shift out
of a reading mode dependent upon imaginative activity – the
inferring, deducing, connecting, fancying, necessary during a first
reading – into one that proceeds from possession of the facts. To

restate this in terms of Chapter 1: the Re-reader ceases to be a Lizzie, whose imaginings colour much of the opening sequence, and becomes a Gaffer Hexam, who 'had no fancies' (I, i, 47) and despised the very thought of them. Gaffer's materialism and social rigidity make him an important exemplar of Podsnappery: the Re-reader, imposing facts upon the text to the exclusion of fancy, also plays a Podsnappic role. There is, however, one crucial difference. Gaffer has always been Gaffer; Podsnap has no past that was not Podsnappic. The reader has a memory that re-reading does not obliterate. He can recall a text that generated imaginative engagement, exciting and creative speculation. Though he becomes Podsnappic, he remains aware of and, so, able to criticise the limitations of that monstrous vision. Both factors, the new reading stance and awareness of the old, are important for the re-reading of the main scenes in which Boffin pretends to be a miser.

At the end of Book the Third, Chapter 4, Bella observes that '"Mr Boffin is being spoilt by prosperity, and is changing every day"' (III, iv, 521). Evidence is forthcoming in the very next chapter, entitled 'The Golden Dustman Falls into Bad Company', when Boffin confronts his secretary with extreme economic and social assertions. Here and in subsequent scenes he develops a coherent, powerful and heartless argument, proceeding from the premise that wealth has two main responsibilities. First, the '"man of property ... is bound to consider the market-price"' (III, v, 523) and so must never be generous. Second, he '"owes a duty to other men of property, and must look sharp after his inferiors"' (III, v, 524). If, like Boffin, he has come up from nothing, then, in addition, he must never forget the harsh lesson of his early struggles: '"you must either scrunch them, or let them scrunch you. If you ain't imperious with 'em, they won't believe in your being any better than themselves, if as good, after the stories (lies mostly), that they have heard of your beginnings"' (III, v, 525–6). '"Money's the article"', continues Boffin, and all should be subjugated to its getting and keeping. The power derived from possessing it is absolute: '"If I pay for a sheep, I buy it out and out. Similarly, if I pay for a secretary, I buy *him* out and out"' (III, v, 524). A person's worth, moral and material, depends upon his wealth: '"A man, being poor, has nothing to be proud of"' (III, v, 523). Thus the poor man deserves little and so receives less. He is not even allowed to have feelings, or human dignity. He is expected to be always '"in attendance"', with no right to any time of his own: '"you can take up a book for a minute or two when you've nothing better to do, though I think you'll a'most always find something useful to do"' (III, v, 524), Boffin grimly informs him. Good-looking women should act similarly, exploiting their looks and money to ensure that '"the money you will have, will be worth money, and you shall make money of that too"' (III, v, 527). Their ambition must be to '"live and die rich"' (III, v, 526).

The scene insists that human behaviour, social living, is and must be governed by the callous conservatism of a tradition of class-based heartlessness and contempt for human feelings. These general principles are then applied by Boffin to relations with an employee, Rokesmith, and, of course, to those with his ward, Bella Wilfer, potentially a woman of means. This combination of the general and the particular structures all three Boffin/Rokesmith confrontations.

The second closes Book the Third, Chapter 5. Boffin's heartless general philosophy is again flaunted and his vision darkened even further through an intensification of its specific application. For Boffin now demands even more from the man who originally volunteered his services to protect Boffin's money from the envious greed of those with less. All Rokesmith's time Boffin now regards as his own; the secretary is required to move into an empty room in the Boffin mansion. To do this a quarter's rent in lieu of notice has to be paid to the Wilfers. This Boffin has to pay and seeks to recoup by encouraging Rokesmith to give him his furniture '"in the light of a set-off against the quarter's rent"' (III, v, 536). '"Recollect,"' says Boffin to his distraught wife, "'we are not our old selves. Recollect, we must scrunch or be scrunched"' (III, v, 537).

The final confrontation with Rokesmith is in Book the Third, Chapter 15. Boffin is miserly even at breakfast: 'His altered character had never been so grossly marked. His bearing towards his Secretary was so charged with insolent distrust and arrogance, that the latter rose and left the table before breakfast was half done' (III, xv, 652). Later that day Rokesmith is dismissed for making advances to Bella, the dismissal scene implicitly restating the heartless economics and rigid money-based social structuring underpinning Boffin's notion of human behaviour. It stresses, explicitly, the relationship between affairs of the heart and monetary status. Again, Boffin's thinking begins with suspicion and cynicism: Bella, with her good looks and material expectations, is, in Boffin's revealing imagery, '"lying in wait ... for money ... looking about the market for a good bid"' (III, xv, 654). The latter, which is also, of course, a further example of commercial imagery, refers to a suitor with appropriate wealth; the penniless, such as Rokesmith, should have no role in this marketplace, even though they try to get their hands on the possessions of unwary wards, as '"Rokesmith, greedy and hungering, begins a-creeping on his hands and knees towards the money"' (III, xv, 656).

He, therefore, receives what he deserves, Boffin depriving him, finally, of all human diginity. He loses what a servant might expect always to retain, the power to walk out, Boffin gruffly insisting, '"Let's have no pretending that you discharge yourself. I discharge you"' (III, xv, 656). Rokesmith, though present, is referred to in a contemptuous third-person, and has his wages simply thrown at him. Above all his capacity for love is denied through ridicule:

> 'Win her affections', retorted Mr Boffin, with ineffable contempt, 'and possess her heart! Mew says the cat, Quack-quack says the duck, Bow-wow-wow says the dog! Win her affections and possess her heart! Mew, Quack-quack, Bow-wow!' (III, xv, 660)

The Re-reader, of course, knows that Boffin is acting a part and so is sufficiently freed from emotional involvement in scenes that appalled on a first reading to appreciate the developing argument they contain. The presence of that argument helps counter Smith's contention that, once the charade is exposed, the scenes cannot be taken seriously. For though the argument does not reflect Boffin's beliefs and attitudes it is not on that or any other account to be rejected. Boffin's adopted view of life as a battle between the haves and have-nots, in which both mercenary opponents seek ruthlessly and cynically to exploit each other – 'scrunch or be scrunched' – is in accord with so many aspects of the text. The way the Lammles behave is one example, Silas Wegg's grasping response to Boffin's kindness, his plan to keep Boffin 'in a state of abject moral bondage and slavery until the time when they should see fit to permit him to purchase his freedom at the price of half his possessions' (III, vii, 561) is another, as is Fledgeby's treatment of Riah and all others in his power, and all Podsnap's conduct and philosophy. When Betty Higden collapses at Rogue Riderhood's lock, his concern to seize her money, and lack of concern for her physical and mental plight is as vicious as any of Boffin's playacting. Further, Boffin's professed fear of the workhouse – '"If I didn't keep my eyes open, and my pockets buttoned, shouldn't I be brought to the workhouse before I knew where I was?"' (III, xv, 655) – which seems so extreme in its distrust of fellow-men and social institutions – may well be justified by events; it is certainly similar to Betty Higden's fear of the Parish that, in itself, is an indictment of Victorian society's treatment of the poor.

Because of this abundant textual support it is impossible, on a re-reading, to reject Boffin's professed sentiments as too extreme. Indeed, the Re-reader tends, to some extent, to agree with them, and is not dissuaded from doing so by the empathetic force and exuberance of Boffin's miserly utterances. But two important scenes prevent the Re-reader from simply adopting Boffin's point-of-view. The first returns us to the confrontation with Rokesmith at the close of Book the Third, Chapter 5. For at the centre of this scene is an apology. Rokesmith is accused by Boffin of profligate use of his employer's money. His protest is rudely interrupted:

> 'Hold your tongue!', said Mr Boffin. 'You oughtn't to like it in any case. There! I didn't mean to be rude, but you put me out so, and after all I'm master. I didn't intend to tell you to hold your tongue. I beg your pardon. Don't hold your tongue. Only, don't contradict.' (III, v, 535)

Momentarily the subterfuge breaks down and the old, the real Boffin is glimpsed. The Re-reader notes the inconsistency but feels that Boffin does not.

The second scene is another kind of seeming inconsistency. At the close of Book the Third, Chapter 14, a repentent Venus informs Boffin of Wegg's scheming and his own part in it. As Boffin walks home alone from Venus's shop he wonders why that strange proprietor should now confess all. Could it be, considers Boffin, that Venus

> 'is setting himself to get the better of Wegg? . . . to have me all to himself and to pick me clean to the bones!'
>
> It was a cunning and suspicious idea, quite in the way of his school of Misers, and he looked very cunning and suspicious as he went jogging through the streets. (III, xv, 650)

This is sometimes cited as an inconsistency: Boffin is only

pretending to be a miser and has no need to pretend when alone. Against this it could be argued that Dickens is making a plausible psychological point in showing Boffin to have lost some of his original innocence through assimilating worldliness from the books he has been made acquainted with and the role he has played. This much is clearly evident in his later treatment of the Lammles. That this loss of innocence leaves his goodness un-affected is evident from the way the whole masquerade is resolved. And what is certain is that the scene does not establish any kind of self-awareness, on Boffin's part, of what has happened to him.

For the Re-reader these two scenes have added significance. They enable Boffin to be judged. The judging establishes the Re-reader's superiority and the fact that he now works out of factual knowledge, a Podsnappic position, plus a very unPodsnap-pic moral awareness. In *Our Mutual Friend* judicial moral aware-ness is, first and foremost, the province of John Harmon, who judges himself and then others, principally Bella Wilfer. For, though the masquerade is the Boffins' idea, there is little doubt it is masterminded by their secretary. Revealing evidence of this con-cerns the books about misers used by Boffin to terrorise Wegg. For though Boffin is illiterate, he has, of the many volumes that he takes to Wegg, a precise knowledge far greater than could, realistically, be obtained from the bookseller from whom they were bought. With hindsight we know it was obtained from Rokesmith in his role as Boffin's reader and adviser, one way in which he is a Victorian version of *Measure for Measure*'s Duke.

The judging Re-reader, then, identifies with John Harmon, and this has a further and important effect on the masquerade scenes. Though Boffin pretends, Harmon-as-Rokesmith does not. His contributions are deeply sincere and acceptable statements, the human response to heartless economics. In this respect the dismis-sal scene in Book the Fourth, Chapter 15 is crucial. Here Rokesmith makes three points. First, he demonstrates a belief in the dignity of labour, in the labourer being worthy of his hire: when Boffin throws Rokesmith's wages on the ground before him and tells him insultingly, '"I dare say you can stoop to pick it up, after what you have stooped to here"', he is quick to respond. '"I have stooped to nothing but this,"' Rokesmith answered as he took it from the ground; '"and this is mine, for I have earned it by the hardest of hard labour"' (III, xv, 659). Second, he is sustained against his master's degradation by his feelings for Bella: '"To be near her, has been a recompense to me from day to day"' (III, xv, 657). Third, an associated point, the gaining and making of money are unimportant beside his desire to '"win her affections and possess her heart"' (III, xv, 660). This last, of course, causes Boffin's reaction to reach the level of hysterical farce.

Even though the vigour and force of Boffin's masquerade allow the Re-reader some empathetic reaction, yet, through the scenes, he identifies more and more strongly with Rokesmith, partly because of the latter's sincerity and humane sentiments, and partly because the Re-reader knows what Rokesmith knows about what is going on. That is, they both know that Wegg's plot will not succeed. But the Re-reader knows what Rokesmith will never know – the full story of Headstone and Wrayburn, for instance – or what he can discover only at the close of the whole sequence, including, for example, Fledgeby's fate, that Wrayburn marries Lizzie, the relationship between Jenny Wren and Sloppy, and Podsnap's temporary discomfiture at the hands of Twemlow. All re-read texts are fatalistically ironic but only the Re-reader knows this.

The reader of *Our Mutual Friend* is an imaginative, emotionally involved, and struggling dupe. The text retains much of its power to grip, move and involve, no matter how many times it is read. But the Re-reader is an ironist, perceiving the ultimate futility of so much human behaviour good and bad, always emotionally involved but more intellectually aware. He is also, in a sense a disappointed ironist, contrasting the new textual world with the old one, which was dominated by imaginative engagement, excitement, suspense and narrative drive. On a first reading the reader identifies with the good characters but also struggles, in a position separate and inferior to the Narrator, to gain an overall understanding of the unfolding mystery. In his new textual world the Re-reader identifies with good and bad characters, such as Gaffer Hexam, John Harmon and Podsnap, and perceives the Narrator's inadequacy before taking up the same position as the implied author. The Re-reader understands the inadequacy of each character's vision and that there is no necessary relationship between moral qualities, good or bad, and social and human perceptiveness. Knowing more makes him more pessimistic. This sense of how the world is now is not lightened by what becomes a complex relationship with that long-gone first reading. Re-reading cannot recapture that early freshness and imaginative involvement.

Rather, it is haunted by the chilling thought that during that initial involvement Boffin's dreadful miserliness, translated into a programme of class-warfare, revengeful human relations, and inhumane conduct as the only expression of strength and the only effective form of self-preservation, was readily accepted because only too plausible in the novel's world as first experienced. Boffin's masquerade becomes ever more darkly sinister the more the text is re-read.

2   DROODIANA AND *THE MYSTERY OF EDWIN DROOD*[6]

The Mystery of Edwin Drood ends at a tantalising point: young Edwin Drood has disappeared and Neville Landless, generally suspected of having killed him, has been forced to leave Cloisterham for London. Jasper pursues Rosa, who flees to her guardian, also in London. There she meets Tartar, whose room in Staple Inn adjoins Neville's. Crisparkle, we see, is attracted towards Helen Landless. Her brother, Crisparkle and Tartar consider counter-moves against Jasper. The mysterious Dick Datchery moves into lodgings in Cloisterham and keeps watch on Jasper. The text, therefore, ends as events gather themselves for a further narrative surge.

Almost all curious and frustrated readers, desperate for clues to the nature of that surge, and turning to the surviving related documentary evidence and to informed speculation, read John Forster's account of Dickens's intentions:

The story ... was to be that of the murder of a nephew by his uncle; the originality of which was to consist in the review of the murderer's career by himself at the close, when its temptations were to be dwelt upon as if, not he the culprit, but some other man, were the tempted. The last chapters were to be written in the condemned cell, to which his wickedness, all elaborately elicited from him as if told of another, had brought him. Discovery by the murderer of the utter needlessness of the murder for its object, was to follow hard upon commission of the deed; but all discovery of the murderer was to be baffled till towards the close, when, by means of a gold ring which had resisted the corrosive effects of the lime into which he had thrown the body, not only the person murdered was to be identified but the locality of the crime and the man who committed it. So much was told to me before any of the book was written; and it will be recollected that the ring, taken by Drood to be given to his betrothed only if their engagement went on, was brought away with him from their last interview. Rosa was to marry Tartar, and Crisparkle the sister of Landless, who was himself, I think, to have perished in assisting Tartar finally to unmask and seize the murderer.[7]

The reliability of this account was stressed by Kate Perugini, Dickens's daughter: it was the information Dickens 'voluntarily gave to Mr Forster, from whom he had withheld nothing for thirty-three years'.[8] This was corroborated in part by Dickens's recorded comment to his illustrator, Luke Fildes, that Jasper strangled Drood with his scarf, and by the cover-design for the monthly-parts wrapper that shows urgently pursuing figures, with Tartar, possibly their leader, pointing at Jasper as he stands in the cathedral choir.

These documents point the reader towards solutions. One other is no more than a distraction. This last is the so-called 'Sapsea fragment', the short manuscript extract found by Forster among Dickens's papers and introducing a character, Poker, who has some affinities with Datchery. Given that Datchery has been firmly established in the text it is hard to accept this fragment as any more than a false start, soon discarded. The only substantial remaining mystery concerns the strange figure appearing out of the darkness to confront Jasper at the bottom of the wrapper-cover design. This might be Edwin Drood come back from the dead; it might be Helen Landless dressed as a man. Its importance might be, as Angus Wilson suggests, simply to confirm 'that Dickens's ideas about the novel ... changed substantially'[9] after he commissioned the first designs.

Of informed, let alone ill-informed, speculation there is, almost, too much to read. What follows refers to a small selection consisting of the two most reliable modern editions of *Edwin Drood* – Margaret Cardwell's standard edition and the more stimulating popular one by Wilson and Cox – and a recent controversial discussion (though equally reliable in its preliminary review of the evidence) of the '*Drood* problem' by W.W. Robson.[10] All three quote the important documents and references. Robson argues, speculatively, that Datchery may be Dickens himself.

To consult the extensive apparatus to the two editions and to read Robson's account, is to gain a sound knowledge of the relevant extra-textual material and of 'state of the art' Droodiana. The open-minded reader must be convinced that Jasper murdered Drood, and that he did so needlessly, given that his jealousy of Edwin Drood was misplaced. Indeed, the potential Re-reader has already received potent indications of how the romantic interest must develop: Rosa and Edwin are no longer betrothed and since Neville Landless will perish it is, to say the least, unlikely that he will be Rosa's new beau; the unfinished text leaves the reader in little doubt about the future course of the relationships between Rosa and Tartar, Helen Landless and Crisparkle. The reader believes Dickens's main interest to be in the exploration of Jasper's psychology, rather than in the 'whodunnit' aspect of the book, and in the development of the romantic couplings. Regarding the first, Kate Perugini's words about her father are readily recalled:

> it was [not] upon the Mystery alone that he relied for the interest and originality of his idea ... [but] ... in what we may call the psychological description the murderer gives us of his temptations, temperament, and character.[11]

The informed Re-reader of *The Mystery of Edwin Drood*, then, moves through the text with expectations conditioned by his extra-textual explorations, his knowledge of relevant documents and speculation. He is in a powerful position, not so much a character implied by the text as one forcing the text to confirm his new role and to conform to those expectations. That is, the text's mysterious narrative thrust is now dominated, for the Re-reader, by confirmatory repetitions.

One begins in the very first paragraph. The opium-dream, freed from factual mystery, is immediately understood as an expression of Jasper's crucial and fateful sensuality and violence:

> What IS the spike that intervenes, and who has set it up? Maybe, it is set up by the Sultan's orders for the impaling of a horde of Turkish robbers, one by one. ... Ten thousand scimitars flash in the sunlight, and thrice ten thousand dancing-girls strew flowers. ... Still ... no writing figure is on the grim spike. ... (i, 1)

When Jasper awakes, the violence continues: curious about his companions' visions he 'pounces on the Chinaman, and, seizing him with both hands by the throat, turns him violently on the bed. The Chinaman clutches the aggressive hands, resists, gasps, and protests' (i, 3). A lingering reminder of this menacing physicality is his ostensibly affectionate response, in Chapter 2, to Edwin Drood's arrival: Jasper 'starts from his chair, and catches a young fellow in his arms', watches him with a 'hungry' (i, 7) affection, and holds Drood's hands until the younger man has to release them. Aggressive behaviour appears in Chapter 5 in his response to Deputy's stone-throwing – '"Hold your hand," cries Jasper, "and don't throw while I stand so near him, or I'll kill you!"' (v, 33) – and to that of 'some half-dozen other hideous small boys' (v, 37). The stone-throwing invariably stimulates Jasper's most violent urgings:

'What! Is that baby-devil on the watch there!' cries Jasper in a fury: so quickly roused, and so violent, that he seems an older devil himself. 'I shall shed the blood of that Impish wretch! I know I shall do it!' Regardless of the fire, though it hits him more than once, he rushes at Deputy, collars him, and tries to bring him across.

The boy breaks loose, wild with 'rage and malice' (xii, 110). Durdles protects him from Jasper's continuing ferocity. Jasper is a frightening '"Monster"' whose presence '"terrifies"' (vii, 52–3) Rosa. In Chapter 8, when Edwin and Neville quarrel viciously, it is not so much that Jasper deliberately aggravates their inflamed feelings as that their rising violence draws him like a game or a performance: 'Mr Jasper's play of eyes between the two, holds good throughout the dialogue, to the end' (viii, 59). Later, in a chilling but slightly careless passage, he watches Neville walking with Crisparkle:

'He takes no note whatever of the Minor Canon, but watches Neville, as though his eye were at the trigger of a loaded rifle, and he had covered him, and were going to fire. A sense of destructive power is so expressed in his face, that even Durdles pauses in his munching. . . . (xii, 104)

For 'trigger' read 'sight', or, more appropriately, for 'eye' read 'finger': 'appropriately' because Jasper's physical menace is in part conveyed by a stress on what the Re-reader believes to be murderous hands. For example, as Mr Tope and a few loiterers

stare at the storm-damaged cathedral tower, 'this cluster is suddenly broken and put aside by the hands of Mr Jasper' (xiv, 131),
coming, panic-stricken, with news of Drood's disappearance. He
writes in his diary that he will not rest until '"I hold the clue to
[Drood's murder] in my hand"' (xvi, 146). That same entry reveals
his desire to destroy, not simply to apprehend the murderer. But,
to return to the 'hand' motif, it is used chillingly, given the
accumulated associations, in the scene in Chapter 19 in which
Jasper declares himself to Rosa: 'He would begin by touching her
hand. . . . This time he does touch her with his outstretched hand'
(xix, 169–70). The 'easy attitude' he preserves makes 'his convulsive
hands absolutely diabolical . . . he stretches out his hand towards
the porch' (xix, 171). Her protestations regarding Neville Landless's advances he 'puts . . . from him with a slighting action of his
hand' (xix, 172). His speech is violent; in its assertion of dark,
obsessive passion – 'In the distasteful work of the day, in the
wakeful misery of the night, girded by sordid realities, or wandering through Paradises and Hells of visions into which I rushed,
carrying your image in my arms, I loved you madly' (xix, 170–71) –
and moments of torrential energy it recalls Bradley Headstone's
equally hopeless passion. Dickens's use, here as with Headstone,
of such aspects of the melodramatic mode as the 'curled lip',
'darkly threatening' expression, and, of course, those 'convulsive
hands absolutely diabolical' (xix, 170–72), help emphasise, through
the melodrama's insistence on extreme external traits, the man's
threatening physicality, the more-than-latent violence sensed, only
too strongly, by Rosa Budd herself.

Mr Grewgious's protestations to Rosa that her lodgings in
Furnival's Inn are proof against the lurking man – '"There is a
stout gate of iron bars to keep him out", said Mr Grewgious,
smiling, "and Furnival's is specially watched and lighted, and *I* live
over the way!"' (xx, 182) – in that they are implicit reminders of
Jasper's lurking menace, are not reassuring. That menace persists
to the end of the incomplete text. Back once more in the opium-
den, a half-drugged Jasper is, the Re-reader now realises, obsessed
with his crime and acts with a 'savage air' (xxiii, 206). His talk of
obtaining relief from a life he cannot bear, expressed with 'extraordinary vehemence, and the snarl of a wolf' (xxiii, 208), now has
special significance. The Re-reader, like the old opium-seller, is
fascinated by him and, unlike that dreadful woman, has moved
beyond suspicion to a recognition that Jasper (like Headstone after

his attack on Wrayburn) returns again and again to the crime he
has committed. Jasper's second visit to the opium-den, taking
place, fortuitously, in the final extant chapter, in returning the
Re-reader to the novel's opening scene, confers a structural unity
on the incomplete text that is, it now seems, far from spurious.

The conditioned Re-reader foregrounds Jasper's violence against
a text full of violent behaviour. Deputy's stone-throwing, that
recurring textual motif, is but one indication of the aggressive
nature of the novel's world. Septimus Crisparkle, amiable and
sensible in his professional life, working off much violent energy in
swimming and shadow-boxing, provides another. Neville Landless
offers a third: his brooding, smouldering violence breaks out
frequently and never more intensely than when he refers to his
dead stepfather as '"a cruel brute as well as a grinding one. It was
well he died when he did, or I might have killed him"' (vii, 47).
Neville has had, he tells Crisparkle, '"from my earliest remembrance, to suppress a deadly and bitter hatred"' of that cruel
stepfather (vii, 49). It is not always suppressed, but breaks out in
the quarrel with Drood and when he resists, bloodily, the men sent
to arrest him after Drood's disappearance. His sister has similar
tendencies: she expresses astonishment that Drood might not be
fascinated by Rosa 'with an earnestness that threatened to blaze
into ferocity if he didn't' (vii, 52). Drood himself, as the quarrel-
scene shows, is easily roused and swept into the scene's surge
towards the violent. Even an infrequent visitor to Cloisterham like
Mr Honeythunder, the philanthropist, contributes, in his case
substantially, to the general atmosphere of violence. Those he
meets are invariably oppressed physically by his presence. His
aggressive behaviour places him in Crisparkle's world through the
use of the imagery of pugilism, philanthropists only differing from
'professors of the Noble Art of fisticuffs' (xvii, 147) in that, unlike
the latter, they ignored the rules to set, directly and unfairly, about
the targets of their philanthropy.

Violence is everywhere, even in end-of-term larks at Miss
Twinkleton's. When Miss Ferdinand plays the comb-and-paper
'until suffocated in her own pillow by two flowing-haired execu-
tioners' (xiii, 112), this light-hearted prevention faintly but effectively recalls what the informed Re-reader knows: Dickens's comment to his illustrator that Jasper's flowing black scarf must be
mentioned in the text because it would be used to strangle Drood.
Again, such a minor character as Grewgious's clerk, Mr Bazzard, is

glimpsed, suddenly and momentarily, as the product of parental assault.

The text moves from instances of personal violence to three indications of a fundamentally violent world. First, in Chapter 11 the Cathedral organ and choir dominate the 'cracked monotonous mutter' of the congregation's responses:

> [they] burst forth, and drowned it in a sea of music. Then, the sea fell, and the dying voice made another feeble effort, and then the sea rose high, and beat its life out, and lashed the roof, and surged among the arches, and pierced the heights of the great tower. (ix, 73)

All readers notice the violent imagery. The Re-reader also sees that violence is endemic in natural forces and that the attempt to drown followed by success through uncontrolled and sadistic violence, these effects attached to Cathedral music that is in part provided by Jasper himself, provide a momentary paradigm of Jasper's crime.

Second, the text contains numerous references to *Macbeth*. These are well-known and vary from hints, as when the drugged Chinaman tries to draw a phantom knife, or via the use of the word 'murky' in a description of the Cathedral (ix, 73), to such substantial allusions as that in Chapter 11 to Macready's version of Macbeth stealing to Duncan's chamber, and the title ('When Shall These Three Meet Again?') of Chapter 14. *Macbeth* lurks Jasper-like in the text, such reminders of Shakespeare's darkest and most murderous play contributing greatly to the atmosphere of desperate violence. Indeed, the fragment ends, once more fortuitously but significantly, with a sequence through which, despite the absence of the Shakespearean imperative, echo, here as elsewhere, some of the play's most barbaric words, – 'Come, seeling night,/ Scarf up the tender eye of pitiful day'[12] – in the repeated construction: 'Comes Mr Tope ... Come Mrs Tope ... Come, in due time ... Come sundry rooks ...' (xxiii, 215).

Third, the storm on Christmas Eve, whose 'violent rushes abate not, but increase in frequency and fury', tear at trees and the Cathedral tower until, early the following morning, 'it begins to lull. From that time, with occasional wild charges, like a wounded monster dying, it drops and sinks; and at full daylight it is dead' (xiv, 130), re-enact, the Re-reader is convinced, Jasper's murderous actions during that same night.

All three sequences combine to demonstrate the darkly unified nature of the world: the often uncontrolled impulse towards violence links natural forces and the human mind. The actions of particular characters enact this fundamental and despairing vision, the exploration of which leads inevitably to the detailed examination of motives. The Re-reader knows the text to be mainly concerned with criminal and extreme psychological states; Jasper's condemned-cell reverie will be the text's inescapable climax.

Constant awareness of the link between the particular and the general is, for the Re-reader, a further conditioning factor. Thus, the abrupt contrasts between the London opium-den and the cathedral-city and between the violence and passions that lurk and express themselves behind the latter's façade of 'oppressive respectability' (iii, 14), force the Re-reader to recognise that division, split personality, the divided life, the calculated concealing act, are basic characterising principles.

Occasionally they are also a source of humour: Miss Twinkleton, we are told, 'has two distinct and separate phases of being. Every night, the moment the young ladies have retired to rest, does Miss Twinkleton smarten up her curls a little, brighten up her eyes a little, and become a sprightly Miss Twinkleton whom the young ladies have never seen' (iii, 15). Miss Twinkleton's method of reading to Rosa, during which 'she cut the love scenes, interpolated passages in praise of female celibacy, and was guilty of other glaring pious frauds' (xxii, 201–2), is equally calculated and deceiving, though well-meant, behaviour. A serious example is the appearance given by Rosa Budd and Drood that they are a happily engaged couple even though their relationship is foundering. The principle is developed further in Chapter 3 when they discuss themselves in the third person (iii, 20–21). Again, Sapsea, with his ecclesiastical air, seems to be 'a credit to Cloisterham, and society' (iv, 24); in reality he is a bombastic and conceited bore. Durdles, who refers to his 'professional' self in the third person, seems never quite sure of his own identity. Crisparkle, as a clergyman loving physically violent sports, is a further instance of the divided self and, on occasion, of pretence in action, as when, for the best of reasons, he encourages his aged mother to wear spectacles by pretending that he also needs them. Mr Honeythunder's aggressive behaviour, it hardly needs to be said, is at odds with his professed philanthropy. Prim Mr Grewgious offers significant comment on the effect of love upon the lover: the latter is a different person in the presence of the loved one, and only then comes to life, so that the lover lives '"'at once a doubled life and a halved life"'' (xi, 95). He himself shows an unexpected romantic side when recalling Rosa's long-dead mother and the Narrator comments: 'there are such unexplored romantic nooks in the unlikeliest men' (xi, 99). Crucially, the divided self is linked to stimulants: Neville Landless stirred to violence by Jasper's drinks; Durdles in his drink- and, we believe, drug-induced sleep, dreaming his strange dream whilst Jasper takes his cathedral keys.

The Re-reader, constantly aware of such divisions, must include Jasper as the prime example. A key passage is in Chapter 2, when through a fraught conversation his 'breathing seems to have stopped . . . [until] . . . Mr Jasper, becoming a breathing man again without the smallest stage of transition between the two extreme states, lifts his shoulders, laughs, and waves his right arm' (ii, 12). In the piano-scene, Jasper's hands seem not to be his own: '[they] had, in the same instant, lifted themselves from the keys' (vii, 51). From the first his sincerity is suspect: when he first meets Drood, after initial enthusiasm he looks carefully at the younger man: 'a look of intentness and intensity – a look of hungry, exacting, watchful, and yet devoted affection – is always, now and ever afterwards, on the Jasper face whenever the Jasper face is addressed in this direction' (ii, 7). For Jasper always plays a part. He listens to Drood describing the relationship with Rosa, watches him closely and 'remains in that attitude after they are spoken, as if in a kind of fascination . . .'. At the close of the exchange he 'dissolves his attitude, and they go out together' (ii, 13). When with Sapsea he is skilfully ingratiating, appealing shrewdly to the former's conceit by praising him fulsomely in front of the Dean through references to 'Mr Sapsea's knowledge of mankind, and power of drawing out whatever is recluse or odd around him' (xii, 101). The wine-drinking scene is a further example of calculation: under the guise of interested conversation he provokes the violent quarrel. His account of the evening to Crisparkle is equally suspect: Jasper describes only Neville's dreadful conduct and the threat to Edwin Drood that it represents and nothing of Drood's reprehensible conduct or, of course, the part played by the drinks he himself plied. Jasper's use of his diary makes a similar point: he shows Crisparkle extracts describing Neville's hostile behaviour towards Drood and another, detailing his conviction that Drood was murdered and that he would not rest until he found and destroyed the murderer. The extracts combine to cast all suspicion on Neville and so to assert a version of events at odds with what the Re-reader knows to be the case. This latter includes, of course, Jasper's terrible response to Grewgious's information that Drood had broken off his engagement with Rosa before his disappearance, a sudden glimpse of Jasper's dark and secret psyche.

One other discernable textual motif is that of imprisonment. The extant text, full of examples, prepares the reader for the final unwritten scene in Jasper's cell. Jasper is imprisoned by his craving for opium and by his obsession with Rosa. Deputy has spent periods in Cloisterham Jail. Durdles searches, always successfully, for walled-up bodies in the Cathedral masonry. Septimus Crisparkle's dining-room closet contains spices, pickles, jams, wines, all safely locked up. His herb-closet, more explicitly, is a 'herbaceous penitentiary' into which the man, if 'convicted . . . of an imperceptible pimple', would, by his doting mother, be 'submissively led' (x, 80). In Mr Grewgious's rooms sparkling wines 'pushed at their corks to help the corkscrew (like prisoners helping rioters to force their gates), and danced out gaily' (xi, 93). Miss Twinkleton, making her end-of-term speech to her young ladies, compares their predicament to that of 'the captive in his dungeon . . . [who] . . . yearned for home' (xiii, 112). Rosa and Edwin, agreeing to part, view the alternative as 'life-long bondage' (xiii, 116). Neville Landless, suspected of killing Drood, has a room at Staple Inn that 'had a prisonous look, and he had the haggard face of a prisoner' (xvii, 152). Mr Tope's home in Cloisterham is a 'cool dungeon' (xviii, 163), placed, symbolically, below Jasper's rooms. Mr Sapsea, as a magistrate, is familiar with 'the secrets of the prison-house' (xviii, 165).

The conditioned Re-reader fastens upon these textual patterns. Like all re-readers he is an ironist, even a malevolent deconstructionist, uncovering layers of meaning unsuspected on a first reading. Thus, in Chapter 2, though the Dean's question, '"And when and how has Mr Jasper been taken . . . ?"', in being completed by '"Poorly"' (ii, 5) refers to Jasper's health, now, on the re-reading, points to Jasper's eventual apprehension. The Dean's slightly later remark about Jasper's feelings for Drood – '"I hope Mr Jasper's heart may not be too much set upon his nephew"' – is open to the same ironical and sinister interpretation, as is his opinion that Drood's arrival will do Jasper '"More good than a dozen doctors"' (ii, 6), given that the Re-reader knows the nephew's arrival will allow Jasper to release his repressed violent urges. Irony is everywhere: in Mrs Tope's words to Drood about his uncle, who is '"too much wrapped up in you"' (ii, 8); in all Jasper's professions of affection for his nephew; in Rosa Budd's question to Edwin, '"Can't you see a happy Future?"' (ii, 23); in the fact that she sings, to Jasper's accompaniment, 'a sorrowful strain of parting' (vii, 51); in the description of the lime-heap near the Cathedral yard as '"quick enough to eat your bones"' (xii, 104), that is a reminder of Forster's synopsis; and, particularly, in the exchange between Grewgious and Jasper about Rosa and Edwin:

'God save them both!' cried Jasper.

'I said, bless them,' remarked the former, looking back over his shoulder.

'I said, save them,' returned the latter. 'Is there any difference?'

(ix, 76)

The romantic interest is more straightforward the second time around. Knowledge of Forster's account of the unwritten part of the lovers' progress highlights Crisparkle's feelings for Helen Landless and Tartar's eager response to Rosa Budd.

All in all, the Re-reader now understands the world of appearances, dramatised by the frequent use of the 'as if' construction, and so possesses more insight than any character. Even Jasper, who knows what has happened, does not know what *will* happen. The Narrator, telling his past-tense tale, presumably does but cannot complete the telling. Only the Re-reader, with his knowledge of extra-textual sources, can begin to do that. But, paradoxically, this beginning has a certain conclusiveness. Believing he knows how things will go, the Re-reader finds a text that confirms his assumptions, a text shaken like a kaleidoscope into a number of immutable patterns. It is not a case of falsely *imposing* upon a text, but of the text, via apprehendable aspects, being made to demonstrate what it contains. This text now has a Re-reader who knows more than it contains. But this is not simply to say that the Re-reader is identical with the author, for the latter had choice. Indeed, in the case of this incomplete text that choice remained, in part, still to be exercised. The Re-reader knows the ending and how it will be reached and so watches in paradoxical helplessness as the characters take part in preordained and often futile man-oeuvres. He is helpless, possessing knowledge without power. That *The Mystery of Edwin Drood*, Dickens's last work, should cast its Re-reader as a version of Tiresias, is a final chilling indication that this great author's vision was mainly dark to the very end.

5

Characterisation and Ideas in *Little Dorrit*: Clennam and Calvinism[1]

'At the very centre of the novel is Mrs Clennam', writes Lionel Trilling.[2] That being so, the centre is very dark. For most of the novel she imprisons herself in her 'old brick house ... within a gateway' (I, iii, 31–2), propped up on her 'black bier-like sofa' (I, iii, 33) or rigid in her wheelchair. Not until five chapters from the end – Book II, Chapter 30 – does she leave her room. But her influence on her son is as deadly as any Biblical plague.

Critics unite in stressing her essentially evil nature. Trilling notes that 'she perverts and prevents [love] by denying all that love feeds on – liberty, demonstrative tenderness, joy and ... art;'[3] to F.R. Leavis she was associated with 'the Calvinistic commercialism of the early and middle Victorian age – the repressiveness towards children, the hard righteousness, the fear of love, the armed rigour in the face of life';[4] J. Hillis Miller emphasises her 'perverted Christianity' and her 'dismal doctrine';[5] Daleski considers her to be a Mr Dombey with religious rather than commercial mania.[6] It is impossible to disagree with such comments but it is also true to say that no critic moves much beyond a generalised antagonism, despite the fact that Dickens accumulates a precise statement of Mrs Clennam's religious beliefs.

'"I justify myself by the authority of these Books"', she cries in Book I, Chapter 15 (176). The 'Books', we learn, include the Old Testament, from which she reads at Arthur's homecoming, and commentaries upon it, to which she refers. The 'Books' provide, for Mrs Clennam, 'a fortification against sweetness of temper, natural affection, and gentle intercourse' (I, iii, 30), and call for the wrath of Old Testament Jehovah to be directed, mercilessly, against the ungodly. The Old Testament sanctions the harsh beliefs that emerge in her response to Arthur Clennam's birth.

He is the illegitimate consequence of Gilbert Clennam's extra-marital affair with an unnamed woman. Mrs Clennam discovers the affair and forces the woman to hand over the baby. The boy is then brought up by Gilbert Clennam and his wronged wife so that '"the presence of Arthur was a daily reproach to his father ... the absence of Arthur was a daily agony to his mother"' (II, xxx, 755). This vicious revenge is, for Mrs Clennam, an expression of religious faith. The fate of both her husband and his former lover was, Mrs Clennam believes,

> the just dispensation of Jehovah. . . . I devoted myself to reclaim the otherwise predestined and lost boy ... to bring him up in fear and trembling, and in a life of practical contrition for the sins that were heavy on his head before his entrance into this condemned world. (II, xxx, 755)

Here are her fundamentals: a belief in original sin and in the world's fallen state. Man moves inevitably to deserved damnation unless he struggles, is made to struggle, constantly against the world's vanities. We are, asserts Mrs Clennam, '"every one, the subject (most justly the subject) of a wrath that must be satisfied, and against which mere actions are nothing"' (I, xxx, 351). Innate sinfulness requires expiation; life is 'reparation' (I, v, 48).

Those who struggle against self and world are sustained by a sense of superior status. As she puts it:

> I take it as a grace and favour to be elected to make the satisfaction I am making here, to know what I know for certain here, and to work out what I have worked out here. My affliction might otherwise have had no meaning to me. (I, xxx, 351)

The 'elect' and only the 'elect' have a sure and certain hope of eventual salvation. Such confidence inspires Mrs Clennam to-wards quasi-Biblical lyricism: '"Are we not all cut down like the grass of the field, and was not I shorn by the scythe many years ago; since when, I have been lying here, waiting to be gathered into the barn?"' (I, xv, 177) From such eager fatalism she derives her fierce strength.

Dickens does not only enunciate the basic tenets of Mrs Clennam's Calvinism; he also analyses the consequences of her belief. The dingy, blackened, Clennam home, 'standing by itself' in a mouldering neighbourhood and propped up by 'gigantic crutches' (I, iii, 31–2) as Mrs Clennam, within, is propped by cushions, her physical paralysis, the unnaturalness of her confined existence so indifferent to night, to day, to the seasons, with the fire always burning and only the vicious Jeremiah and the half-daft Affery in attendance, all dramatise the cost of her rejecting the world. Further, we are made to see that this rejection – and Mrs Clennam's belief – has, as a cause, a tragic lack of sympathetic imagination: 'Great need had the rigid woman of her mystical religion, veiled in gloom and darkness, with lightnings of cursing, vengeance, and destruction, flashing through the sable clouds', because she demanded of her Creator, 'do Thou as I would do' (I, v, 45). Mrs Clennam's creed perverted 'the making of man in the image of his Creator to the making of his Creator in the image of an erring man' (I, xiii, 158). Again, through her life 'she . . . abided by her old impiety – still reversed the order of Creation, and breathed her own breath into a clay image of her Creator' (II, xxx, 754). With this twisted view of God came a similar view of the world. The isolated house seemed unchanging and

> the invalid within it turned the same unvarying round of life. Morning noon and night, morning, noon, and night, each recurring with its accompanying monotony, always the same reluctant return to the same sequences of machinery, like a dragging piece of clockwork.

As the Narrator comments:

> to suppose mankind stricken motionless, when we were brought to a stand-still; to be unable to measure the changes beyond our view, by any larger standard than the shrunken one of our own uniform and contracted existence; is the infirmity of many invalids, and the mental unhealthiness of almost all recluses. (I, xxix, 333)

Mrs Clennam, he insists, is no exception.

She can conceive of neither love nor affection nor tenderness, but though her imaginative shortcomings are important they only partly explain her rejection of the world. Dickens, in a profound exploration of the psychology of the religious recluse, stresses two other points. Mrs Clennam derives masochistic delight even from the unnaturalness of her predicament: '"All seasons are alike to me", she returned, with a grim kind of luxuriousness. "I know nothing of summer and winter, shut up here. The Lord has been pleased to put me beyond all that"' (I, iii, 34). She is, she considers, again with some satisfaction, '"justly infirm and righteously afflicted"' (I, v, 45). Secondly, to reject the world is also to escape from it: for Mrs Clennam it is some '"compensation"' that she is '"also shut up from the knowledge of some things that I may prefer to avoid knowing"' (I, xv, 180).

But, in a novel much concerned with desperate aimlessness she is sustained by an overwhelming sense of purpose: '"I shape my course by pilots, strictly by proved and tried pilots, under whom I cannot be shipwrecked – can not be"' (I, xxx, 350). Hence her strength, her willpower, her ability to outface even the fierce Flintwinch, the 'certain air [she has] upon her of resolute waiting' (II, xvii, 607).

That sense of purpose, of course, stultifies Arthur Clennam's childhood. It receives more complex expression in the traditional link between Calvinism and capitalism. The Calvinist's investment in mortification and rejection in the certain hope of future celestial dividends is a paradigm of capitalist behaviour; it is no accident that the Clennams run a finance-house. In Mrs Clennam's case the extent of her hatred and distrust of the world has undermined even that business. The firm has declined. As Arthur Clennam recognises: '"We have never shown much confidence, or invited much; we have attached no people to us; the track we have kept is not the track of the time; and we have been left far behind"' (I, v, 44). Nonetheless, the core of Calvinism is dramatised through persisting business attitudes. Mrs Clennam is only comfortable with the returned Arthur when they confine themselves to the business implications of his withdrawal from the family firm. She evaluates his advice in terms of business efficacy: when he warns her that Rigaud has been in prison accused of murder, she rejects that warning because his informant lacks respectable commercial credentials. Above all, her relations with God mirror those with the world, in offering a version of reparation-with-a-view-to-eventual-salvation suitable for the dingiest Lombard Street: 'she [was] always balancing her bargain with the Majesty of heaven, posting up the entries to her credit, strictly keeping her set-off, and claiming her due' (I, v, 50). 'Business' becomes a chilling metaphor for loveless, heartless relations with man and with God.

One point remains to be noted: despite her strength and conviction, Mrs Clennam is vulnerable to Rigaud's assault on her implacability. He penetrates her world and holds her to ransom; he does so without much difficulty because he has demystified – and threatens to expose – the dark secret at the heart of Mrs Clennam's life. Her vulnerability leads to an undermining of her Calvinism for her life and her religion centre on mysteries that cannot survive too-close examination. She rejects Rigaud only by trying to abandon her faith.

Critics are generally in agreement about the effects upon Clennam of his Calvinistic upbringing. Such effects are heavily stressed during the first thirteen chapters, from his entry into the text until he asks his overwhelming question:

> 'From the unhappy suppression of my youngest days, through the rigid and unloving home that followed them, through my departure, my long exile, my return, my mother's welcome, my intercourse with her since, down to the afternoon of this day with poor Flora', said Arthur Clennam, 'what have I found!' (I, xiii, 158)

and the answer comes unexpectedly from the doorway: '"Little Dorrit."'

In these early chapters he is earnest and dejected, without momentum or purpose. When he first appears in the text he is slow to acquire a name, a significant portent of a persisting lack of assertive identity. He is overwhelmed by a strong but undefined sense of guilt that finds an obsessive outlet in unsupported suspicions about the Clennam business: its dealings may have disadvantaged others, may have wronged someone. The occasional presence of Little Dorrit in his mother's house may be a gesture of reparation. Clennam longs for a vague justice, for a shadowy restitution. He longs to initiate positive action as a counter to his helplessness; he feels life has passed him by, that he is incapable of loving and does not deserve love. '"I am",' he considers, '"... liable to be drifted where any current may set. . . . I have no will"' (I, ii, 19–20).

Clennam, we see, despite the psychological scarring, is not Mrs Clennam's clone. From the first he is capable of fellow-feeling: quarantined in Marseilles he has '"had so much pleasure"' (I, ii, 18) even in Mrs Meagles's company. And he does try to shatter the rigidity of his life by questioning the work he does. In withdrawing from the Clennam business he tries to channel some of the guilt and dissatisfaction into beneficial action. For even though his nature 'had been disappointed from the dawn of its perceptions' it 'had not quite given up all its hopeful yearnings yet' (I, iii, 33). Unlike his mother, Clennam has retained a capacity for imagining. He recalls the lost possibilities for romance and 'began to dream. For, it had been the uniform tendency of this man's life – so much was wanting in it to think about, so much that might have been better directed and happier to speculate upon – to make him a dreamer, after all' (I, iii, 40). He remains a dreamer

> because he was a man who had deep-rooted in his nature, a belief in all the gentle and good things his life had been without . . . this had rescued him to be a man of honourable mind and open hand . . . to have a warm and sympathetic heart . . . to judge not, and in humility to be merciful, and have hope and charity.
>
> And this saved him still from the whimpering weakness and cruel selfishness of holding that because such a happiness or such a virtue had not come into his little path, or worked well for him, therefore it was not in the great scheme, but was reducible, when found in appearance, to the basest elements. A disappointed mind he had, but a mind too firm and healthy for such unwholesome air. Leaving himself in the dark, it could rise into the light, seeing it shine on others and hailing it. (I, xiii, 158)

Such a passage, in its strategically important position immediately before Little Dorrit's appearance in Clennam's doorway at the close of Book I, Chapter 13, allows a hopeful interpretation of his position: he has freed himself from the business, from lingering romantic hopes of Flora, and from similar thoughts of Pet Meagles. Even though he encounters later problems, such as his sad obtuseness about Little Dorrit, the implacability of the Circumlocution Office, and his losing of Doyce's capital, it has been possible to regard the jettisoning of past ties and delusions as a necessary prelude to events that lead to eventual happy recovery. Daleski, for example, stresses that Clennam takes the 'decisive step of becoming Doyce's partner' because Doyce is, for Clennam, a 'liberating force', particularly at the end. More obviously, Little Dorrit provides 'another kind of liberation'.[7] More recently and by a different

route Garrett Stewart has reached broadly similar conclusions:
'Arthur Clennam fares better "after all", but he must suffer for it'
before being 'saved by Little Dorrit'.[8] Even F.R. Leavis, who writes
more suggestively than anyone of the lingering influence upon
Clennam of his early years, is close to Daleski in his accounts of
Clennam's relationships with Doyce and with Little Dorrit.

This present study, from this point, makes use of Trilling's
observation that with Clennam's characterisation we become
aware of a 'certain formality of pattern'.[9] It argues that Clennam's
textual life, through its patterns, its structures, demonstrates
persisting Calvinism to an extent not previously recognised. To
become aware of such structures is to make previous analyses of
the work's ending – and hence, our understanding of Clennam
and of the novel – much in need of radical revision.

One such pattern dramatises directly Clennam's inability wholly
to free himself from Mrs Clennam's influence. The characterisation
is structured on repeated visits to his mother and her household.
Only during the first visit – the sad reunion after twenty years
when he withdraws from the business and suspects previous
injustice linked vaguely to Little Dorrit – does he stay for even one
night in the dreary house that was once his home. Thereafter he
moves into lodgings and effects his severance from the business by
attending Mrs Clennam only during business hours. In Book I,
Chapter 16, still obsessed with reparation, he calls unexpectedly,
not to see his mother but to ask Affery whether Mrs Clennam
knows of Little Dorrit's history; the servant refuses even to come
near him. His 'regular visits to his mother's dull sickroom' (II, viii,
503) continue, cease during his preoccupation with the Circumlocution Office, then recommence in Book II, Chapter 10. This visit
coincides with that of Blandois. Clennam is repelled and angered
by the latter's threatening arrogance and familiarity but when he
objects in support of his mother she turns on him, cites Blandois'
impeccable business credentials – he carries introductions from
'"highly esteemed and responsible correspondents"' (II, x, 529) –
and orders Clennam to leave. Affery shows him out and still
refuses to respond. As a consequence he is 'depressed and made
uneasy by the late occurrence at his mother's' (I, xiii, 562); the
events lie 'heavy on his lonely mind' (I, xiii, 566). When he learns
from John-Baptist that Blandois was once imprisoned as a suspected murderer he pays another visit to his old home. He hopes
that Affery, despite her previous lack of cooperation, can explain

Blandois' connection with the business, and that he can alert his mother to Blandois' criminal record. But Affery still refuses to talk. His mother, once again, rejects his help: in her eyes his information is suspect because his informant lacks commercial standing. Before Clennam can call again Merdle dies and the Marshalsea beckons.

In this short summary it might appear that the sequence of visits in itself dramatises the extent of Clennam's new-found spiritual freedom: the two scenes involving Blandois could show Clennam's human concern wholly at odds with his mother's commercialism. But the sequence also dramatises the displacing of the personal by the commercial, apparent in the observing of 'daily business hours' (I, v, 57). And the effect of continuing exposure to commercialism is all too evident in the very fibre of Clennam's attitudes even in the 'Blandois' scenes. For when he learns about Blandois his reaction is not a simple one: 'It was like the oppression of a dream, to believe that shame and exposure were impending over her and his father's memory' (II, xxiii, 659). Mingled with admirable morality is a businessman's concern for the firm's reputation. He is impelled to appeal to her:

> 'Mother, shall I do nothing to assist you?'
> 'Nothing.'
> 'Will you entrust me with no confidence, no charge, no explanation? Will you take no counsel with me? Will you not let me come near you?'
>
> (II, xxiii, 663)

She, of course, refuses. Though Clennam's closing sentence hints at some slight emotional involvement his speech is dominated by the language of commerce. The exchange is more one between a businessman and his partner than, as Clennam believes, between a son and his mother.

Clennam has withdrawn but is still involved. He still thinks and speaks like a businessman which, in this work, means like a Calvinist. We are not surprised when he moves from the family business only to find a similar position – in financial management – as part of Doyce and Clennam, and that he is attracted towards Daniel Doyce. Part of this attraction is, we know, admiration for Doyce's qualities and, consequently, a desire to assist him. But it is more significant that Doyce has some resemblance to Mrs Clennam: he, too, endures the slings and arrows of a world unworthy of him, finds a strange consolation in his treatment – ' "'it's a certain sort of relief to know that I might have counted on this'" ' (I, x, 116) – and in a startling application of the idea of the 'elect' becomes, for a foreign power, 'one of the chosen' (II, xxii, 652). Doyce and the job he provides for Clennam help fill the psychological vacuum caused by the latter's rejection of his mother's world. Put another way, Doyce offers new opportunities for Clennam to continue moving through habitual and stultifying thought-patterns. Clinching evidence of these last is provided by his succumbing to the lure of investment. When Pancks stimulates his interest in Merdle's empire Clennam's thought-sequence is predictable: he is tempted by the ingrained belief that present investment will yield certain future dividends and by a failure to stand aloof from shared faith in seemingly divine omnipresence (here, Merdle) typical of those used to living within a narrow sect.

For Clennam, attempting to make a new life, apparent difference only masks more of the same. A further example is his general restlessness, of which his visits to his mother are only one instance. He may lack psychological momentum but physically he is rarely still. On his first appearance in the text, with Meagles in Marseilles, as he talks he walks 'backward and forward in the shade of the wall' (I, ii, 17). A pattern is set. Thereafter he follows Little Dorrit through streets and over bridges, or walks with her 'through the miserable muddy streets, and among the poor mean shops ... jostled by the crowds of dirty hucksters usual to a poor neighbourhood' (I, ix, 95). He moves obsessively to and from the Circumlocution Office and makes regular visits on foot to Twickenham. Clennam not only moves to and from buildings but within them also: through his grim home, the Marshalsea, and the labyrinthine department of government. Book I, Chapter 10, offers a typical sequence: Clennam makes his 'fifth enquiry one day at the Circumlocution Office' (I, x, 103), is directed by Barnacle Junior to see his father at Mews Street, Grosvenor Square, returns to the Office, is sent from department to department within it, meets Meagles and Doyce and walks with them to Doyce's factory in Bleeding Heart Yard, from which, in Chapter 12, he rides with Mr Plornish to the Marshalsea.

More than anyone else in this novel of pilgrimage Clennam is one of the 'restless travellers through the pilgrimage of life' (I, ii, 26). His movements are pointless, thwarted, or misconceived, whether they are to the Circumlocution Office, to visit Pet, or to see a Little Dorrit whom he excludes from his heart. But one might wish to say, once again, that these movements in themselves indicate a kind of freedom, albeit a problematical one, consequent upon an escape from the old rigidities represented by his mother and her predicament into a world that is, at the very least, one of possibilities.

Mrs Clennam's life is pointless because thwarted by circumstances and ultimately unsuccessful; in that it continues to be an expression of spiritual dissatisfaction, her son's new life is not wholly dissimilar from the old. And Mrs Clennam herself is not simply paralysis opposed to questing. She is confined to her room and, within it, to sofa and wheel-chair, yet she enacts, as it were in miniature, her son's wanderings in the outside world; her small movements, intense with emotion, are her equivalent of Clennam's physical ranging. Though the Narrator tells us of her stony demeanour, she is rarely wholly still. Her hands motion, move food, open and close books, adjust spectacles, move from lap to desk; her arms gesture; she shakes her head, turns her face, shapes her lips. These constant, small, highly-charged movements indicate the tense, repressed existence from which, on occasion, emotion can break with such sudden power that even her wheel-chair is forced to move 'from time to time, a little on its wheels' (I, v, 47). When Clennam voices his suspicions of past dealings anger mobilises her: 'By a swift and sudden action of her foot, she drove her wheeled chair rapidly back to [the bell-rope] and pulled it violently' (I, v, 47). Pushed by Flintwinch – once by Arthur Clennam – she makes a daily journey from sofa to desk and 'tall cabinet' (I, v, 43). Like Clennam's visits to the Circumlocution Office and to Twickenham hers, to her desk, to judge from the decline in the business, are equally futile.

Eventually, of course, stirred by Blandois' revelations and financial demands she rises out of paralysis: 'She put her two hands to her head again, uttered a loud exclamation, and started to her feet. She staggered for a moment, as if she would have fallen; then stood firm. . . . It was . . . almost as if a dead woman had risen.' (II, xxx, 762). She puts on outdoor clothes and, in the famous sequence, runs 'wildly through the courtyard and out at the gateway' (II, xxx, 765) to rush through the streets to find Little Dorrit. Though she confesses to her that she had once cheated her out of a legacy, and though she asks Little Dorrit for forgiveness, for Mrs Clennam it is too late for redemption. The house collapses, the shock strikes her down; now, dumb and completely paralysed, she lingers for three long years.

From the Clennam house to the Marshalsea is a way much trodden by Arthur Clennam. In breaking out of confinement to follow in her son's footsteps Mrs Clennam forges another link between their two worlds. Instead of appreciating differences between Clennam's restless world and the old rigidities, more and more the reader is made to feel their essential connecting similarities, a feeling intensified by the aesthetic symmetry of the continuing relationship: Mrs Clennam lives confined and then escapes to Little Dorrit, whilst Arthur Clennam also lives in continuing confinement – the Circumlocution Office, Doyce's counting-house, the Marshalsea, succeeding the earlier spiritual prison – before escaping to (and with) Little Dorrit at the close.

One other pattern of behaviour links mother and son. Clennam recalls his religion not as an inspiration or consolation but as an interrogator whose methods are represented by the 'horrible tract which commenced business with the poor child by asking him in its title, why he was going to Perdition?' (I, iii, 30). When he dreams of Mrs Clennam justifying her existence in the face of discovered past dishonesty, the interrogatory mode is an essential part of the memory: '"He withers away in his prison; I wither away in mine; inexorable justice is done; what do I owe on this score!"' (I, viii, 86). Indeed, the question is, for Mrs Clennam, in itself an important way of relating to the world. For example, to Flintwinch's own enquiries about Little Dorrit she responds with her own chilling questions:

> Mr Flintwinch lighted the candle briskly, and said, as he put it down upon the table:
> 'What are you going to do with Little Dorrit? Is she to come to work here for ever? To come to tea here for ever? To come backwards and forwards here, in the same way, for ever?'
> 'How can you talk about "for ever" to a maimed creature like me? Are we not all cut down like the grass of the field, and was not I shorn by the scythe many years ago; since when, I have been lying here, waiting to be gathered into the barn?'
>
> (II, xv, 177)

When he asks where Little Dorrit lives, she denies knowing and fends him off with more demands: '"Could I not have asked her

... why do you goad me? ... why should you, of all men, grudge me that relief [of escaping the world]? ... Is it so much, that you torment me like an evil spirit"' (I, xv, 178).

When Rigaud attacks through revelations of her past, Mrs Clennam again retorts with queries. She asks about Clennam's real and long-dead mother: '"And what was the repentance that was extorted from the hardness of her heart and the blackness of her depravity? ... I ask, what was the penitence, in works, that was demanded of her?"' (II, xxx, 754–5) Rigaud's taunts press upon her but do not subdue her constant cross-examining.

Of course she cross-examines herself as much as others. In this sense her questions dramatise the self-doubt that, eventually, sends her in search of forgiveness. Equally, they demonstrate her hatred of the 'non-elect' world by substituting defensive conflict for communication: her exchange with Flintwinch is the prime instance of conversation being replaced by the tactics of repulsion. Each remains in a prison-house of questioning utterances.

Clennam, too, is a questioner. He always 'want to know'. His questions begin in that first conversation with Meagles in Marseilles, when he asks about Tattycoram's name and Meagles's family circumstances. In response to Mr Meagles's queries about the future he asks questions about himself: '"What is to be expected from *me* in middle life? Will, purpose, hope? ... (I, ii, 20). His first meeting with Flintwinch, naturally enough after twenty years, begins with more. In exchanges with Mrs Clennam there are disturbing echoes of the latter's encounters with Flintwinch:

'Does it snow?'
  'Snow, mother? And we only yet in September?'

(I, iii, 34)

He asks Pancks about his work, John-Baptist about his origins, Mrs Chivery about John Chivery's intentions. He cross-questions Affery about Mrs Clennam and about Little Dorrit. The latter – the mystery that surrounds her, as well as the girl herself – is a source of constant speculation. Clennam's meetings with her lead to numerous queries: he interrogates Little Dorrit about her history, about her connection with Mrs Clennam, about her father and his creditors. All the while he interrogates himself. When he talks of being too old for love he asks – of himself, of her:

'Why do I speak of this to Little Dorrit? Why do I show you, my child, the space of years that there is between us, and recall to you that I have passed, by the amount of your whole life, the time that is present to you? . . . Why have you kept so retired from me? . . . Have you no secret you could entrust to me, with hope and comfort, if you would?' (I, xxxii, 374)

Clennam searches for answers to mysteries that include his personal dilemmas. His questioning of Little Dorrit also demons-trates the nature of that relationship: as interrogator he retains what he considers to be a superior position – parent to child, teacher to pupil – and so distances himself from her. To put this another way: his interrogatory stance, here as elsewhere, disables him from satisfying human involvement. It is a constant reminder of his psychological inadequacy implicit in his failure to open himself to another and reminds us that *de facto*, if not by birth, he is Mrs Clennam's son.

The fact that he remains so is made clear to us not only through the persisting patterns of his behaviour, but also through the nature of his textual life *per se*, considered in the most basic way, in terms of his presence and absence in the work. In Book I he appears in eighteen chapters, in Book II in eleven. As has been noted, though he is much on the move he is invariably unsuccess-ful, thwarted, disappointed or depressed. He gets nowhere in his investigations of guilt; he fails to further Doyce's cause with the Circumlocution Office and then ruins him by investing in Merdle; his mother refuses his help; he misunderstands Little Dorrit. Without him the Clennam business proceeds much as before; Pancks and Rugg secure William Dorrit's inheritance and conse-quent release from prison; Doyce's eventual success owes nothing to Clennam's efforts; Mrs Clennam herself renders Blandois's actions innocuous before divine retribution and/or social neglect collapses the Clennam house upon him. Indeed, as the novel proceeds, Clennam's presences become more and more ineffectual as he moves from disengagement with the business to the ruining of Doyce, to imprisonment and illness. Clennam's inability to impose himself upon circumstances is only to be expected follow-ing a childhood dominated by Calvinistic fatalism.

As has been seen, his readiness to invest is equally unsurprising; when Merdle's enterprises fail, Clennam's reactions remain pre-dictable. What begins as contrition swiftly wells over into self-flagellation:

'I . . . who have ruined my partner! Pancks, Pancks, I have ruined Doyce! The honest, self-helpful, indefatigable old man, who has worked his way all through his life; the man who has contended against so much disappointment, and who has brought out of it such a good and hopeful nature; the man I have felt so much for, and meant to be so true and useful to; I have ruined him – brought him to shame and disgrace – ruined him, ruined him!' (II, xxvi, 692)

Despite obvious differences – the comparative lack of control, the concern for another – in Clennam's words is a reminder of his mother punishing herself. The Narrator's comment is that Pancks was desperately upset because 'the agony into which the reflection wrought [Clennam's] mind was so distressing to see' (II, xxvi, 692): in the failure of 'wrought' wholly to free itself from connotations of 'crafted', of being deliberately 'worked up', is a suggestion of Clennam's self-indulgence. He shares with Mrs Clennam the same masochistic streak, and for the same reason.

His overwhelming sense of guilt causes him to abandon his life to expiation:

'My course,' said Clennam, brushing away some tears that had been silently dropping down his face, "must be taken at once. What wretched amends I can make must be made. I must clear my unfortunate partner's reputation. I must retain nothing for myself. I must resign to our creditors the power of management I have so much abused, and I must work out as much of my fault – or crime – as is susceptible of being worked out, in the rest of my days.' (II, xxvi, 693)

This central belief in life as penance leads him, naturally and eagerly, to the language of his childhood faith: a public statement of his absolute culpability would be, he insists, 'the only real atonement within his power; was a better atonement to the particular man than it would be to many men; and was therefore the atonement he had first to make' (II, xxvi, 695). The restrictions of his 'mind-forg'd manacles' are implicit in the chilling repetition.

From this point onwards Clennam reverts, more and more, to his mother's way. The obsessive sense of guilt that makes him desire punishment combines with fatalistic passivity: '"My only wish"', he tells Rugg, '"is, that it should be over. I will go on, and take my chance."' He waits for his creditors to invoke the full rigour of the law and will do nothing to ameliorate its effect. Indeed, he seems to want the worst: '"I would rather,"' he continues to the protesting Rugg, '"be taken to the Marshalsea than to any other prison"' (II, xxvi, 697).

Most significant of all is his refusal to accept Little Dorrit's help, despite the depth and passion of her appeal to him to use her money to escape the debtors' prison and retrieve his fortunes:

> 'I have no use for money, I have no wish for it. It would be of no value at all to me, but for your sake. I could not be rich and you here.... Dear Mr Clennam, make me of all the world the happiest, by saying Yes! Make me as happy as I can be in leaving you here, by saying nothing to-night, and letting me go away with the hope that you will think of it kindly; and that for my sake – not for yours, for mine, for nobody's but mine! – you will give me the greatest joy I can experience on earth, the joy of knowing that I have been serviceable to you, and that I have paid some little of the great debt of my affection and gratitude.... But pray, pray, pray, do not turn from your Little Dorrit, now, in your affliction!' (II, xxix, 738)

Only a hard heart – or one corrupted by old dogma – could remain immune. Clennam's is the latter. Little Dorrit sees money as nothing in itself, as deriving value only from what it can do, and from Clennam's acceptance of it as a source of mutual happiness and fulfilment. His reply is revealing: '"I must not hear of such a sacrifice. Liberty and hope would be so dear, bought at such a price, that I never could support their weight, never bear the reproach of possessing them."' He assails himself bitterly for missed opportunities, for his own deficiencies. When she again appeals to him his language becomes more extreme: '"I am disgraced enough, my Little Dorrit. I must not descend so low as that, and carry you – so dear, so generous, so good – down with me"' (II, xxix, 739). He insists that all is over between them.

Clennam has hardly listened carefully to her appeal: she has stressed that giving would not be a sacrifice, that his acceptance would not seem disgraceful to her. But then, despite what he now knows of her feelings for him – he has been informed, of course, by young John Chivery, let alone by Little Dorrit herself – he remains at his most obtusely patronising. Despite his disclaimers, she is still

his 'child', still his '"dearest girl"' (II, xxix, 739). He still conducts –
a further backward link – the relationship as one between ardent
disciple and reproving authority. Above all, in refusing Little
Dorrit's money, Clennam has returned to the core of Calvinism, to
the very heart of loss. The central image of his reply, drawn from
commercial accounting, is a vivid reminder of Mrs Clennam doing
deals with her Maker. And as she 'breathed her own breath into a
clay image of her Creator' (II, xxx, 754), so Clennam suffers a failure
of the sympathetic imagination: he sees Little Dorrit and her offer,
he sees the world, wholly from his own point of view.

Most critics agree that through the inspirational qualities of Little
Dorrit, Arthur Clennam eventually escapes from these depths. J.
Hillis Miller's view of the novel's closing stages is mainly typical:

> The novel, then, ends happily with the usual Dickensian scene
> of reciprocal love, as Arthur Clennam and Little Dorrit leave the
> Marshalsea for the last time to be married. But here there is even
> less emphasis than usual on the completeness of the lovers'
> escape from the shadow, and there is a firm assertion that their
> happiness is limited to themselves alone and leaves the selfish,
> restless, and deluded multitudes still locked in the prison of the
> world.[10]

Miller's first and third points are widely echoed. For example,
Daleski notes that 'the shadow of the Marshalsea that falls on
Clennam may be transformed by Little Dorrit's brightness, but
there is no suggestion that the shadow it casts on a whole society
will be transformed'.[11] F.R. Leavis stresses that though the ending
may be 'right and happy', in that it solves 'the personal problem of
each',[12] it has little wider relevance. Barickman also agrees: the
couple ultimately achieve a quiet, modest, secure resolution of
their personal dilemmas'.[13]

But Miller's second point, that Dickens does not insist on the
'completeness of the lovers' escape', is not fully articulated and
suggests that he is not wholly at ease with his account of the
ending. This unease is shared by Daleski when the latter writes of
the 'tentative' nature of Dickens's vision of 'the transforming
power of love' and that 'at the end of *Little Dorrit* . . . Dickens seems
less hopeful than in *Bleak House*'.[14] More recent writers, though
perpetuating the notion that Clennam finds 'salvation'[15] and that
the book is ultimately affirmative,[16] remain uncertain about the

extent to which Clennam's achievement of personal success convinces.[17]

The present writer is wholly unconvinced by the general agreement that, despite some moments lacking in persuasiveness, in the end Clennam is redeemed. For such a reading neglects two basic points. Firstly, it has been argued, above, that Clennam cannot free himself from the persisting thought-patterns of Calvinism inculcated by his upbringing; indeed, in his new life, in his plunge into crisis as well as in the suffered consequences, he is more and more possessed by the old religion. Because of this the reader becomes embroiled in an associated and powerful psychological sequence, in what Iser has called an 'increasing complexity of expectation'.[18] To give one example, when Mrs Clennam and Arthur both break out of their respective confinements towards Little Dorrit, the reader gains aesthetic satisfaction from perceiving the comparison. Mrs Clennam's escape is too late: Little Dorrit can only suggest the possibility of redemption but cannot halt the retributive sequence of the collapsing house, the paralysis and loss of speech. The reader expects the comparison to be completed and so is, as it were, aesthetically compelled to expect Little Dorrit to fail Clennam as she 'fails' Mrs Clennam. A second example concerns Clennam's textual presence: it is always synonymous with ineffectiveness and so generates expectations that attend his return to the text in the closing sequence. As patterns are perceived, as they unfold and combine, all readings of the ending are affected by the accumulating force of such expectations. The later scene derives its power from such links and connotations. Further – the second basic point – such reader-expectations do not, here, exist in tension with the text itself. In important ways the ending *does* provide what the reader now expects to find.

In Book II, Chapter 29, Clennam dreams, or seems to dream, in his prison cell, that 'some abiding impression of a garden stole over him. . . . Beside the tea-cup on his table he saw, then, a blooming nosegay: a wonderful handful of the choicest and most lovely flowers.' They delight and reinvigorate him. Then comes Little Dorrit 'with her knees upon the floor at his feet, and with her lips raised up to kiss him, and with her tears dropping on him as the rain from Heaven had dropped upon the flowers' (II, xxix, 735–6).

It is a famous scene but it is not, to this reader at least, an imaginatively compelling one. In the description of the flowers the triteness of 'a blooming nosegay' is typical of the thinness of the language. Such writing does not demand the reader's assent, does not force the reader into aesthetic involvement. Paradoxically, this is an advantage: the reader is able to stand back, to respond, as it were, intellectually to the scene and, in particular, to relate it to previous similar scenes.

For Little Dorrit is not the first girl in this novel to be associated with gardens and flowers. In Book I, Chapter 16, when Clennam first visits the Meagleses at Twickenham, the garden becomes an emblem of Pet's situation, 'as fresh and beautiful in the May of the Year, as Pet now was in the May of her life' (I, xvi, 186). More importantly and precisely, when Clennam makes a further visit he is met on the riverbank by Pet with 'some roses in her hand' (I, xxviii, 236). She gives him a few, then weeps over them when she tells him of her forthcoming marriage to Henry Gowan. When Little Dorrit gives Clennam his 'nosegay', flowers carry connotations of unhappiness and unfulfilled hopes. Further, in the river-bank scene Clennam can only look on helplessly as Pet Meagles turns away from him; in the prison scene – for some critics a scene wholly of renewal – he is equally passive as Little Dorrit kneels not *to* him but in order to comfort him.

Any sense the reader might have of Clennam awakening to life is at least partly countered by a potent context that generates an awareness of persisting contrary attitudes. It is fitting that the flowers-scene is followed by Clennam's rejection of Little Dorrit's money, for that, as has been said, is the gesture that reveals most clearly the manacles on Clennam's wrists.

The final chapter opens with a description of autumn that, though initially suggestive of reinvigorative change, reveals itself to be full of images of decline and decay: 'the summer fruits had ripened and waned ... the green perspectives of hops had been laid low ... the yellowing foliage'. The season has moved beyond Keatsian lushness to offer 'glimpses of the hardy winter that was coming' (II, xxxiv, 790). Sadness is the keynote as life and beauty fade. And through this description we are brought back to Mrs Clennam's insistent question. To repeat: '"Are we not all cut down like the grass of the field, and was I not shorn by the scythe many years ago: since when, I have been lying here, waiting to be gathered into the barn?"' (I, xv, 177) In both passages any sense of harvest as a symbol of fruition and gain yields to harvest as part of the destructive process.

Even the momentary liveliness of the sea gives way to 'little sails on the horizon, drifting away like autumn-tinted leaves that had drifted from the trees' (II, xxxiv, 790), as the prose, in tone always sad, modulates into elegiac cadences. The repeated verb-form – 'drifted . . . drifting' – recalls Clennam's hopeless words to Meagles in Marseilles: '''I am such a waif and stray everywhere, that I am liable to be drifted where any current may set''' (I, ii, 19).

A similar effect is created by the juxtaposed scene of Little Dorrit reading to the convalescing Clennam. On the one hand the 'tones of the voice that read to him' remind him constantly of the finer things of life, of 'every merciful and loving whisper that had ever stolen to him (II, xxxiv, 790); on the other hand the scene is a reminder – because a partial re-enactment – of earlier scenes and times when his mother read so vindictively from the Bible. Here, as always through these closing pages, the scene's positive suggestiveness is swiftly undermined.

Certainly such undermining helps preserve to the bitter end the presence of Mrs Clennam and all she represents. Two further examples stress the point. When she has finished reading, Little Dorrit confesses that her money has been lost, that she can offer Clennam only herself. Thus reduced and lacking material support, she is now acceptable to the man. The Calvinists welcome a world changed because separated from Mammon. In accepting a Little Dorrit stripped of worldly goods Clennam continues to function within the old parameters. Again, in late autumn, when Meagles makes his final appearance he enquires whether he had been expected sooner. Arthur Clennam replies:

'I did . . . but Amy told me—'
   'Little Dorrit. Never any other name.' (It was she who whispered it.)

(II, xxxiv, 796)

Clennam is quickly put in his place or, rather, back in his place. His attempt to shed his old – and patronising – obtuseness, to move to a relationship with Little Dorrit that is more one of equals, simply fails. That the girl's mild objection is enough, that Clennam reverts so readily to the old procedure, betrays the weakness of his desire for or ability to change and prepares the reader for the novel's final pages.

With Meagles is Doyce, back in Britain to give Clennam his old job back. Through Doyce's good offices he will continue old patterns and procedures in the counting-house in a factory in which the 'sequences of machinery' echo the earlier imagery of his mother's isolation, and where he will devote much of his life to filling ledgers similar to those that cram the collapsed cellars of the ruined Clennam home. The reader's recollection of earlier imagery once more helps darken his sense of the ending; here Clennam, on his return home, recalls 'that old workshop where the loom of his youth had stood' (I, iii, 40).

As for the wedding-day: it begins with Clennam as interrogator, questioning Little Dorrit about the burning of the folded paper given her by the contrite Mrs Clennam. It continues with further suggestions that in Clennam's textual end is his textual beginning. For after he burns the paper to Little Dorrit's orders he fades from the text, never again to be named. Momentarily he is 'her husband', before being subsumed in 'they'.

Nameless, he ends as he began, so completing another pattern of pessimism. The apprehension of such patterns, of such characterising structures and symmetries, reveals Clennam's persisting and fundamental Calvinism. The final paragraph itself demonstrates the main consequence of his inability to be born again to life. For the couple 'went down' into a life dominated by Little Dorrit's *own* actions: she it is who gives 'a mother's care ... to Fanny's neglected children no less than to their own', and who becomes Tip's 'tender nurse and friend' (II, xxxiv, 801). In these last few lines Clennam, in his impregnable prison, is annihilated.

6

Characterisation and Structure: John Harmon in *Our Mutual Friend*

Our mutual friend in *Our Mutual Friend* has received much attention from the critics.[1] John Harmon's part in the 'disguises' or 'resurrection' or 'identity' theme, his testing of Bella Wilfer, his role as a positive force for goodness and love, have been the main areas of discussion. But – it might now seem inevitably – despite his centrality as a character, that attention has not been much directed towards the way in which the characterisation is structured, the way in which that characterisation, in turn, helps structure the novel, and how such apprehension has interpretative force. The key to understanding Harmon is the 'secretarial metaphor', used by Dickens both to present the character and to relate it to the novel's concern with documents. Even though John Harmon may be like the Duke in *Measure for Measure* and the Prince Charming of the Cinderella story[2] it is of at least equal importance that, for much of *Our Mutual Friend*, he is Boffin's Secretary.

Harmon's textual career is in three distinct parts, each characterised in terms of the relationship between him and the documents and papers he constantly encounters. In the first part, the opening fourteen chapters, the pre-Secretary stage, Harmon's actions are all consequent upon his association with the novel's most important document, the Harmon Will. His agitation, furtiveness, and 'repressed' (I, viii, 141) manner, all indicate his failure completely to come to terms with the situation this document has created. Further, within this Will-created world, other papers press upon him: the handbill with news of his own 'death' compels him to visit the police-station mortuary, an agreement has to be signed before he can lodge at the Wilfers'. Crucially, in both these scenes, the man is identified, both to the other characters and to the reader, in the same way: the 'stranger' becomes 'Julius Handford' and the 'gentleman' 'John Rokesmith' only when such names are written down, the former on the Inspector's paper and the latter on the lodging-agreement. Such actions can be linked to the 'stranger's' seeming shiftiness when unable to produce his card for the Inspector and the establishing of the drowned man's name by means of the papers found in his pocket. On each occasion a full identity can be asserted only via the production, creation, or completion of written material. That such identities and impressions are false is important in pointing to what becomes a recurring concern in the novel, the frequent use of documents and papers as supporters of subterfuge, the confusers of appearance with reality. Even more important is the fact that documents dominate, that in this pre-Secretary stage the man is subservient to them.

Harmon is also subservient to those who act the secretary-part, such as the Night-Inspector, 'with a pen and ink, and ruler, posting up his books in a whitewashed office' (I, iii, 66), whose order and efficiency contrasts with and dominates the disturbed and harassed Handford, and, even, R. Wilfer, the 'cherubic scribe' preparing the lodging agreement 'in duplicate', whose position as landlord gives him at least the final power of decision that his family would insist he exercise. To this general subservience there is a single and important exception. When Harmon refuses R. Wilfer's request, backed by Bella, for a reference – '"a reference is not necessary. . . . I require no reference from you. . . . Indeed, I show the greater confidence . . . for I will pay in advance whatever you please and I am going to trust my furniture here"' (I, iv, 82) – he is reacting to a request for further documents by expressing a paper-free faith in human virtues. The scene emphasises the way in which characters are evaluated in terms of their attitudes to documents (Bella hinting at the desirability of a reference makes her seem unduly suspicious in comparison with Harmon, an early pointer to the latter's future role as Bella's moral touchstone) and, in that Harmon asserts himself against documentary domination, prepares us for his career as Boffin's Secretary.

The second part of Harmon's progress begins in Book the First, Chapter 15:

'Now, for instance – come!' said Mr Boffin, in his pouncing way. 'If you entered my employment, what would you do?'

'I would keep exact accounts of all the expenditure you

sanctioned, Mr Boffin. I would write your letters, under your direction. I would transact your business with people in your pay or employment. I would', with a glance and a half-smile at the table, 'arrange your papers – . . . .'

Relinquishing his hat and gloves, Mr Rokesmith sat down quietly at the table, arranged the open papers into an orderly heap, cast his eyes over each in succession, folded it, docketed it on the outside, laid it in a second heap, and, when that second heap was complete and the first gone, took from his pocket a piece of string and tied it together with a remarkably dexterous hand at a running curve and a loop ... [and] ... read his abstracts aloud. They were all about the new house. . . .

Then came correspondence. Acceptance of Mr Boffin's offer of such a date and to such an effect. Rejection of Mr Boffin's proposal of such a date and to such an effect. Concerning Mr Boffin's scheme of such another date to such another effect. All compact and methodical.

(I, xv, 227–8)

The scene reverses our main sense of the character up to that point in the text. Harmon's quiet efficiency and confidence contrasts with his earlier agitation, embarrassment, and brooding silence; his clerical and manual dexterity follows descriptions of his 'tremulous hand' (I, iii, 69) in the police-station, his 'hesitating hand' (I, iv, 83) and general awkwardness at the Wilfers' home; his candid examination of Boffin's papers is opposed to previous stealthiness; his ability to free Boffin from 'Care and Complication' (I, xv, 226) succeeds a tendency to arouse only suspicion and unease. Most importantly, he is now able to dominate and order the documentary world to which he was previously subservient.

As Secretary, Harmon masters his work and gains 'the power of knowledge; the power derivable from a perfect comprehension of his business' (I, xvi, 241). Such power finds expression in two types of secretarial activity: to protect the Boffins, Harmon successfully struggles against the 'dismal swamp' of begging-letters, frauds, and avaricious tradesmen, evil designs countered by efficient office-management; and, secondly, Harmon himself originates documents motivated by kindness and able to do good. The cloud over Harmon's memory is dispersed by the written retraction obtained from Riderhood; Harmon suggests and writes the letter to be carried by the wandering Betty Higden '"stating, in the names of Mr and Mrs Boffin, that they are your friends"' (I, xiv, 447); he writes to Headstone to arrange for Sloppy to be educated. This last action (a minor one) apart, Harmon's secretarial work includes some of the novel's most effective expressions of goodness in an antagonistic world. His protection of the Boffins better allows their childlike virtue to influence events. The retraction obtained from Riderhood not only comforts Lizzie, to whom Harmon sends it, and links, sustains, or reassures many of the novel's positives, such as Jenny Wren, Riah, Abbey Potterson, and the Boffins, all of whom see and read it, but is also described by Lightwood at the Lammles' anniversary breakfast, the satirical reactions of the 'social chorus' being a further instance of the latter's moral self-exposure. Similarly, Betty Higden's letter, surviving Riderhood's 'reading', at the old lady's death is found by Lizzie Hexam, whose subsequent contacting of the Boffins leads to the meeting between Lizzie and Bella Wilfer at which the former's influence on the latter plays a large part in the redemption of Bella that leads to her marriage to Harmon.

Whilst circulating documents propagate goodness, Dickens offers Harmon's own recapitulation of the events leading up to his appointment as Secretary. The account reinforces the contrast between the first and the second part of Harmon's career in reminding the reader even more forcibly of Harmon's earlier relationship to documents. Thus the Will is clearly seen as a threat to his peace of mind and basic virtue: the power of the handbill, forcing him '"in a wild, incautious way"' (II, xiii, 428) to the Thames-side police-station, is further emphasised, as is the dependence of personal identity upon documents, the papers found on the dead man both misleading the police and supporting Harmon's subterfuge. Our sense of Harmon's emergence from a dark world of antagonistic documents is strengthened by the fact that the whole sequence of murder and disappearance began on board ship when, Harmon recalls, a '"clerk . . . tapped me on the shoulder, and said 'Mr Radfoot, look here', referring to some papers that he had in his hand"' (II, xiii, 423). Whereas, in the recapitulation, papers brought to him began a train of evil or undesirable events, now, as Secretary, Harmon neutralises such papers with efficiency and despatch and initiates counters of permeating value.

Dickens is very concerned to suggest Harmon's *development*: the rejection of references foreshadowed his secretarial attitudes. That is, as Secretary, Harmon not only effects good via papers but also does so directly in his frequent stirring of Bella's conscience, thus preparing us for the post-Secretary phase. But contrast remains the central characterising principle, hence the importance of the description of Harmon's room as observed by Bella Wilfer:

> It was tastefully though economically furnished, and very neatly arranged. There were shelves and stands of books, English, French, and Italian; and in a portfolio on the writing-table there were sheets upon sheets of memoranda and calculations in figures, evidently referring to the Boffin property. On that table also, carefully backed with canvas, varnished, mounted, and rolled like a map, was the placard descriptive of the murdered man who had come from afar to be her husband. She shrank from this ghostly surprise, and felt quite frightened as she rolled and tied it up again. Peeping about here and there, she came upon a print, a graceful head of a pretty woman, elegantly framed, hanging in the corner by the easy chair. (III, iii, 511)

Here is a further indication of Harmon's role as a symbol of desirable order and the scene has, also, an important summarising function. It alludes to Harmon's past, now controlled and in its place, the placard mounted and rolled-up from view; to his present concern for Boffin's welfare, the memoranda and calculations easily accessible to the curious visitor; and to still-cherished hopes, the print of Bella's likeness, wholly open to view with, significantly, the future, represented by a picture, dissociated from documents and papers.

Yet the scene basically contributes to the system of contrasts between the first two parts of Harmon's career and within the second part itself. As regards the latter, the description of Harmon's room is followed immediately by Boffin's masquerade. That is to say, our sense of Harmon as a symbol of order and control is juxtaposed with Harmon harassed and subservient. The contrast is repeated in the relationship between the scene, already discussed, in which Boffin appoints a Secretary, and that in which Harmon is dismissed; the former redolent of selfless kindness and mastery, the latter emphasising the possible and, as Chapter 4 demonstrates, only-too-believable results of Podsnappery, its heartless economics, lack of proper human relationships, contempt for decent human feelings, and uncontrolled suspicion, and the extent to which they affected Harmon's dominance.

Paradoxically, Harmon's dismissal makes him even more powerful. In the third part of his career, the post-Secretary phase, his acts of stealthy goodness still continue: Riderhood's retraction still circulates, the collusion with Boffin still obtains. Documents no longer require mastering for they no longer trouble him at all, a fact well illustrated by Harmon's imperturbability when the Inspector identifies his hand-writing as that of Julius Handford. The third phase sees the development of the direct influence previously seen in his encounters with Bella. Harmon has moved, as it were, from his office at headquarters into the paper-free field of his marriage to Bella, influencing her for good and making her happy through his presence and action. We are prepared for his final appearances.

Book the Fourth, Chapter 12, ends the masquerade. Harmon and Bella make the mysterious journey to the Boffins' house and its new delights:

> It was only her husband's encircling arm . . . that prevented Bella from stopping at the foot of the staircase. As they ascended, it was seen to be tastefully ornamented with most beautiful flowers. . . .
>
> Going on a little higher, they came to a charming aviary, in which a number of tropical birds, more gorgeous in colour than the flowers, were flying about; and among those birds were gold and silver fish, and mosses, and water-lilies, and a fountain, and all manner of wonders. . . .
>
> And on Bella's exquisite toilette table was an ivory casket, and in the casket were jewels the like of which she had never dreamed of, and aloft on an upper floor was a nursery garnished as with rainbows. . . . (IV, xii–xiii, 838, 848–9)

This is a passage open to objections. It is certainly an uneasy mixture of realism and fairy-tale symbolism. But so far as the internal patterning of Harmon's character is concerned, such details are exactly right: they effect a link and complete a contrast with the imagery, also tropical, of the 'dismal swamp' of earlier days. That world of sharks and alligators and 'breast-high' (I, xvii, 261) quicksands, of 'crawling, creeping, fluttering, and buzzing creatures, attracted by the gold dust' (I, xvii, 257), with the avaricious Wegg hopping about 'like some extinct bird' (I, xvii, 262), is replaced by a new, watery and bejewelled world of nature ordered, beautified, and beautiful. The 'dismal swamp' was a metaphor for documentary harassment, referring back to the secretarial world; the later symbolism looks outward, away from papers, to a very different world of growth, vigour, beauty, and hope. The contrast reflects Harmon's new power: whereas he struggled against the swamp, the new-found delights are in his gift and under his control. It is the most glittering expression of Harmon's transformation.

Three scenes remain. The first is Mrs Boffin's recognition of John Harmon, part of the explanation to Bella of the pretence at miserliness:

> 'My Noddy wanted a paper out of his Secretary's room, and I says to Noddy, "I am going by the door, and I'll ask him for it."
> ... He chanced to look up with a pleased kind of smile ... and then in a single moment every grain of the gunpowder that had been lying sprinkled thick about him ever since I first set eyes upon him as a man at the Bower, took fire!' (IV, xiii, 840–41)

Here is another link and contrast, the end of the whole mystery with the scene that began it; the clerk with papers mistaking Harmon for Radfoot, the friend desiring papers discovering Rokesmith to be Harmon. Secondly, we have a final and full flowering of Harmon's powers: in the conclusive scene with Wegg, Harmon offers both direct action, the face-to-face confrontation and disposal of that villain and, his last secretarial act, counters a document of evil intent (the Will in Wegg's possession) with one (the Dutch-bottle Will) supporting the forces of goodness. Harmon's last brief appearance is as master of the house and host to the Wrayburns, the complete antithesis of the secretarial role.

Such an outline makes us aware of the dominant quality of the Harmon characterisation, the extent to which it is a careful arrangement of contrasts and developing traits. And it is this sense of careful arrangement, the patterning, the obvious schematisation, of which we are most conscious. Too conscious, some might argue, and 'diagrammatic' is the adverse comment of at least one recent critic.[3] But this is to miss the point; the patterning and, in particular, patterning in terms of secretarial activity, contributes crucially to Dickens's presentation of Harmon as a symbol of order set against a particular chaos best exemplified by part of Dickens's description of London's springtime desolation:

> That mysterious paper currency which circulates in London when the wind blows, gyrated here and there and everywhere. Whence can it come, whither can it go? It hangs on every bush, flutters in every tree, is caught flying by the electric wires, haunts every enclosure, drinks at every pump, cowers at every grating, shudders upon every plot of grass, seeks rest in vain behind the legions of iron rails. (I, xii, 191)

Apart from exhibiting the obvious analogy with banknotes the passage reminds us of another equally important sense in which 'bits of paper, whirled by the cold wind'[4] are fundamental to the novel's world. *Our Mutual Friend* is dominated by documents: Wills, certificates, contracts, promissory notes, authorisations, registers, letters, notes, visiting-cards, secretarial *bric-à-brac*, bills of sale or of exchange or on walls, recur constantly.[5] Lizzie Hexam and her papermaking colleagues in the mill at Plashwater Weir have much to answer for. The whirling paper is both linked to and controlled by the wind, that recurring Dickensian symbol of hostility and, indeed, the direct hostility of documents is frequently encountered. Characters are threatened by bills of exchange or notes of hand, auction notices are instruments of public humiliation, placards threaten discovery, and the 'dismal swamp' of begging-letters and scheming visiting-cards seeks to drag down the virtuous. Other documents work more insidiously but with no less hostility. Thus the Harmon Will threatens to corrupt John Harmon and Bella Wilfer and *does* corrupt Silas Wegg by offering the last-named the illusory promise of wealth and power, this last making us aware of a special kind of insidiousness: the dishonesty of so many of the novel's documents in offering mainly appearance, rarely reality.

Thus, when the Lammles marry, Dickens describes the 'little flourish' Veneering

> has prepared for the trumpets of fashion, describing how that on the seventeenth instant, at St James's Church, the Reverend Blank Blank, assisted by the Reverend Dash Dash, united in the bonds of matrimony, Alfred Lammle Esquire, of Sackville Street,

Piccadilly, to Sophronia, only daughter of the late Horatio Akershem, Esquire, of Yorkshire. Also how the fair bride was married from the house of Hamilton Veneering, Esquire, of Stucconia, and was given away by Melvin Twemlow, Esquire, of Duke Street, St James's, second cousin to Lord Snigsworth, of Snigsworthy Park. (I, x, 163)

The 'flourish' imposes a surface respectability and appearance of devotion very different from the reality, the 'happy pair' (I, x, 173), as we swiftly realise, being united only in bitterness and deceit. Similarly, when the Podsnaps are informed of the Lammles' designs on their daughter, Podsnap's note, restrained yet decisive and indicating a parent's concern for Georgiana, suggests a very different Podsnap from the grossly vulgar and oppressive parent we know him to be. The appointments-book that imposes the pretence of activity on to the void of Lightwood's legal practice; Mrs Veneering's invitations (the effectiveness of which contrasts absolutely with her ineffective presence); Headstone's 'certificate' of respectability which masks his buried life of violent and instinctive passion; Miss Peecher's slate-bound fantasisings about love; the selectivity of Jenny Wren's letters; Charlie Hexam's first note to Mortimer that seems to provide a neat ending to the latter's after-dinner story yet, in reality, continues and complicates it; even Milvey's note to Mrs Boffin, 'the kindest note possible . . . offering to find me another little child' (II, x, 388), but which causes the old lady much heart-searching; all these, like the Will found by Wegg, are deceptive alternatives to how things really are.

When they are not directly or insidiously hostile, 'papers' are, nonetheless, often a function of the novel's pessimism. That Riah *needs* to produce account-books and papers in order to prove his honesty; that only a documented retraction forced out of a recalcitrant Riderhood can restore Hexam's posthumous reputation; that, only too often, documentary-links serve as poor substitutes for personal relationships, as when Bella's letter informs her mother of her marriage or when Fledgeby's vindictive note dismisses Riah (a contrast with Boffin's firing of Harmon, which at least is face-to-face); that, repeatedly, the sense of class-separation is emphasised by bills and placards that seem the only contact between the ordered and policed and the dark regions of riverside brutality and murder; all point to serious failures in social and personal relationships, as alienation is dramatised by documents.

Given the importance of documents and papers in the novel, attitudes to them are equally important and, to develop an earlier point, become a criterion of a person's moral worth or, occasionally, a person's understanding of the world. Here again John Harmon, with his deep awareness both of the power and of the limitations of documents, is the point of reference. Perception of such limitations is a mark of virtuous potential: Lightwood telling the tale of 'the Man from Somewhere' and referring to the death of John Harmon's sister, comments:

> 'I must refer you to the Registrar of the District in which the humble dwelling was situated, for the certified cause of death; but early sorrow and anxiety may have had to do with it, though they may not appear in the ruled pages and printed forms.' (I, ii, 56)

R. Wilfer implies the same when, present whilst Harmon and Bella Wilfer declare their love in the office of Chicksey, Veneering, and Stobbles, he remarks of that place of paper-pushing: '"that anything of a tender nature should come off here, is what tickles me. To think that ever I should have seen my Bella folded in the arms of her future husband, *here*, you know!"' (III, xvi, 674)

But the novel's two consummate villains, Rogue Riderhood and Silas Wegg, regard documents, favourably and uncritically, as sources of money and power. The former's belief in 'the binding powers of pen and ink and paper' and in the desirable ability of documents to impose themselves on facts, are reflected in his attempts 'to take an Alfred David' (I, xii, 195–6) and so turn malicious suspicion into damaging proof of Hexam's murderous activities, and to obtain from Lightwood a favourable reference for the post of lock-keeper. Equally reprehensible is Wegg's search for Harmon-documents and his eagerness to use the newfound Will against Boffin and his Secretary. Equally uncritical, though naive rather than reprehensible, is Georgiana Podsnap's belief that '"by signing something somewhere"' (IV, ii, 715) the Lammles can be saved.

Two points emerge and merge: Harmon's role as symbol of order in a world of documentary and moral chaos and his function as moral touchstone so far as attitudes to documents are concerned, combine to stress that 'relating to Harmon' is one of the central organising principles of the novel. An important example is the recurring symbol of 'desk-work'. At one (positive) extreme is Harmon in the 'appointment' scene, ordering and dominating Boffin's papers in a spirit of selfless endeavour. Elsewhere in the text is a series of similar scenes, involving other characters. Some approximate to Harmon's, as does that already mentioned, the Night-Inspector in his 'office' (I, iii, 66) and, in the same riverside locality, Miss Abbey Potterson's 'little desk in the corner where Miss Abbey filed her receipts and kept her sample phials (customers' scores were interdicted by the strict administration of the Porters)' (III, ii, 499), both characters resembling Harmon in that they stand for order and moral worth in a dark region of the city, but differing in that their attempts at imposing such qualities on *their* surroundings are less effective, less wide-ranging, than are those of Boffin's Secretary.[6] Again, after her marriage, Bella also exhibits some of her husband's secretarial qualities: 'Her letter folded, sealed, and directed, and her pen wiped, and her middle finger wiped, and her desk locked up and put away, and these transactions performed with an air of severe business sedateness . . .' (IV, v, 754). The letter is to Lizzie, Bella continuing and sustaining a morally beneficial relationship in a hostile world in the manner of Secretary Harmon, but without his power and force.

As for her father:

'You see that little desk in the corner?'

'In the dark corner, furthest both from the light and from the fireplace? The shabbiest desk of all the desks?'

'Now, does it really strike you in that point of view, my dear?' said her father, surveying it artistically with his head on one side: 'that's mine. That's called Rumty's Perch.'

'Whose Perch?' asked Bella with great indignation.

'Rumty's. You see, being rather high and up two steps they call it a Perch. And they call *me* Rumty.'

(III, xvi, 669–70)

His desk-activities involve little more than struggles against ridicule. When he signs 'R. Wilfer' in response to 'dear Rumty' he is initiating a documentary counter to papers essentially hostile to personal dignity. In this his activities are similar to Harmon's but are far from effective and involve only himself.

Contrasting more completely with Harmon-at-work is Wrayburn, in his statement to Lightwood:

'Do me the favour to step into my bedroom. Secrétaire, you see, an abstruse set of solid mahogany pigeon-holes, one for every letter of the alphabet. To what use do I devote them? I receive a bill – say from Jones. I docket it neatly at the secrétaire, JONES, and I put it into pigeon-hole J. It's the next thing to a receipt and is quite as satisfactory to *me*.' (II, vi, 337)

We might well be reminded of Pip and Herbert keeping their accounts in *Great Expectations*. There as here, desk-work is a form of evasion, literally a shelving of commitments. In its false order, its dishonesty and contempt for others, it is directly opposed to John Harmon's kind of secretarial order and inimical to it in its satirical tone. Similarly, Fledgeby's inspection of Riah's books and papers, vindictive and solely concerned with personal gain – the evil use of the secretarial activity – is also in direct opposition to and actively hostile towards the work of Boffin's Secretary.

This use of the 'desk-work' symbol points to the recurring scene (and not only this one) as a main means of unifying this huge and diverse novel, again stressing John Harmon's importance as a structural point of reference. Equally important is his role as modifying summary: through his characterisation Harmon illustrates one of the main movements of the novel, the escape, accomplished by so many of the more morally positive characters, including Boffin and Bella, from antagonistic circumstances much of whose threatening quality proceeds from documentary hostility. Even though Harmon's modifying role is expressed through the fact that he *develops* away from initial circumstances in a more convincing and complex way than other characters, his summarising function is another way in which he becomes a recurring and unifying device.

But his complexity, though it does not, of course, disqualify him from being a point of reference, does set him apart from the other figures in Dickens's story in the same way as his patterned and schematic characterisation contrasts with the less-obviously-regular structures of the other textual lives, and his plainer speech and narrative context differ so abruptly from the livelier, often brilliant idiolects that vary from Mr Boffin's 'cockney sparkle' to Wrayburn and Lightwood's 'aimless sophistication of indolent absurdity'.[7]

Thus John Harmon's textual function is essentially paradoxical: he is at once a contrast *and* a comparison, at once apart from and a part of the society of Dickens's tale. He is thus prevented from ever achieving a foregrounded and firm-edged social position. Despite his power he remains an uncertain figure, an apt reminder of the vulnerability of goodness and its shifting, tense relationship with *Our Mutual Friend's* dark world. The contrast with Podsnap's solidity and unequivocal social progress and permanence, despite Twemlow's small final triumph, helps make this point.

In the final analysis 'contrast' is a key word and a reminder that it is at times too extreme to be meaningful. To put this another way, there are areas of the novel where Harmon's writ does not run and where his efforts have no effect – the Headstone/Wrayburn sequence being the important instance. His effectiveness is pessimistically qualified by our sense of a world of dark and uncontrollable emotion and violence, unsusceptible to order or to virtuous influence. So that, ultimately, John Harmon's influence is limited and our pessimism is deepened by the main consequence of it ending. R. Wilfer's appointment as Boffin's next Secretary is hardly a source of reassurance.

7

Story and Text

As we stand and look back at a Dickens novel, the general movement we remember – the decisive movement – is a hurrying seemingly random passing of men and women, each heard in some fixed phrase, seen in some fixed expression: a way of seeing men and women that belongs to the street. There is at first an absence of ordinary connection and development. These men and women do not so much relate as pass each other and then sometimes collide. Not often in the ordinary way do they speak to one another. They speak at or past each other, each intent above all on defining through his words his own identity and reality; in fixed self-descriptions, in voices raised emphatically to be heard through and past other similar voices. But then as the action develops, unknown and unacknowledged relationships, profound and decisive connections, definite and committing recognitions and avowals are as it were forced into consciousness. These are the real and inevitable relationships and connections, the necessary recognitions and avowals of any human society. But they are of a kind that are obscured, complicated, mystified, by the sheer rush and noise and miscellaneity of this new and complex social order.[1]

Raymond Williams's brilliant account, part of which was cited in an earlier chapter,[2] of the consequences for character of Dickens's urban vision, reaches to the very heart of his portrayal of people. The keynotes are alienation, loneliness, social antagonism, the difficulty of communicating and the failure to do so in a clear, understanding and sustaining way. Forced back upon themselves, the men and women of Dickens's works become obsessed with asserting personal identity against the onrush of hostile circumstances, an obsession that results in a desperate solipsism that fuels the sense of alienation and so often expresses itself in strident hostility. But, as Williams also shows, they are basically helpless, enmeshed in the web of society, with 'relationships and connections' forced upon them, and disorientated, colliding, almost literally and certainly psychologically and socially, as they seek to pass through a confusing, obscuring, and mystifying world.

Such a pessimistic account of Dickens's vision finds support in much of this present study. From the very first Dickens's characters are found to be flawed and trapped beings. Even the simplicities of *Sketches By Boz* are disturbing gestures made by reactionary and prejudiced Members of Parliament; the socially disconnected Reader in 'Shabby-Genteel People'; the self-obsessed Cymon Tuggs, so completely trapped by the inculcated attitudes of his upbringing that he is unable to learn from experience and so incapable of change; and the dehumanised Simmons, that willing agent of harsh, unfeeling authority. The faults of character apparent in *Sketches By Boz* are similar in kind, though not, of course, in degree of depth and complexity, to those found in the characters, major and minor, of the later writings, the great fiction in particular. Thus most of the characters examined in previous chapters do not present a cheering prospect. From the negativity of the socially isolated Fat Boy and Young Bailey's disturbing amorality and inability to achieve self-knowledge to Gaffer Hexam's rigid and immutable Podsnappery, our sense is of all three as society's victims. Re-readers, whether of *Our Mutual Friend* or *Edwin Drood*, are initially deceived and later become controlled and disappointed ironists; Clennam is trapped in a tangled and complex web of Calvinistic thinking imposed upon him during his dreadful childhood. And if we include in this present study all Dickens's other works there are all-too-many opportunities to confront the strange, the distorted and the unhappy, from Mrs Bardell to Quilp, Pecksniff, Heep, Gradgrind, Carton, Headstone and so many of the rest. Certainly those named are, all else apart, imprisoned within the confines of socially-induced thinking; in important respects each has become a version of Clennam.

But Raymond Williams's Dickens is not wholly pessimistic, for he also quotes the famous passage from *Dombey and Son* that begins:

> Oh for a good spirit who would take the house-tops off, with a more potent and benignant hand than the lame demon in the tale, and show a Christian people what dark shapes issue from amidst their homes, to swell the retinue of the Destroying Angel as he moves forth among them. . . .[3]

and comments: 'That potent and benignant hand . . . is the hand of the novelist; it is Dickens seeing himself.'[4] Williams is not concerned, here, to distinguish between author and Narrator, but it is perhaps ironical that his optimistic gesture points implicitly to a narrative presence that imposes order and insight on experience, for I contend that it is in this area, the Narrator as character, that the least optimism is to be found. My view is much closer to that of Kate Flint's in her fine introduction to Dickens's work. In engaging with Raymond Williams's argument and with the same quotation from *Dombey and Son* Flint notes that Dickens's narrative presence (which she is careful to distinguish from Dickens himself) aims to suggest 'comprehensive organisation'; but she also insists, what is surely the case, that the tone of the 'good spirit' passage is 'wishful, conditional and . . . somewhat apocalyptic'.[5] This is a part of her developed argument that the Dickens Narrator, and certainly the Narrator of *Dombey and Son*, 'does not speak with a constant, confident, all-knowing voice',[6] and through his 'mode of narration, alternately certain and unsure'[7] the Narrator has a disquieting effect on the reader.

In this present study I look away from Williams and towards but past Flint: its bleakest sections are several of those on Narrators regarded as dark and troubled figures who range from the urban being whose attempts to be streetwise are undermined by persistent uncertainty about 'Shabby-Genteel People' in that sketch by Boz to the prejudiced, misogynistic writer of letters, the negative-thinking, alienated traveller in Italy, the patronising and repressed sentimentalist in *A Christmas Carol*, the commercially trapped Mr Pirrip, and the Podsnappic presence who narrates *Our Mutual Friend*. Here is a world in which personal free will is overcome by fate that, up to a point, is socially determined; in which society invariably triumphs over the individual, confusing and ultimately hostile discrepancies occur between image and reality, and social repressions negate individual power.

This sombre visionary is not everybody's Dickens. 'His leading quality was Humour',[8] wrote his closest friend and literary adviser, and, to be sure, we must remember there is much of that. And though we also need to remember the cliché that the greatest comedy always has a serious purpose this is not enough to explain the disturbing *basis* of much of it. One aspect of this has already been explored in the discussion of the class-based humour purveyed by the Narrator of *Our Mutual Friend*.[9] It is basically similar to that found in *David Copperfield*: in the latter also David, the older man telling his story, gears his tonal stance to the social standing of his characters. But in this earlier novel he directs the most ridicule and the most vicious humorous satire, respectively, towards those, Traddles and Uriah Heep, whose ambitions and progress most nearly resemble his own. Unlike the Narrator of *Our Mutual Friend*, he reserves more humour for those – the Micawbers, Barkis, the Peggottys – *below him* on the social scale, the humour dwindling through Betsy Trotwood and Mr Dick until, so far as Doctor Strong, the Wickfields, Mr Spenlow and his daughter (bearing in mind that the humour of courtship and marriage is invariably directed by David against himself), let alone the Steerforth entourage, are concerned, those on an equal or superior social footing to himself are treated seriously.

Of course Dickens creates positive characters, or, at least, characters with positive qualities: in *David Copperfield* Peggotty is one and Mr Micawber becomes another. Bung, the new Beadle in *Sketches By Boz*, is humane and caring, a favourable contrast to the dead Simmons; John Harmon is the benevolent Machiavel who puts private worlds to rights; Gaffer Hexam, a fascinating example of Dickens's attenuated but persisting optimism, preserves finer feelings about family and work amidst the deepening darkness of the last completed novel. But, even in these instances, our sense of them as positives is qualified by sharp delimiting that weakens the power for goodness: Bung's empathetic writ does not extend to the widow and her dying son; nor, as has also been noted, Harmon's to Headstone's terrible nihilistic world; nor can Gaffer's inviolable core influence the socially-induced Podsnappic prejudice ingrained in himself and others.

But, to use another quotation from Flint, this time her keynote statement: 'Dickens's writing is full of contradictions'.[10] This chapter thus far is evidence of that. His work is dominated by character; he can hardly write a letter, report on his travels, let alone create fiction, without playing a role or in other ways creating character. It is inconceivable that there could ever be a G. Wilson Knight of Dickens studies, that is, a critic who can sensibly, indeed brilliantly, and centrally conceive of the works, in particular of the novels, almost wholly in terms of symbolised moral arguments and thematically potent patterns of imagery. All writers on Dickens are forced to confront his characters and engage with characterising problems.

Yet, despite this deep and all-abiding concern with people, Dickens's stories do not assert their power or, with few exceptions, celebrate their good qualities. There are obvious dangers in generalising from any set of particulars, but the characters examined in this present study, a deliberate *selection* from Dickens's output, do comprise a substantial group. Even if characters from sketches, letters, travel-writing and Christmas novellae are excluded, here are vehicles for interpreting more than half of the published novels. Dickens's fictional treatment of these characters and those from the minor works, the parts they play in the stories, is invariably pessimistic.

But amongst the most important of all seeming contradictions are the relationships between story and text and, consequently, between character and characterisation. As Rimmon-Kenan insists, characterisation is the sum of 'various character-indicators distributed along the text-continuum'.[11] She is concerned with *describing* those various character-traits; this present study is concerned with what these characterisations *do*, with how they function in the text. However helpless they may be in the story, however dark and despairing may be Dickens's characters in general, in the text the situation is very different. Characterisations organise, summarise and modify thematic material; characterisations provide an all-pervading narrative presence that unifies disparate action and controls its availability to the reader; characterised readers offer an implied response to a text that often modifies and deepens meaning; characterisations shape and develop ideas; characterisations structure works.

The distinctions between story and text and between character and characterisation are theoretical. Both parts of each pair are experienced simultaneously in the reading process. This process, therefore, is essentially deconstructive in its nature. For even when characters in a story are at their most pessimistic, most helpless in the face of a cudgelling social or metaphysical fate, their textual presence, their characterisation, asserts opposing, countering ideas. In the cases of one or two novels – *Nicholas Nickleby*, perhaps, which sprawls in neo-picaresque style, or *The Old Curiosity Shop*, possibly, with its false start as part of *Master Humphrey's Clock* – character-based unifying systems are difficult to find and describe, but, generally speaking, as previous chapters have demonstrated, the text of a Dickens novel is an ordered, unified and coherent fictive world. Even *Oliver Twist*, which is also an early novel and in which the story moves with apparent lack of ease from the superb accounts of Fagin and the thieves' kitchen to the watery sentimentality of the Rose Maylie sequences, is *textually* satisfying because of the coherent system of structuring relationships established between those two parts of the book, effected most strongly via a character, such as Oliver himself, who is common to both parts. To make the point again by repeating an example: when in *Little Dorrit*, Amy brings flowers to Clennam in prison, that scene as part of the story lacks imaginative force; textually, however, it links persuasively with the use of flowers during Clennam's earlier visit to Pet Meagles at Twickenham.

The ordered, resolvable world of Dickens's text insists that characters (characterisations) have definite, ascertainable functions invariably performed successfully. Characterisations are invariably positive and optimistic constructs in that they invariably possess aesthetically satisfying textual power. As this book has demonstrated, that power is always great and can be enormous. It is far greater than that possessed by other textual traits, such as structuring patterns of language, recurring symbolism, or other such motifs, because it controls every area of the reading experience. Dickens's textual world is, in one way, a light-year's distance from the dark vision of his story. The fictive, formally self-enclosed and essentially non-realistic nature of that world is not, in itself, evidence of any consoling or idealistic humanism but, paradoxically, as will be seen, enjoys an influential relationship with the story.

The nature of that relationship is a paradigm of that between the real and the ideal in Dickens's fiction, clearly summed up in two quotations from *Little Dorrit*. The first is from the close of the opening chapter: 'the stars came out in the heavens, and the fire-flies mimicked them in the lower air, as men may feebly imitate the goodness of a better order of beings' (I, i, 14). The second is an even more famous passage describing the Marshalsea prison:

> Black, all night, since the gate had clashed upon Little Dorrit, its iron stripes were turned by the early-glowing sun into stripes of gold. Far aslant across the city, over its jumbled roofs, and through the open tracery of its church towers, struck the long bright rays, bars of the prison of this lower world. (II, xxx, 741)

These quotations, central as they are to Dickens's vision, demonstrate, of course, the element of aspiration mixed with longing in

Dickens's work. The point does not need to be laboured. What needs to be stressed is our constant awareness of the textual world which characterisation dominates, imposes upon, orders, shapes and clarifies, and so asserts, always, the textual power of people. This world, such impressions, self-contained though they appear to be, can never wholly free themselves from mimesis and the story. As Dickens's vision darkens through his literary career and his works grow more complex so our sense of formal, textual satisfaction increases through our solving of more difficult critical and analytical problems. In this way, at least, even through the bleakest parts of the stories we keep in mind a sense of the power and achievement of characterisations. This last, the textual life of Dickens's characters, cannot be dissociated from the characters themselves. That textual life is a persisting reminder of the humane possibilities at the very heart of Dickens's dark world.

Notes

1 Introduction – Some *Sketches By Boz*

1. Quoted in S. Rimmon-Kenan, *Narrative Fiction: Contemporary Poetics* (London and New York: Methuen, 1983), p. 29.
2. J. Culler, *The Pursuit of Signs* (London and Henley: Routledge & Kegan Paul, 1981), pp. 5–6.
3. Rimmon-Kenan, p. 3.
4. Aristotle, *On the Art of Poetry*, trans. Ingram Bywater (Oxford: Clarendon Press, 1920), p. 37.
5. Quoted in M. Allott (ed.), *Novelists on the Novel* (London: Routledge & Kegan Paul, 1959; reprinted 1975), pp. 290–91.
6. R. Barthes, *Image Music Text*, trans. Stephen Heath (London: Fontana/Collins, 1977), p. 107.
7. Ibid., 106.
8. *The Life of Charles Dickens*, ed. A.J. Hoppé (London: Dent, 1966), II, 278.
9. R. Garis, *The Dickens Theatre* (Oxford: Clarendon Press, 1965), p. 68.
10. P. Collins, 'Charles Dickens', *Victorian Fiction: A Second Guide to Research*, ed. George H. Ford (New York: The Modern Language Association of America, 1978), pp. 65–7.
11. J. Weinsheimer, 'Theory of Character: *Emma*', *Poetics Today*, I (1979), 208–10.
12. S. Chatman, *Story and Discourse: Narrative Structure in Fiction and Film* (Ithaca and London: Cornell University Press, 1978; reprinted 1980), pp. 117–18.
13. Ibid., p. 118.
14. Weinsheimer, 'Theory', op. cit., p. 195.
15. E.M. Eigner, *The Metaphysical Novel in England and America* (Berkeley, Los Angeles and London: University of California Press, 1978), p. 69
16. Quotations are from *Sketches By Boz*, *The Works of Charles Dickens*, Authentic edition, Vol. XVI (London and New York: Chapman & Hall, Charles Scribner's Sons, 1903). 'A Parliamentary Sketch' is on pp. 118–27.
17. Ibid., pp. 206–9.
18. See J.H. Miller, 'The Fiction of Realism: *Sketches By Boz*, *Oliver Twist*, and Cruikshank's Illustrations', *Dickens Centennial Essays*, ed. Ada Nisbet and Blake Nevius (Berkeley, Los Angeles & London: University of California Press, 1971), pp. 87–8, for a related discussion of the use of 'we'.
19. *The English Novel from Dickens to Lawrence* (London: Chatto & Windus, 1970; reprinted St Albans: Paladin, 1974), pp. 28–9.
20. *Sketches*, pp. 266–82.
21. 'On Some of the Old Actors', *The Essays of Elia*, World Classics edition (London: Oxford University Press, 1951), p. 198.
22. *Sketches*, pp. 1–37.

2 Modifying Summaries

1. Quotations are from *The Pickwick Papers*, ed. James Kinsley, The Clarendon Dickens (Oxford: Clarendon Press, 1986).
2. B. Hardy, *The Moral Art of Dickens* (London: Athlone Press, 1970) p. 95.
3. J.R. Kincaid, *Dickens and the Rhetoric of Laughter* (Oxford: Clarendon Press, 1971), p. 29.
4. C. Dickens, *The Posthumous Papers of the Pickwick Club*, ed. Robert L. Patten (Harmondsworth: Penguin Books, 1972), p. 24.
5. G. Stewart, *Dickens and the Trials of Imagination* (Cambridge, Mass.: Harvard University Press, 1974), pp. xvi–xvii. Stewart's italics.
6. Quotations are from *Martin Chuzzlewit*, ed. Margaret Cardwell, The Clarendon Dickens (Oxford: Clarendon Press, 1982).
7. B.B. Pratt, 'Dickens and Freedom: Young Bailey in *Martin Chuzzlewit*', *Nineteenth-Century Fiction*, XXX (1975–6), p. 197.
8. See S. Marcus, *Dickens: from Pickwick to Dombey* (London: Chatto & Windus, 1965), pp. 213–68, and G. Stewart, *Dickens and the Trials of Imagination*, op. cit., *passim*.
9. A.E. Dyson, *The Inimitable Dickens* (London: Macmillan, 1970), p. 81.
10. Kincaid, *Dickens and the Rhetoric of Laughter*, op. cit., p. 160.
11. Hardy, *The Moral Art of Dickens*, op. cit., p. 116.
11A. J.H. Miller, *Charles Dickens: the World of His Novels* (Cambridge, Mass. and London: Harvard University Press and Oxford University Press, 1958), p. 135.
11B. H.M. Daleski, *Dickens and the Art of Analogy* (London: Faber & Faber, 1970), p. 98.
12. R. Barickman, 'The Subversive Methods of Dickens's Early Fiction: *Martin Chuzzlewit*', *Charles Dickens: New Perspectives*, ed. Wendall Stacy Johnson (Englewood Cliffs, NJ: Prentice-Hall, 1982), pp. 41, 46.
13. Pratt, 'Dickens and Freedom', op. cit., p. 197.
14. C. Dickens, *The Life and Adventures of Martin Chuzzlewit*, ed. P.N. Furbank (Harmondsworth: Penguin Books, 1968; reprinted 1981), p. 17.
15. Marcus, *Dickens: from Pickwick to Dombey*, op. cit., p. 214.
16. Pratt, 'Dickens and Freedom', op. cit., p. 190.
17. Here and in subsequent chapters, quotations are from *Our Mutual Friend*, ed. Stephen Gill (Harmondsworth: Penguin Books, 1971).
18. See, e.g. R.D. McMaster, 'Birds of Prey: A Study of *Our Mutual Friend*', *Dalhousie Review*, XL (1960–61), 372–81; R.A. Lanham, '*Our Mutual Friend*: The Birds of Prey', *Victorian Newsletter*, XXIV (Fall, 1963), 6–11; A.M. Patterson, '*Our Mutual Friend*: Dickens as the Compleat Angler', *Dickens Studies Annual*, ed. R.B. Partlow, Jr., I (1970), 252–64.
19. Stewart, *Dickens and the Trials of Imagination*, op. cit., p. 178.

3 Narrators

1. Quotations are from *The Letters of Charles Dickens*, Pilgrim edition, Vol. I, ed. Madeline House and Graham Storey (Oxford: Clarendon

Press, 1965); *The Letters of Charles Dickens*, Pilgrim edition, Vol. II, ed. Madeline House and Graham Storey (Oxford: Clarendon Press, 1969).

2. Quotations are from *Bleak House*, ed. Norman Page (Harmondsworth: Penguin Books, 1971; reprinted 1980).
3. See *Letters*, II, 66–7 and footnotes.
4. Leigh Hunt, *Selected Essays* (London: Dent, 1929), pp. 339, 341.
5. M. Bakhtin, *Problems of Dostoevsky's Poetics*, ed. & trans. Caryl Emerson (Manchester: Manchester University Press, 1984), p. 6.
6. Quotations are from *Pictures from Italy*, ed. David Paroissien (London: André Deutsch, 1973).
7. *The Letters of Charles Dickens*, Pilgrim edition, Vol. III, ed. Madeline House, Graham Storey and Kathleen Tillotson (Oxford: Clarendon Press, 1974), 587.
8. Ibid., 162.
9. Ibid., vii.
10. M. Praz, *The Hero in Eclipse in Victorian Fiction*, trans. Angus Davidson (London: Oxford University Press, 1956), p. 446.
11. J. Carey, *The Violent Effigy* (London: Faber & Faber, 1973), p. 152.
12. A. Wilson, *The World of Charles Dickens* (Harmondsworth: Penguin Books, 1972), pp. 184ff.
13. W. Burgam, 'Little Dorrit in Italy', *Nineteenth-Century Fiction*, XXIX (1974–5), 393–411.
14. F. Kaplan, *Dickens and Mesmerism* (Princeton, NJ: Princeton University Press, 1975), pp. 216ff.
15. Quotations are from *The Christmas Books*, Vol. I, ed. Michael Slater (Harmondsworth: Penguin Books, 1971; reprinted 1976).
16. The coloured illustrations and the woodcuts, superbly reproduced, are most conveniently found in Charles Dickens, *A Christmas Carol: a facsimile of the manuscript in The Pierpont Morgan Library* (New York: James H. Heineman, 1967).
17. R. Browning, *Poetical Works 1833–1864*, ed. Ian Jack (London: Oxford University Press, 1970; reprinted 1975), pp. 645, 568, 373.
18. A. Sinfield, *Dramatic Monologue* (London: Methuen, 1977), p. 7.
19. G.K. Chesterton, *Charles Dickens* (London: Methuen, 1906), p. 170.
20. E. Johnson, *Charles Dickens: His Tragedy and Triumph*, Revised & Abridged edition (Harmondsworth: Penguin Books, 1986), p. 256.
21. C. Dickens, *Selected Short Fiction*, ed. Deborah A. Thomas (Harmondsworth: Penguin Books, 1976), p. 23.
22. G. Holderness, 'Imagination in *A Christmas Carol*', *Études Anglaises*, XXX (1979), p. 40.
23. Ibid., p. 44.
24. Quotations are from *Bleak House*, ed. Norman Page (Harmondsworth: Penguin Books, 1971; reprinted 1980).
25. *Bleak House* (London: Edward Arnold, 1974), p. 13.
26. R. Donovan, 'Structure and Idea in *Bleak House*', *ELH*, XXIX (1962), 175–201.
27. K. Flint, *Dickens* (Brighton: The Harvester Press, 1986), p. 53.
28. C.A. Senf, '*Bleak House*: Dickens, Esther, and the Androgynous

Mind', *The Victorian Newsletter*, No. 64 (Fall, 1983), 21–7.

29. Flint, *Dickens*, op. cit., p. 55.
30. III, ii, 46.
31. *Proverbs* 13:12.
32. Quotations are from *Great Expectations*, ed. Angus Calder (Harmondsworth: Penguin Books, 1965; reprinted 1985).
33. R.B. Partlow, Jr., 'The Moving I: A Study of the Point of View in *Great Expectations*'; *Hard Times, Great Expectations*, and *Our Mutual Friend: A Casebook*, ed. Norman Page (London: Macmillan, 1979), p. 119.
34. John O. Jordan, 'The Medium of *Great Expectations*', *Dickens Studies Annual*, II (1983), 78.

4 Two Re-readers

1. W. Booth, *The Rhetoric of Fiction* (Chicago and London: University of Chicago Press, 1961; reprinted 1975).
2. W. Iser, *The Implied Reader* (Baltimore: Johns Hopkins University Press, 1974), *passim*.
3. See, e.g., S. Fish, 'Literature in the reader: affective stylistics', *New Literary History*, II (1970), 123–62.
4. G. Smith, *Dickens, Money and Society* (Los Angeles: University of California Press, 1968).
5. Wilson, *The World of Charles Dickens*, op. cit., p. 280.
6. Quotations are from *The Mystery of Edwin Drood*, ed. Margaret Cardwell, The Clarendon Dickens (Oxford: Clarendon Press, 1972). This edition has good reproductions of all the relevant illustrative material.
7. Hoppé (ed.), *The Life of Charles Dickens*, op. cit., II, 366.
8. *The Mystery of Edwin Drood*, ed. Cardwell, p. xx.
9. *The Mystery of Edwin Drood*, ed. A. Cox, intro. Angus Wilson (Harmondsworth: Penguin Books, 1974; reprinted 1976), p. 21.
10. 'The Mystery of Edwin Drood: the solution', *The Times Literary Supplement* (11 November 1983), pp. 1246, 1259. For subsequent correspondence: *TLS* (25 November 1983), p. 1321; (2 December 1983), p. 1347; (9 December 1983), p. 1372; (30 December 1983), 1457; (20 January 1984), p. 61.
11. *The Mystery of Edwin Drood*, ed. Cardwell, p. xx.
12. *Macbeth*, III, ii, 46–7.

5 Characterisation and Ideas in *Little Dorrit*: Clennam and Calvinism

1. Quotations are from *Little Dorrit*, ed. Harvey Peter Sucksmith, The Clarendon Dickens (Oxford: Clarendon Press, 1979).
2. L. Trilling, 'Little Dorrit', *Charles Dickens: A Critical Anthology*, ed. Stephen Wall (Harmondsworth: Penguin Books, 1970), p. 371.
3. Ibid., p. 371.
4. F.R. and Q.D. Leavis, *Dickens the Novelist* (Harmondsworth: Penguin Books, 1972), p. 285.

5. Miller, *Charles Dickens: The World of His Novels*, op. cit., p. 238.
6. Daleski, *Dickens and the Art of Analogy*, op. cit., p. 219.
7. Ibid., pp. 232–3.
8. Stewart, *Dickens and the Trials of Imagination*, op. cit., pp. 184–5.
9. Trilling, 'Little Dorrit', op. cit., p. 375.
10. Miller, *Charles Dickens: The World of His Novels*, op. cit., p. 247.
11. Daleski, *Dickens and the Art of Analogy*, op. cit., p. 235.
12. F.R. and Q.D. Leavis, *Dickens the Novelist*, op. cit., p. 323.
13. R. Barickman, 'The Spiritual Journey of Amy Dorrit and Arthur Clennam: "A Way Wherein There Is No Ecstasy"', *Dickens Studies Annual*, ed. R.B. Partlow, Jr., VII (1978), p. 163.
14. Daleski, *Dickens and the Art of Analogy*, op. cit., p. 235.
15. D. Walder, *Dickens and Religion* (London: George Allen & Unwin, 1981), p. 184.
16. J.L. Larsen, *Dickens and the Broken Scripture* (Athens, Georgia: University of Georgia Press, 1985), pp. 177–279 *passim*.
17. See Walder, *Dickens and Religion*, op. cit., and Larsen, *Dickens and the Broken Scripture*, op. cit. See also e.g. Dianne F. Sadoff, 'Storytelling and the Figure of the Father in *Little Dorrit*', *PMLA*, XCV (1980), 234–45.
18. W. Iser, *The Act of Reading* (London: Routledge & Kegan Paul, 1978), p. 118.

6 Character and Structure

1. There is too much to be listed here. Two standard accounts, Daleski (*Dickens and the Art of Analogy*, op cit., pp. 330–36) and J.H. Miller (*Charles Dickens: The World of His Novels*, op. cit., Chapter 11, *passim*), are of particular interest.
2. Respectively: R. Garis, *The Dickens Theatre* (Oxford: Clarendon Press, 1965), p. 247, and A.E. Dyson, *The Inimitable Dickens*, p. 254.
3. J. Gribble, 'Depth and Surface in *Our Mutual Friend*'. *Essays in Criticism*, XXV (1975), 197.
4. T.S. Eliot, 'Burnt Norton', *The Complete Poems and Plays* (London: Faber & Faber, 1970), p. 174.
5. Such a list makes it difficult to agree with Richard D. Altick's comment that 'In *Our Mutual Friend* . . . the paper that is thematically and dramatically important is both printed and public' ('Education, Print, and Paper in *Our Mutual Friend*; *Nineteenth-Century Literary Perspectives*, ed. Clyde de L. Ryals (Durham, NC: Duke University Press, 1974, pp. 252–3). Harmon's Wills are the most important and obvious exceptions to that statement.
6. Altick (p. 247) describes both the police-station and public house as having 'the air of a schoolroom', a comment applicable to several other 'desk-work' scenes. His article, in relating some of the references also used in this present essay to the novel's treatment of education and literacy, offers a complementary and absorbing account of *Our Mutual Friend* that deepens our sense both of the novel's complexity and Dickens's unifying powers.

7.   R. Golding, *Idiolects in Dickens* (London: Macmillan, 1985), pp. 184–99.

7 Story and Text

1.   Williams, *The English Novel from Dickens to Lawrence*, op. cit., pp. 28–9.
2.   See above, p. 11.
3.   *Dombey and Son*, ed. A. Horsman, The Clarendon Dickens (Oxford: Clarendon Press, 1974), xlvii, 620.
4.   Williams, *The English Novel from Dickens to Lawrence*, op. cit, pp. 29–30.
5.   Flint, *Dickens*, op. cit., p. 71.
6.   Ibid., p. 82.
7.   Ibid., p. 84.
8.   *The Life of Charles Dickens*, ed. Hoppé, op cit., II, 272.
9.   See above, pp. 107ff.
10. Flint, *Dickens*, op. cit., p. 5.
11. Rimmon-Kenan, *Narrative Fiction*, op. cit., p. 59.

Select Bibliography

1. EDITIONS OF DICKENS

Sketches By Boz, The Works of Charles Dickens, Authentic edition, Vol. XVI (London and New York: Chapman & Hall, Charles Scribner's Sons, 1903).

The Pickwick Papers, ed. James Kinsley, The Clarendon Dickens (Oxford: Clarendon Press, 1986.

The Posthumous Papers of the Pickwick Club, ed. Robert L. Patten (Harmondsworth: Penguin Books, 1972).

Martin Chuzzlewit, ed. Margaret Cardwell, The Clarendon Dickens (Oxford: Clarendon Press, 1982).

The Life and Adventures of Martin Chuzzlewit, ed. P.N. Furbank (Harmondsworth: Penguin Books, 1968; reprinted 1981).

The Christmas Books, ed. Michael Slater, Vol. I (Harmondsworth: Penguin Books, 1971; reprinted 1976).

A Christmas Carol: a facsimile of the manuscript in The Pierpont Morgan Library (New York: James H. Heineman, 1967).

Pictures from Italy, ed. David Paroissien (London: André Deutsch, 1973).

Dombey and Son, ed. A. Horsman, The Clarendon Dickens (Oxford: Clarendon Press, 1974).

David Copperfield, ed. Nina Burgis, The Clarendon Dickens (Oxford: Clarendon Press, 1981).

Bleak House, ed. Norman Page (Harmondsworth: Penguin Books, 1971; reprinted 1980).

Little Dorrit, ed. Harvey Peter Sucksmith, The Clarendon Dickens (Oxford: Clarendon Press, 1979).

Great Expectations, ed. Angus Calder (Harmondsworth: Penguin Books, 1965; reprinted 1985).

Our Mutual Friend, ed. Stephen Gill (Harmondsworth: Penguin Books, 1971).

The Mystery of Edwin Drood, ed. Margaret Cardwell, The Clarendon Dickens (Oxford: Clarendon Press, 1972).

The Mystery of Edwin Drood, ed. A. Cox, intro. Angus Wilson (Harmondsworth: Penguin Books, 1974; reprinted 1976).

Selected Short Fiction, ed. Deborah A. Thomas (Harmondsworth: Penguin Books, 1976).

The Letters of Charles Dickens, Pilgrim edition, ed. Madeline House, Graham Storey, Kathleen Tillotson, etc. (Oxford: Clarendon Press, 1965ff).

2. DICKENS: SECONDARY MATERIAL
This section is restricted to works wholly on Dickens and directly relevant to this present study.

Altick, Richard D., 'Education, Print, and Paper in *Our Mutual Friend'*, *Nineteenth-Century Literary Perspectives,* ed. Clyde de L. Ryals (Durham, NC: Duke University Press, 1974), pp. 337–54.

Axton, William F., '*Great Expectations* Yet Again', *Dickens Studies Annual*, ed. Robert B. Partlow, Jr., II (1972), 278–93.

Barickman, Richard, 'The Spiritual Journey of Amy Dorrit and Arthur Clennam: "A Way Wherein There is No Ecstasy"', *Dickens Studies Annual*, ed. Robert D. Partlow, Jr., VII (1978), 163–189.

Barickman, Richard, 'The Subersive Methods of Dickens's Early Fiction: *Martin Chuzzlewit*', *Charles Dickens: New Perspectives*, ed. Wendall Stacy Johnson (Englewood Cliffs, NJ: Prentice-Hall, 1982), pp. 37–50.

Baumgarten, Murray, 'Calligraphy and Code: Writing in *Great Expectations*, *Dickens Studies Annual*, ed. Robert B. Partlow, Jr., XI (1983), 61–72.

Blain, Virginia, 'Double Vision and the Double Standard in *Bleak House*: A Feminist Perspective', *Literature and History*, XI (1985), 31–46.

Breslow, Julian W., 'The Narrator in *Sketches By Boz*', *English Literary History*, XLIV (1977), 127–49.

Browning, Robert, '*Sketches By Boz*', *Dickens and the Twentieth Century*, ed. John Gross and Gabriel Pearson (London: Routledge & Kegan Paul, 1962; reprinted 1966), pp. 19–34.

Burgam, William, 'Little Dorrit in Italy'. *Nineteenth-Century Fiction*, XXIX (1974–5), 393–411.

Butt, John and Tillotson, Kathleen, *Dickens at Work* (London: Methuen, 1957; reprinted 1968).

Carey, John, *The Violent Effigy* (London: Faber & Faber, 1973).

Chesterton, G.K., *Charles Dickens* (London: Methuen, 1906)

Collins, Philip, 'Charles Dickens', *Victorian Fiction: A Second Guide to Research*, ed. George H. Ford (New York: The Modern Language Association of America, 1978), pp. 34–113.

Connor, Stephen, *Charles Dickens* (Oxford: Basil Blackwell, 1985).

Cox, C.B., 'Comic Viewpoints in *Sketches By Boz*', *English*, XII (1958–9), 132–5.

Daleski, H.M., *Dickens and the Art of Analogy* (London: Faber & Faber, 1970).

Davies, James A., 'Boffin's Secretary', *Dickensian*, lxxii (1976), 148–57.

Davies, James A., 'Negative Similarity: The Fat Boy in *The Pickwick Papers*', *Durham University Journal*, LXX (1977–8), 29–34.

DeVries, Duane, *Dickens's Apprentice Years: The Making of a Novelist* (Hassocks & New York: Harvester Press and Barnes & Noble, 1976).

Dyson, A.E., *The Inimitable Dickens* (London: Macmillan, 1970).

Feltes, N.N., 'The Moment of *Pickwick*, or the Production of a Commodity Text', *Literature and History*, X (1984), 203–17.

Fielding, K.J., *Charles Dickens: A Critical Introduction*, 2nd edition (London: Longman, 1966).

Flint, Kate, *Dickens* (Brighton: Harvester Press, 1986).

Forster, John, *The Life of Charles Dickens*, ed. A.J. Hoppé, 2 vols (London: Dent, 1966).

Garis, Robert, *The Dickens Theatre* (Oxford: Clarendon Press, 1965).

Gervais, David, 'The Prose and Poetry of *Great Expectations*', *Dickens Studies Annual*, ed. Robert B. Partlow, Jr., XIII (1984), 84–114.

Gilbert, Elliot L., '"In Primal Sympathy": *Great Expectations* and the Secret Life', *Dickens Studies Annual*, ed. Robert B. Partlow, Jr., XI (1983), 89–113.

Golding, Robert, *Idiolects in Dickens* (London: Macmillan, 1985).

Gribble, Jennifer, 'Depth and Surface in *Our Mutual Friend*', *Essays in Criticism*, XXV (1975), 197–214.

Grillo, Virgil, *Charles Dickens's Sketches By Boz: End in the Beginning* (Boulder, Colorado: Colorado Associated University Press, 1974).

Gross, John and Pearson, Gabriel (eds.), *Dickens and the Twentieth Century* (London: Routledge & Kegan Paul, 1962; reprinted 1966).

Hardy, Barbara, *The Moral Art of Dickens* (London: Athlone Press, 1970).

Holderness, Graham, 'Imagination in *A Christmas Carol*', *Études Anglaises*, XXX (1979), 28–45.

Hollington, Michael, *Dickens and the Grotesque* (London, Sydney, and Totowa, NJ: Croom Helm and Barnes & Noble, 1984).

Holloway, John, 'Dickens and the Symbol', *Dickens 1970*, ed. Michael Slater (London: Chapman & Hall, 1970), pp. 53–74.

House, Humphrey, *The Dickens World* (London: Oxford University Press, 1941; reprinted 1965).

Johnson, Edgar, *Charles Dickens: His Tragedy and Triumph*, Revised and Abridged edition (Harmondsworth: Penguin Books, 1986).

Jordan, John O., 'The Medium of *Great Expectations*', *Dickens Studies Annual*, ed. Robert B. Partlow, Jr., XI (1983), 73–88.

Kaplan, Fred, *Dickens and Mesmerism: The Hidden Springs of Fiction* (Princeton, NJ: Princeton University Press, 1975).

Kincaid, James R., *Dickens and the Rhetoric of Laughter* (Oxford: Clarendon Press, 1971).

Knoepflmacher, U.C., *Laughter and Despair* (Berkeley, Los Angeles and London: University of California Press, 1971).

Lanham, Richard A., '*Our Mutual Friend*: The Birds of Prey', *Victorian Newsletter*, No. 24 (Fall, 1963), 6–11.

Larson, Janet L., *Dickens and the Broken Scripture* (Athens, Georgia: University of Georgia Press, 1985).

Leavis, F.R. and Q.D., *Dickens the Novelist* (Harmondsworth: Penguin Books, 1972).

Lucas, John, *The Melancholy Man* (London: Methuen, 1970).

Marcus, Stephen, *Dickens: from Pickwick to Dombey* (London: Chatto & Windus, 1965).

McMaster, R.D., 'Birds of Prey: A Study of *Our Mutual Friend*', *Dalhousie Review*, XL (1960–61), 372–81.

Miller, J. Hillis, *Charles Dickens: the World of his Novels* (Cambridge, Mass. and London: Harvard University Press and Oxford University Press, 1958).

Miller, J. Hillis, 'The Fiction of Realism: *Sketches By Boz, Oliver Twist*, and Cruikshank's Illustrations', *Dickens Centennial Essays*, ed. Ada Nisbet and Blake Nevius (Berkeley, Los Angeles and London: University of California Press, 1971), pp. 85–153.

Mundhenk, Rosemary, 'The Education of the Reader in *Our Mutual Friend*', *Nineteenth-Century Fiction*, XXXIV (1979–80), 41–58.

Newsom, Robert, *Dickens on the Romantic Side of Familiar Things: Bleak House and the Novel Tradition* (New York: Columbia University Press, 1977).

Partlow, Jr., Robert B., 'The Moving I: A Study of the Point of View in *Great Expectations*', *College English*, XXIII (1961–2), 122–6. Reprinted in *Hard*

Times, Great Expectations and Our Mutual Friend: A Casebook, ed. Norman Page (London: Macmillan, 1979), pp. 118–24.

Patterson, A.M., '*Our Mutual Friend*: Dickens as the Compleat Angler', *Dickens Studies Annual*, ed. R.B. Partlow, Jr.

Pratt, Branwen Bailey, 'Dickens and Freedom: Young Bailey in *Martin Chuzzlewit*', *Nineteenth-Century Fiction*, XXX (1975–6), 185–99.

Robson, W.W., 'The Mystery of Edwin Drood: the solution', *The Times Literary Supplement*, 11 November 1983), pp. 1246, 1259. See also *TLS* 25 November 1983, p. 1321; 2 December 1983, p. 1347; 9 December 1983, p. 1372; 30 December 1983, p. 1457; 20 January 1984, p. 61.

Sadoff, Dianne F., 'Storytelling and the Figure of the Father in *Little Dorrit*', *PMLA*, XCV (1980), 234–45.

Sadrin, Amy, *Great Expectations* (London: Unwin Hyman, 1988).

Senf, Carol A., '*Bleak House*: Dickens, Esther, and the Androgynous Mind', *The Victorian Newsletter*, No. 64 (Fall, 1983), 21–7.

Schwarzbach, F.S., *Dickens and the City* (London: Athlone Press, 1979).

Smith, Grahame, *Dickens, Money and Society* (Berkeley, Los Angeles and London: University of California Press, 1968).

Smith, Grahame, *Charles Dickens: Bleak House* (London: Edward Arnold, 1974).

Stewart, Garrett, *Dickens and the Trials of Imagination* (Cambridge, Mass.: Harvard University Press, 1974).

Stoehr, Taylor, *Dickens: The Dreamer's Stance* (Ithaca, NY: Cornell University Press, 1965; reprinted 1966).

Tillotson, Kathleen, 'The Middle Years from the *Carol* to *Copperfield*', *Dickens Memorial Lectures 1970* (London: The Dickens Fellowship, 1970).

Tracey, Robert, 'Reading Dickens' Writing', *Dickens Studies Annual*, ed. Robert B. Partlow, Jr., XI (1983), 37–60.

Trilling, Lionel, 'Little Dorrit', *Little Dorrit*, Oxford Illustrated edition (London: Oxford University Press, 1953), pp. v–xvi. Reprinted in *Charles Dickens*, ed. Stephen Wall (Harmondsworth: Penguin Books, 1970), pp. 363–75.

Walder, Dennis, *Dickens and Religion* (London: George Allen & Unwin, 1981).

Westburg, Barry, *The Confessional Fiction of Charles Dickens* (Dekalb, Ill.: Northern Illinois University Press, 1977).

Wilson, Angus, *The World of Charles Dickens* (Harmondsworth: Penguin Books, 1972).

Woodring, Carl, 'Change in Chuzzlewit', *Nineteenth-Century Literary Perspectives*, ed. Clyde de L. Ryals (Durham, NC: Duke University Press, 1974), pp. 211–18.

3. THEORETICAL AND OTHER WORKS

Allott, Miriam, *Novelists on the Novel* (London: Routledge & Kegan Paul, 1959; reprinted 1975).

Anderson, Howard, Daghlian, Philip B., Ehrenpreis, Irvin, *The Familiar Letter in the Eighteenth Century* (Lawrence, Kansas: University of Kansas Press, 1966).

Arac, Jonathan, *Commissioned Spirits* (New Brunswick, NJ: Rutgers University Press, 1979).

Aristotle, *On the Art of Poetry*, trans. Ingram Bywater (Oxford: Clarendon Press, 1920).

Bakhtin, Mikhail, *Problems of Dostoevsky's Poetics*, ed. and trans. Caryl Emerson (Manchester: Manchester University Press, 1984).

Barthes, Roland, *Image Music Text*, trans. Stephen Heath (London: Fontana/Collins, 1977).

Bayley, John, *The Characters of Love* (London: Constable, 1960; reprinted 1962).

Booth, Wayne C., *The Rhetoric of Fiction* (Chicago and London: University of Chicago Press, 1961; reprinted 1975).

Bradbury, Malcolm, 'Towards a Poetics of Fiction: An Approach Through Structure', *Towards a Poetics of Fiction*, ed. Mark Spilka (Bloomington and London: Indiana University Press, 1977).

Bronzwaer, W., 'Implied Author, Extradiegetic Narrator and Public Reader. Gérard Genette's Narratological Model and the Reading Version of *Great Expectations*', *Neophilologus*, LXII (1978), 1–18.

Browning, Robert, *Poetical Works 1833–64*, ed. Ian Jack (London: Oxford University Press, 1970; reprinted 1975).

Chatman, Seymour, *Story and Discourse* (Ithaca and London: Cornell University Press, 1978; reprinted 1980).

Culler, Jonathan, *The Pursuit of Signs* (London and Henley: Routledge & Kegan Paul, 1981).

Docherty, Thomas, *Reading (Absent) Character* (Oxford: Clarendon Press, 1983).

Eigner, Edwin M., *The Metaphysical Novel in England and America* (Berkeley, Los Angeles and London: University of California Press, 1978).

Eliot, T.S., *The Complete Poems and Plays* (London: Faber & Faber, 1969; reprinted 1971).

Ferrara, Fernando, 'Theory and Model for the Structural Analysis of Fiction', *New Literary History*, V (1973), 245–68.

Fish, Stanley, 'Literature in the Reader: Affective Stylistics', *New Literary History*, II (1970–71), 123–62.

Freund, Elizabeth, *The Return of the Reader* (London & New York: Methuen, 1987).

Garrett, Peter K., *The Victorian Multiplot Novel* (New Haven and London: Yale University Press, 1980).

Gilmour, Robin, *The Idea of the Gentleman in the Victorian Novel* (London: Allen & Unwin, 1981).

Harvey, W.J., *Character and the Novel* (London: Chatto & Windus, 1965; reprinted 1970).

Hochman, Baruch, *The Test of Character* (London & Toronto: Associated University Presses, 1983).

Holub, Robert C., *Reception Theory: A Critical Introduction* (London and New York: Methuen, 1984).

Hunt, Leigh, *Poetical Works*, ed. H.S. Milford (London: Oxford University Press, 1923).

Hunt, Leigh, *Selected Essays* (London, Toronto and New York: Dent, Dutton, 1929).

Iser, Wolfgang, *The Implied Reader* (Baltimore and London: Johns Hopkins University Press, 1974).

Iser, Wolfgang, *The Act of Reading* (London and Henley: Routledge & Kegan Paul, 1978).

Lamb, Charles, *The Essays of Elia and The Last Essays of Elia* (London: Oxford University Press, 1946; reprinted 1951).

McCarthy, Mary, 'Characters in Fiction', *Partisan Review*, XXVIII (March–April 1962), 171–91.

Praz, Mario, *The Hero in Eclipse in Victorian Fiction*, trans. Angus Davidson (London: Oxford University Press, 1956).

Price, Martin, *Forms of Life* (New Haven and London: Yale University Press, 1983).

Rimmon-Kenan, Shlomith, *Narrative Fiction: Contemporary Poetics* (London and New York: Methuen, 1983).

Sinfield, Alan, *Dramatic Monologue* (London & New York: Methuen and Barnes & Noble, 1977).

Swinden, Patrick, *Unofficial Selves* (London: Macmillan, 1973).

Todorov, Tzvetan, *The Poetics of Prose*, trans. Richard Howard (Oxford: Blackwell, 1977).

Tompkins, Jane P. (ed.), *Reader–Response Criticism* (Baltimore and London: Johns Hopkins University Press, 1980).

Weinsheimer, Joel, 'Theory of Character: *Emma*', *Poetics Today*, I (1979), 185–211.

Weinstein, Philip, *The Semantics of Desire* (Princeton, NJ: Princeton University Press, 1984).

Williams, Raymond, *The English Novel from Dickens to Lawrence* (London: Chatto & Windus, 1970; reprinted St Albans: Paladin, 1974).

Index